P9-CQH-094

*North End
and the
Waterfront*

*Beacon
Hill and
West End*

*Old Boston
and the
Financial
District*

*Chinatown
and the
Theater District*

**NORTH END AND
THE WATERFRONT**
Pages 66–77

**OLD BOSTON AND THE
FINANCIAL DISTRICT**
Pages 54–65

EYEWITNESS TRAVEL
BOSTON

EYEWITNESS TRAVEL

BOSTON

MAIN CONTRIBUTORS:
TOM BROSS, PATRICIA HARRIS, AND DAVID LYON

LONDON, NEW YORK,
MELBOURNE, MUNICH AND DELHI
www.dk.com

PROJECT EDITOR Marcus Hardy
ART EDITOR Nicola Rodway
EDITOR Simon Hall
U.S. EDITOR Mary Sutherland
DESIGNERS Elly King, Nikala Sim
MAP CO-ORDINATORS Dave Pugh, Casper Morris
DTP Maite Lantaron
PICTURE RESEARCHER Brigitte Arora
PRODUCTION Michelle Thomas

CONTRIBUTORS
Tom Bross, Brett Cook, Patricia Harris, Carolyn Heller,
David Lyon, Juliette Rogers, Kem Sawyer

PHOTOGRAPHERS
Demetrio Carrasco, Linda Whitwam

ILLUSTRATORS
Stephen Conlin, Gary Cross, Richard Draper,
Chris Orr & Associates, Robbie Polley, John Woodcock

MAPS
Ben Bowles, Rob Clynes, Sam Johnston,
James Macdonald (Colourmap Scanning Ltd)

Reproduced by Colourscan, Singapore
Printed and bound by South China Printing Co. Ltd., China

First American Edition, 2001
09 10 9 8 7 6 5 4 3 2 1

Published in the United States by DK Publishing,
375 Hudson Street, New York, New York 10014

Reprinted with revisions 2003, 2004, 2005, 2006, 2007, 2008, 2009

Copyright © 2001, 2009 Dorling Kindersley Limited, London

ALL RIGHTS RESERVED.
WITHOUT LIMITING THE RIGHTS UNDER COPYRIGHT RESERVED ABOVE, NO PART OF
THIS PUBLICATION MAY BE REPRODUCED, STORED IN OR INTRODUCED INTO A
RETRIEVAL SYSTEM, OR TRANSMITTED, IN ANY FORM, OR BY ANY MEANS
(ELECTRONIC, MECHANICAL, PHOTOCOPYING, RECORDING, OR OTHERWISE) WITHOUT
THE PRIOR WRITTEN PERMISSION OF BOTH THE COPYRIGHT OWNER AND THE ABOVE
PUBLISHER OF THIS BOOK.

Published in Great Britain by Dorling Kindersley Limited.

A CATALOG RECORD IS AVAILABLE FROM THE LIBRARY OF CONGRESS.

ISSN 1542-1554
ISBN 978-0-75662-577-1

*Front cover main image: Paul Revere statue and
Old North Church, Boston, Massachusetts*

We're trying to be cleaner and greener:
- -
• we recycle waste and switch things off

• we use paper from responsibly managed
forests whenever possible

• we ask our printers to actively reduce
water and energy consumption

• we check out our suppliers' working
conditions – they never use child labour
- -
**Find out more about our values and
best practices at www.dk.com**

**The information in every
DK Eyewitness Travel Guide is checked regularly.**
Every effort has been made to ensure that this book is as up-to-date
as possible at the time of going to press. Some details, however,
such as telephone numbers, opening hours, prices, gallery hanging
arrangements, and travel information are liable to change. The
publishers cannot accept responsibility for any consequences arising
from the use of this book, nor for any material on third party
websites, and cannot guarantee that any website address in this
book will be a suitable source of travel information.
We value the views and suggestions of our readers very highly.
Please write to: Publisher, DK Eyewitness Travel Guides,
Dorling Kindersley, 80 Strand, London WC2R 0RL, Great Britain.

◁ **Rowes Wharf, part of new development along Boston's waterfront**

CONTENTS

HOW TO USE THIS GUIDE 6

**Tiffany window in the Arlington
Street Church, Back Bay**

INTRODUCING BOSTON

FOUR GREAT DAYS IN BOSTON 10

PUTTING BOSTON ON THE MAP 12

THE HISTORY OF BOSTON 16

**Federal-style houses, Beacon Hill
district *(see pp42–5)***

View of the Back Bay skyline, with the John Hancock Tower *(see p97)*

**Pumpkins for sale, a
regular sight in the fall**

**Memorial Church steeple,
Harvard Yard** *(see pp110–11)*

Trinity Church, Back Bay
(see pp94–5)

HOW TO USE THIS GUIDE

This guide will help you get the most from your visit to Boston, providing expert recommendations and detailed practical information. The opening section, *Introducing Boston*, maps the city and sets it in its geographical, historical, and cultural context. *Boston at a Glance* is an overview of the city's main attractions. Section two, *Boston Area by Area*, starts on page 38 and describes all the important

Window at First Baptist Church
(see p92)

sights plus three recommended walks, using maps, photographs, and detailed illustrations. The sights are arranged in two groups: those in Boston's central districts, and those a little farther afield. Tips for hotels, restaurants, shopping, entertainment, and sports can be found in *Travelers' Needs*, while the final section, *Survival Guide*, contains practical advice on everything from public transportation and telephones to personal safety.

FINDING YOUR WAY AROUND THE SIGHTSEEING SECTION

Each of the six sightseeing areas is color-coded for easy reference. Every chapter opens with an introduction to the area it covers, describing its history and character. For central districts, this is followed by a

Street-by-Street map illustrating a particularly interesting part of the area; for sights farther away, by a regional map. A simple numbering system relates sights to the maps. Important sights are covered by several pages.

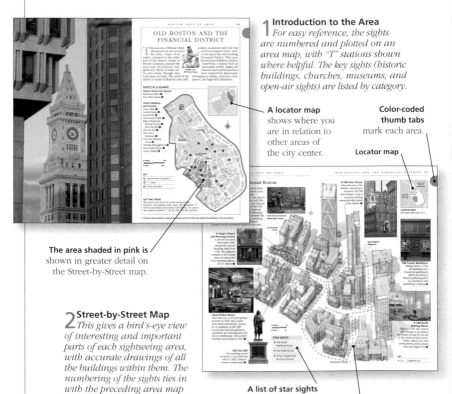

1 Introduction to the Area
For easy reference, the sights are numbered and plotted on an area map, with "T" stations shown where helpful. The key sights (historic buildings, churches, museums, and open-air sights) are listed by category.

A locator map shows where you are in relation to other areas of the city center.

Color-coded thumb tabs mark each area.

Locator map

The area shaded in pink is shown in greater detail on the Street-by-Street map.

2 Street-by-Street Map
This gives a bird's-eye view of interesting and important parts of each sightseeing area, with accurate drawings of all the buildings within them. The numbering of the sights ties in with the preceding area map and with the fuller descriptions on the pages that follow.

A list of star sights recommends the places that no visitor should miss.

Suggested walking route

BOSTON AREA MAP

The colored areas shown on this map *(see inside front cover)* are the five main sightseeing areas of central Boston (excluding the *Farther Afield* section.) Each is covered in a full chapter in the *Boston Area by Area* section *(pp39–127)*. The areas are also highlighted on other maps throughout the book. In *Boston at a Glance (pp26–37)*, for example, they help you to locate the most important sights that no visitor should miss. The maps' colored borders match the colored thumb tabs at the top corner of each page.

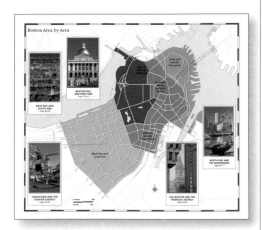

Numbers refer to each sight's position on the area map and its place in the chapter.

Practical information lists all the information you need to visit every sight, including a map reference to the *Street Finder* maps *(pp186–191)*.

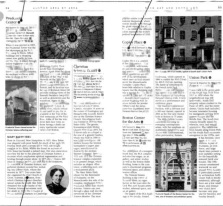

3 Detailed information on each sight

All the important sights are described individually. They are listed to follow the numbering on the area map at the start of the section. The key to the symbols summarizing practical information is on the back flap.

A visitors' checklist provides the practical information you will need to plan your visit.

Story boxes provide details on famous people or historical events.

4 Boston's Major Sights

These are given more extensive coverage, sometimes two or more full pages. Historic buildings are dissected to reveal their interiors; museums and galleries have color-coded floor plans to help you find important exhibits.

Stars indicate the most interesting sights.

Captions provide more detailed information about specific sights.

INTRODUCING BOSTON

FOUR GREAT DAYS IN BOSTON

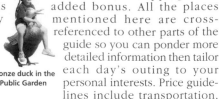

As well as being compact and walkable, Boston also has an extensive subway system (the "T"), which makes neighboring Cambridge easily accessible. These four suggested days offer morning and afternoon opportunities to enjoy the city's prime historical and cultural attractions,

Bronze duck in the Public Garden

with eclectic shopping as an added bonus. All the places mentioned here are cross-referenced to other parts of the guide so you can ponder more detailed information then tailor each day's outing to your personal interests. Price guidelines include transportation, food, and admission charges.

Bell tower and steeple of Old North Church

HISTORIC BOSTON

- Historic North End
- A walk along the waterfront
- Elegant Old State House
- King's Chapel

TWO ADULTS allow at least $75

Morning

Start in the **North End** *(see pp68–9)*, Boston's oldest neighborhood. Hanover Street is full of Italian cafés and bakeries and east from here is the **Paul Revere Mall** *(see p72)*, where an equestrian statue commemorates the patriot. Continue to the lovely 18th-century **Old North Church** *(see p71)*, followed by a stroll through **Christoper Columbus Park** *(see p73)* for great harbor vistas. For lunch, head to **Quincy Market** *(see p64)* or **Durgin-Park** *(see p143)*, with its local specialties.

Afternoon

Refreshed, head to the **Old State House** *(see pp60–61)*, the one-time seat of the British colonial government. Nearby is the simple **King's Chapel and Burial Ground** *(see p58)*. Continue to the **Old South Meeting House** *(see p59)*, where rousing speeches led to The Boston Tea Party *(see p75)*. End the day relaxing in popular **Boston Common** *(see pp46–7)*.

CULTURE & FRESH AIR

- Impressive Trinity Church
- Masterpieces in the Museum of Fine Arts
- Isabella Stewart Gardner Museum
- Boston skyline from Back Bay Fens parkland

TWO ADULTS allow at least $95

Morning

Start the day on the lovely open space that constitutes **Copley Square** *(see p96)*, which is dominated by the beautiful 1877 Neo-Romanesque **Trinity Church** *(see pp94–5)*, with its soaring interior spaces richly decorated with murals and stained-glass windows. Then, for a bit of morning retail therapy, walk a short distance to either of two upscale urban malls: **Copley Place** *(see p99)* or the **Prudential Center**

Stained glass, Trinity Church

(see p98), where all your needs are catered for under one roof. In addition, **Boylston Street** *(see p96)* and parallel **Newbury Street** *(see p93)* also overflow with some of the city's most stylish stores and fashion boutiques. At the Copley "T" station, board a train for the **Museum of Fine Arts** *(see pp104–7)*, the largest art museum in New England, with collections ranging from the ancient world to the 20th century. After allowing ample time to roam the galleries, head to the upper level of the West Wing to enjoy a leisurely lunch in Bravo, the MFA's classy restaurant with walls, as one might expect, adorned with a rotating exhibition of some of the museum's contemporary artworks.

Afternoon

After lunch, head to another Boston cultural treasure nearby: the **Isabella Stewart Gardner Museum** *(see p103)*. Here, European masterpieces are among the

Boston Symphony Orchestra performing

highlights of the collection. After all this culture, take a breath of fresh air and enjoy a stroll amid the waterways, marshes, and footbridges of Back Bay Fens, one of the jewels of the area known as **The Emerald Necklace** *(see p103)*. This rambling parkland also has enchanting views of Boston's soaring skyline. If you would like to extend this cultural day into the evening, make your way to Symphony Hall, the acoustically fine-tuned home of the acclaimed **Boston Symphony Orchestra** *(see p160)*, for a classical music fest. Or, just a block away, audiences regularly fill Jordan Hall for concerts and recitals presented by students of the **New England Conservatory of Music** *(see p160)*. Alternatively, if you are in the mood for drama, Boston University's **Huntington Theatre** *(see p160)* stages first rate productions, while the **Colonial Theater** *(see p160)*, in the Theater District, presents tours of recent Broadway hits.

CAMBRIDGE ACADEMIA

- Bustling Harvard Square
- Harvard Yard architecture
- European masterpieces in the Harvard University Museums
- MIT campus and museums

TWO ADULTS allow at least $90

Morning
Catch a Red Line train across the river to the college town of **Cambridge** *(see p108)*, emerging at Harvard Square. This is the site of the nation's oldest and most prestigious university. Immerse yourself in the scholarly atmosphere by visiting **Harvard Yard** *(see pp110–11)*, surrounded by lecture halls and dormitories that cover a broad spectrum of American architecture. From here head to the eminent **Harvard University**

Grand architecture at Harvard Yard

Museums *(see p112–14)*. Head to the Sackler, a museum dedicated to Asian and Near Eastern art that is currently housing a selection of exhibits from all of the Harvard art museums until the Fogg reopens in 2012 or 2013. Make your way back to Harvard Square, where **Sandrine's Bistro** *(see p149)* offers a good-value lunch

John Harvard Statue

Afternoon
After lunch, visit the Harvard Museum of Natural History to see the scientifically accurate glass flowers. For another cultural experience, ride a No. 1 bus to the **MIT Campus** *(see p121)* to savor avant-garde 20th-century architecture and Alexander Calder's 12-m (40-ft) high stabile *La Grande Voile*. Catch the subway back to central Boston from Kendall Station.

A FAMILY DAY

- **Get wet on the Boston Duck Tour**
- **Swan Boat lagoon "cruise"**
- **Tropical fish in the New England Aquarium**
- **Hand's-on fun in the Children's Museum**

FAMILY OF FOUR allow $125

Morning
Get children acquainted with this kid-friendly city by joining **Boston Duck Tours** *(see p175)*, which provides narrated sightseeing tours in World War II-era amphibious vehicles. The downtown tour includes the Charles River, an exciting way to view the city's skyline. Then stroll through the **Boston Public Garden** *(see pp46–7)*, locale of bronze duck sculptures. Real ducks also swim on the park's lagoon, and you can join them aboard a pedal-powered Swan Boat. Take the subway from Arlington "T" station to Aquarium "T" station, where the **New England Aquarium** *(see pp76–7)* has a huge tank full of tropical fish, sharks and stingrays. For lunch, enjoy a sandwich on home-made bread from **Sel de la Terre** *(see p144)*.

Afternoon
Walk across the bridge to the highly interactive **Children's Museum** *(see p75)*. Permanent features include a rock-climbing wall, a construction zone, a maze, and a science playground.

Swan boats in Boston Public Garden

Putting Boston on the Map

Boston is situated along the United States' northeastern Atlantic coast on Massachusetts Bay. Founded in the early 17th century around a large natural harbor at the mouth of the Charles River, the modern city now covers an area of 49 sq miles (127 sq km) and has a population of 600,000. Boston is the capital of Massachusetts and a major center of American history, culture, and learning.

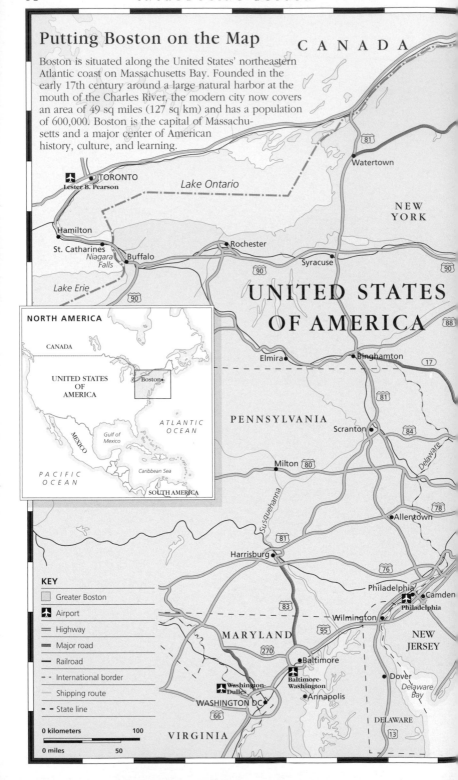

CANADA

Watertown

Lester B. Pearson
TORONTO

Lake Ontario

NEW YORK

Hamilton

St. Catharines
Niagara Falls
Buffalo

Rochester

Syracuse

Lake Erie

UNITED STATES OF AMERICA

Elmira

Binghamton

NORTH AMERICA

CANADA

UNITED STATES OF AMERICA

Boston

MEXICO

Gulf of Mexico

ATLANTIC OCEAN

Caribbean Sea

PACIFIC OCEAN

SOUTH AMERICA

PENNSYLVANIA

Scranton

Milton

Susquehanna

Delaware

Allentown

Harrisburg

Philadelphia
Camden
Philadelphia

Wilmington

NEW JERSEY

KEY

	Greater Boston
	Airport
	Highway
	Major road
	Railroad
	International border
	Shipping route
	State line

MARYLAND

Baltimore

Washington-Dulles
Baltimore-Washington
WASHINGTON DC

Annapolis

Dover
Delaware Bay

DELAWARE

0 kilometers   100

0 miles   50

VIRGINIA

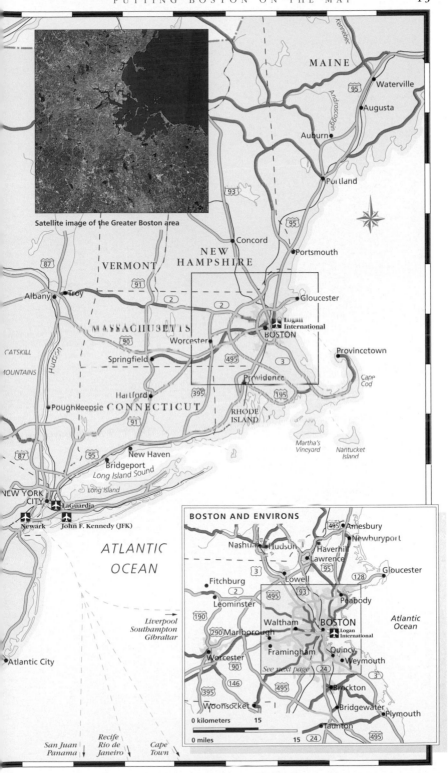

Satellite image of the Greater Boston area

MAINE

Waterville

Augusta

Androscoggin

Auburn

Kennebec

Portland

95

93

95

Concord

Portsmouth

NEW
HAMPSHIRE

VERMONT

Gloucester

87

91

Albany Troy

2

2

MASSACHUSETTS

Logan
International

90

Worcester BOSTON

CATSKILL
MOUNTAINS

Springfield

495

Provincetown

Hudson

3

Cape
Cod

Poughkeepsie CONNECTICUT

Hartford

395

Providence

195

91

RHODE
ISLAND

87

95

New Haven

Bridgeport

Long Island Sound

Martha's
Vineyard

Nantucket
Island

NEW YORK
CITY LaGuardia

Newark John F. Kennedy (JFK)

Long Island

ATLANTIC
OCEAN

Liverpool
Southampton
Gibraltar

Atlantic City

San Juan
Panama

Recife
Rio de
Janeiro

Cape
Town

BOSTON AND ENVIRONS

495 Amesbury

Newburyport

Nashua Hudson

Haverhill

Lawrence

3

95

Fitchburg

Lowell

128 Gloucester

2

190

Leominster

495

93

Peabody

Atlantic
Ocean

Waltham

BOSTON

Logan
International

290 Marlborough

Framingham

Quincy

Weymouth

Worcester

90

See next page

24

3

395

146

495

Brockton

Woonsocket

Bridgewater

Plymouth

Taunton

24

495

0 kilometers   15

0 miles   15

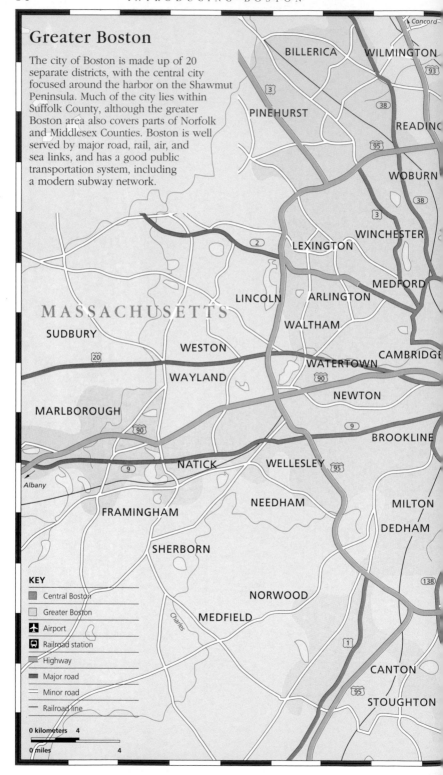

Greater Boston

The city of Boston is made up of 20 separate districts, with the central city focused around the harbor on the Shawmut Peninsula. Much of the city lies within Suffolk County, although the greater Boston area also covers parts of Norfolk and Middlesex Counties. Boston is well served by major road, rail, air, and sea links, and has a good public transportation system, including a modern subway network.

Concord

BILLERICA

WILMINGTON

93

3

38

PINEHURST

95

READING

WOBURN

38

3

WINCHESTER

2

LEXINGTON

MEDFORD

LINCOLN

ARLINGTON

M A S S A C H U S E T T S

WALTHAM

SUDBURY

WESTON

CAMBRIDGE

20

WATERTOWN

WAYLAND

90

NEWTON

MARLBOROUGH

90

9

BROOKLINE

NATICK

WELLESLEY

95

Albany

9

NEEDHAM

MILTON

FRAMINGHAM

DEDHAM

SHERBORN

138

KEY

■	Central Boston
□	Greater Boston
✈	Airport
🚌	Railroad station
▬	Highway
▬	Major road
=	Minor road
—	Railroad line

NORWOOD

Charles

MEDFIELD

1

CANTON

95

STOUGHTON

0 kilometers 4

0 miles 4

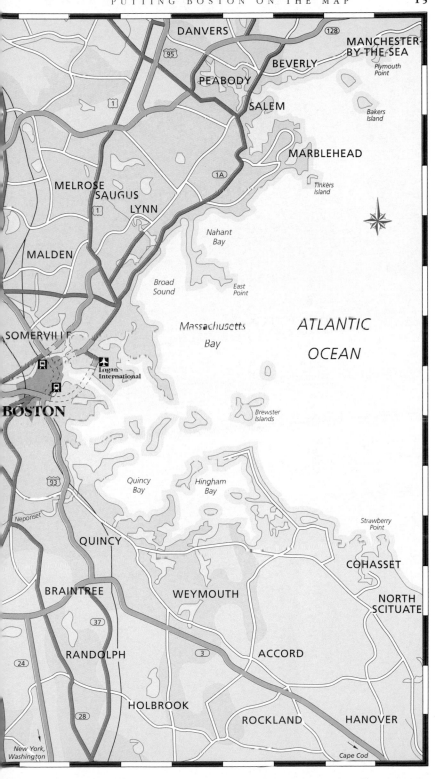

THE HISTORY OF BOSTON

Evidence of human occupation in Massachusetts dates from around 7500 B.C. By around A.D. 500 Algonquin Indians were widespread in the region. Hunter-gatherers, they fished, farmed beans and pumpkins, and hunted moose and deer. They were made up of seven tribes, the closest geographically to present-day Boston being the Massachusetts, Wampanoags, and Nipmucks

Other tribes in the region included the Nausets around Cape Cod, the Pennacooks farther north, and Pocumtucs and Mohicans to the west. Their dialects came from the same language, and their physical features were similar. Each tribe lived in close-knit communities of approximately 250 people.

Artist's impression of the Viking Leif Erikson's ship

THE FIRST EUROPEANS

During the Age of the Vikings, Norsemen from Scandinavia adventured far from home, reaching North America. The coastal land of Vinland discovered by Leif Erikson in around A.D. 1000 may well have been on the Massachusetts coast. French and Spanish fishermen fished here in the mid-15th century and the Italian-born explorer John Cabot led an English expedition to the New England coast once in 1497 and again in 1498. A few years later Miguel Cortereal sailed from Portugal to Massachusetts, where his ship was wrecked. His name was found carved on a granite rock with the year 1511. Throughout the 16th century, the English, French, Portuguese, Spanish, and Italians explored the East Coast, whaling, fishing, and trading with the natives. In 1602 the Englishman Bartholomew Gosnold sailed to Massachusetts, landing on the peninsula he called Cape Cod and traversing the island he would name Martha's Vineyard after his daughter. He returned to England with furs from the natives and sassafras to be used medicinally. In 1607 James I of England offered land in the New World to two companies. What is now Virginia he gave to the London company, led by Captain John Smith. To a group from Plymouth, England, he assigned New England and land as far south as what is now Delaware. The Plymouth Company set out in 1607 to found a colony along the Kennebec River in present-day Maine, but the harsh winter led the company to return to England. John Smith's Virginia expedition was more successful. In May 1607 he arrived in Jamestown, where he founded a permanent colony.

TIMELINE

A.D. 500	1000	1500
Viking casket	**1497** John Cabot leads English expedition to New England coast	**1608** Puritan separatists flee England for the Netherlands
500 Algonquin tribes inhabit land stretching from Canada to Florida	**1511** Portuguese Miguel Cortereal explores Massachusetts	**1607** James I assigns land to Plymouth Company
1000 Viking explorer Leif Erikson is thought to have reached Massachusetts	**1602** English explorer Bartholomew Gosnold names Cape Cod and Martha's Vineyard	

◁ **Inhabitants of Boston watching the Battle of Bunker Hill (see p20)**

The first Thanksgiving at Plymouth, Massachusetts, celebrated by the Pilgrim Fathers in 1621

THE PILGRIM FATHERS

In 1614 John Smith traveled to the northeast and published his findings in a book entitled *A Description of New England*. This land would become a haven for people who were victims of religious persecution, especially Puritans, who did not adhere to all the beliefs and rituals of the Church of England. One group of Puritan separatists had already left England to seek greater freedom in The Netherlands, but had faced economic hardship there. Lured by Captain Smith's reports, they returned to England to seek a grant for land in the New World. Joining other Puritans led by William Bradford, they set out from Plymouth in two ships, the *Mayflower* and the *Speedwell*. Quickly discovering that the *Speedwell* was leaking, they returned to Plymouth, crammed into the *Mayflower*, and set sail again on September 16, 1620.

Meeting of John Winthrop with local native in around 1630

Two months later the 102 Pilgrims arrived at Cape Cod. Before disembarking, they formulated the "Mayflower Compact," agreeing to govern themselves democratically with "just and equal laws...for the general good of the colony." The Pilgrims named their new home Plymouth and soon made friends with the natives. On April 1, 1621, Governor John Carver and Chief Massasoit signed a peace treaty. They celebrated the first Thanksgiving that year sharing provisions with their native hosts.

FOUNDING OF BOSTON

Charles I assigned land 40 miles (65 km) north of Plymouth colony, near the Charles River, to the Massachusetts Bay Company, a large group of Puritans. In the spring of 1630 over 1,000 Puritans departed in 11 ships bound for Massachusetts. Some settled in Salem and other communities along the Massachusetts Bay. The vast majority,

TIMELINE

1614 Captain John Smith explores the Northeast

1630 John Winthrop and Puritans settle in Boston

1636 Harvard University is founded

1652 First American coin produced in Boston

Pine-tree shilling, the first U.S. coin

1686 James II appoints Sir Edmund Andros as governor

1610	1630	1650	1670

1620 The Pilgrims land at Plymouth

1621 Governor John Carver and Chief Massasoit sign peace treaty

1635 Boston Latin School opens

1640 First English-language book printed in America

1638 Anne Hutchinson banished from Boston for religious beliefs

1660 Quaker Mary Dyer hanged on Boston Common

1684 Charles II nullifies the Massachusetts Bay Charter

however, followed John Winthrop, their newly appointed governor, to the mouth of the Charles River. Across the river lived a recluse, an Anglican clergyman, William Blackstone. He learned that disease was rampant among the Puritans due to the scarcity of fresh drinking water, and invited them to move their settlement over the river. Winthrop and his followers were quick to accept. They first called this new land Trimountain, but soon renamed it Boston after the town in England they had left behind. In 1635 they established the Boston Latin School, the first public school in the British colonies. A year later the Puritans founded a university, named subsequently after John Harvard, who had bequeathed it his library.

Although the Puritans had come to Massachusetts in pursuit of religious freedom, they often proved intolerant of others. Anne Hutchinson was driven out of Boston in 1638 for not conforming to the Puritan tradition. Many Quakers were also beaten, fined, or banished. The Quaker preacher Mary Dyer was hanged for religious unorthodoxy on June 1, 1660 on Boston Common. In 1692 after several girls in the town of Salem accused three women of witchcraft, mass hysteria broke out throughout Massachusetts, and many innocents were tried, and hanged. No one felt safe until Governor William Phips put an end to the trials in 1693.

Mary Dyer with other condemned Quakers, before being hanged in 1660

SEEDS OF REBELLION

The British had passed the Navigation Acts to encourage the colonists to trade only with them, but when the colonists refused to obey, Charles II withdrew the Massachusetts Bay Charter in 1684, putting the colony under the control of the king. His successor James II appointed Sir Edmund Andros as royal governor. After James II lost power, the colonists arrested their governor and in 1689 established their own government. But in 1691 William and Mary granted a new charter to the Massachusetts Colony, combining the Massachusetts Bay and Plymouth colonies and recognizing a bicameral legislature. Later, the British and French started a long series of battles over New World territory. France finally ceded control of Canada and the American West, but the cost of war had taken its toll on the British, and the colonists were asked to pay their share in taxes. The seeds of rebellion were sown.

View of the commercial port of Boston in about 1730

1691 William and Mary grant new charter to Massachusetts Colony

Execution for witchcraft at Salem in 1692

1763 France cedes control of Canada and the West

| 1690 | 1710 | 1730 | 1750 |

1692 Women in Salem accused of witchcraft

1754 French and Indian Wars between the French and the British begin

1689 Colonists oust Governor Andros

Revolutionary Boston

It was in Boston, the most important city in the 13 British colonies, that ideas for independence were nurtured and the American Revolution born. The colonists' main quarrel with Britain lay in taxation. The Stamp Act of 1765, and the later Townshend Acts, which placed duties on imports, inflamed colonists because they had no vote. "No taxation without representation" became a common cry. The so-called "Sons of Liberty," led by Samuel Adams, demanded and received the repeal of the Stamp Act. However, attempts to enforce the Townshend Acts led to the Boston Massacre, a tragedy which signaled increasingly poor relations between Britain and its colonies.

Samuel Adams

The Boston Tea Party (1773)
In protest at taxation, Boston patriots boarded three British East India Company ships and threw their cargoes of tea into Boston Harbor (see p75).

THE BOSTON MASSACRE (1770)
At the time of the Townshend Acts, British troops were sent to Boston to protect customs commissioners. Bostonians often scoffed at the soldiers and threw stones. On March 5, 1770 the jeering got out of hand. Shots were fired and five Americans fell.

Old State House (see pp60–61)

Five Americans were killed when British troops shot into the crowd.

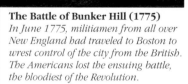

The Battle of Bunker Hill (1775)
In June 1775, militiamen from all over New England had traveled to Boston to wrest control of the city from the British. The Americans lost the ensuing battle, the bloodiest of the Revolution.

TIMELINE

1765 British Parliament passes the Stamp Act

British Revenue stamp

1773 Tea Act gives British East India Company monopoly. Boston Tea Party

1765

1770

1767 Townshend Acts place duties on imports

1766 Repeal of the Stamp Act

1770 Five Americans killed in Boston Massacre

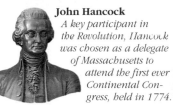

Evacuation of Boston 1776
Following the Battle of Bunker Hill, Boston remained under British control. For almost a year American troops lay siege to the city, until in March 1776 George Washington master-minded a strategy that led the British finally to evacuate.

John Hancock
A key participant in the Revolution, Hancock was chosen as a delegate of Massachusetts to attend the first ever Continental Congress, held in 1774.

British soldiers were sent to protect customs commissioners.

Declaration of Independence (1776)
Events surrounding the Battle of Bunker Hill and the evacuation of Boston inspired insurrection throughout the 13 colonies. This led, in July 1776, to the signing of the Declaration of Independence. Freedom from Britain finally came in 1781.

PAUL REVERE'S RIDE

On April 18, 1775 the British planned to march to Lexington to capture Samuel Adams and John Hancock, and then on to Concord to seize arms. To warn of the arrival of British troops, sexton Robert Newman hung lanterns in the tower of the Old North Church (*see p71*) and, so legend has it, Paul Revere undertook his "midnight ride." Revere's ride is immortalized in Longfellow's epic 1863 poem *Tales of a Wayside Inn*. During the ensuing skirmish at Lexington Green, eight American militiamen were killed – the first battle of the American Revolution had been fought.

Warning lights in the Old North Church

1774 Intolerable Acts passed; Boston Harbor is closed

1776 Siege of Boston ends. Declaration of Independence adopted by Continental Congress

1781 General Cornwallis surrenders at Yorktown, Virginia

1775

1780

1775 Midnight ride of Paul Revere

1777 U.S. victory at Battle of Saratoga is the turning point of the war

Grand Union, America's first national flag

1783 U.S. and Britain sign Treaty of Paris

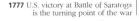

ATHENS OF AMERICA

With the end of the Revolutionary War, Boston's population began to grow and its economy flourish. Its port boomed, and trade, with China in particular, flourished. Some Bostonians made their fortunes at sea; others started profitable textile mills. A number of old Boston families – the Cabots, the Lowells, the Lodges – rose to great prominence boasting of their lineage, their wealth, and their Yankee independence. The United States elected not one but two members of the Adams family (both Boston residents) to the presidency: John Adams (1797–1801) and his son John Quincy Adams (1825–1829). John Adams' wife Abigail, one of the nation's most revered first ladies, made an early call for women's rights when she admonished her husband to "remember the Ladies," for "we …will not hold ourselves bound by any law in which we have no voice, or representation."

Abigail Smith Adams (1744–1818)

Boston soon earned a reputation as the intellectual capital of the new United States. The Boston Athenaeum (*see p49*), both a museum and library, was first organized in 1807 "for the promotion of literary and scientific learning." Eminent Bostonians (*see pp30–31*) at this time included the essayist Ralph Waldo Emerson, who formed the Transcendental Club, naturalist Henry David Thoreau, novelist Nathaniel Hawthorne, poet Henry Wadsworth Longfellow, whose epic poem made famous the midnight ride of Paul Revere (*see p21*), James Russell Lowell, the first editor of the *Atlantic Monthly*, and poet, diarist and educational reformer Oliver Wendell Holmes (*see p45*) . The Boston Public Library, the oldest free library in the U.S., was founded in 1852.

Initially most of Boston's European settlers came from England, but from 1846 Boston attracted thousands of immigrants driven out of Ireland by the potato famine. When the Irish first arrived they settled in overcrowded tenements along the city's waterfront and faced discrimination from the city's residents, especially its social elite, the Boston Brahmins (*see p45*). Signs went up

The Boston Athenaeum, first organized in 1807 but later housed in this building, which was designed in 1846

TIMELINE

George Washington (1732–99)

1787 Constitutional Convention held in Philadelphia

1789 Inauguration of George Washington as president

1786 Daniel Shay's rebellion

1796 John Adams elected as second president

1800

1812 War with England

1807 Boston Athenaeum is founded

1820

1825 William Ellery Channing founds American Unitarian Association

Irish immigrants, who poured into mid 19th-century Boston

around the city with the words "No Irish Need Apply." But despite these obstacles, the Irish rose in stature and by the end of the 19th century would dominate Boston politics and other areas of the city's life.

THE ABOLITION MOVEMENT

Some of America's most vehement anti-slavery sentiment originated in Boston. William Lloyd Garrison *(see p30)* published the first issue of *The Liberator* on January 1, 1831 calling for the unconditional abolition of slavery: "I will not equivocate ... I will not excuse ... I will not retreat a single inch ... and I will be heard." Not all Bostonians sympathized with his cause. To escape from angry mobs he once had to seek safety for the night in a Boston jail. Garrison and other abolitionists (Charles Sumner, Wendell Phillips, Frederick Douglass) gave rousing anti-slavery speeches in Faneuil Hall *(see p63)*, and accounts of their fiery oratory spread across the United States. The city also played an active role in the underground railroad. Fugitive slaves were assured a safe haven,

and popular stopping-off points were the Second African Meeting House, the home of Lewis Hayden (a former slave), and John J. Smith's barbershop on the corner of Howard and Bulfinch Streets. When the first shots of the Civil War were fired on Fort Sumter on April 12, 1861, President Abraham Lincoln immediately asked volunteers to enlist. The state of Massachusetts answered the call first, sending 1,500 men within four days. As soon as African Americans were admitted to the Union forces, black soldiers started training in Boston. The Boston Brahmin, Colonel Robert Gould Shaw *(see p30)* led these men (the 54th Regiment of the Massachusetts Volunteer Infantry) in an assault on Fort Wagner, South Carolina – Shaw and 62 members of the regiment lost their lives. The battle is still remembered for the role played by African Americans, and a monument *(see p47)* to it on Boston Common was dedicated on May 31, 1897.

Attack on Fort Wagner by black soldiers of the 54th Massachusetts

1846 First influx of Irish immigrants into Boston	**1852** Boston Public Library founded	**1861** First shots at Fort Sumter begin Civil War
1840		**1860**
1831 First issue of William Lloyd Garrison's abolitionist newspaper, *The Liberator*	*Mural in the Boston Public Library*	**1863** The 54th Massachusetts leads assault on Fort Wagner
		1865 General Robert E. Lee surrenders. The Union is preserved. President Abraham Lincoln is assassinated

GROWTH AND DESTRUCTION

The end of the Civil War in 1865 led to a decline in shipping, but the Industrial Revolution, specifically in cotton and wool manufacturing, enabled Boston to thrive again and grow both in size and population. The Back Bay had been filled and some of the neighboring towns already annexed. However, on November 9, 1872, Boston suffered a terrible setback as flames from a fire that started in a dry goods store spread to warehouses downtown,

The Great Fire of Boston, November 9, 1872

destroying 765 buildings. Newspaper headlines declared a loss of $250 million with "rich men beggared in a day." The city recovered quickly, though, rebuilding and revitalizing textile and shoe manufacturing.

Public institutions also continued to flourish. The Museum of Fine Arts *(see pp104–7)* was opened in 1876, and the Boston Symphony Orchestra *(see p160)* founded in 1881. The first subway in the United States, the "T," opened in 1897. In Boston and the surrounding areas educational establishments such as Harvard, Radcliffe, the Massachusetts Institute of Technology (M.I.T.), the New England Conservatory of Music, and Boston University all played their part in making the city a mecca for young students. The renowned collector of art Isabella Stewart Gardner *(see p103)*, a rich, famously outspoken, and well-connected woman, opened her house to the public on New Year's Day, 1903.

THE EARLY 20TH CENTURY

Following World War I, changing political and cultural attitudes across the U.S. increasingly left government clashing violently with the wishes of the people. Life in Boston was no exception. The Boston Police Strike of 1919 marks one of the most dramatic chapters in the U.S. Labor movement. As many as 1,290 policemen filed complaints over low wages, unsanitary stations, and lack of overtime compensation and sought affiliation with the American Federation of Labor (A.F.L.). When the strike started, mobs smashed windows and looted stores. After a skirmish with state militia, in which two were wounded and nine killed, A.F.L. president Samuel Gompers persuaded the police to return to work.

However, this was not just a time of conflict, but also

Harvard University students rowing on the Charles River, 1896

TIMELINE

Museum of Fine Arts exhibit

1872 The Great Fire of Boston

1876 Museum of Fine Arts opened

1881 Boston Symphony Orchestra formed

1884 First Irish mayor, Hugh O'Brien, elected

1897 The "T," the U.S.'s first subway, opens.

1905 "Honey Fitz" elected mayor

1903 Isabella Stewart Gardner opens her house to the public

1912 Fenway Park opens

1914 James Michael Curley elected mayor for the first time

1919 Boston Police Strike results in riots

1875	1900	1925

one when popular culture came to the fore. One way this manifested itself was in spectator sports, which began to enjoy unparalleled popularity. Fenway Park in Boston, home to the Boston Red Sox, had opened on April 20, 1912. The Boston Red Sox won the World Series four times before 1918. Supposedly cursed by the sale of slugger Babe Ruth to the New York Yankees, they did not win the World Series again until 2004.

Prominent politicians from this time included John F. Kennedy's grandfather, John F. Fitzgerald, or "Honey Fitz," as he was known, who was elected mayor in 1905. The flamboyant James Curley, son of Irish immigrants, who became mayor, congressman, and governor, and spent time in jail for fraud, became a legend in his own lifetime.

Babe Ruth (1895–1948) in an ad for chewing gum

John F. Kennedy, perhaps the most famous of all American politicians, born of Boston Irish stock

CITY RENAISSANCE

In the late 20th and early 21st centuries, Boston built a prosperous economy based on finance, medicine, and higher education, revitalizing the city's cultural life and gentrifying historic neighborhoods. In 2004 the Boston Red Sox broke their curse and won baseball's World Series, transforming Boston's ethos from resignation to aspiration. The Big Dig – a 20-year, $15-billion project to bury the I-93 highway – finally ended in 2005, providing new tunnels and bridges.

POST-WAR POLITICS

The most famous Boston-born politician was John F. Kennedy, the great-grandson of an Irish potato famine immigrant. In 1960 he became the U.S.'s first Catholic, and youngest elected, president. His brother, Robert, served as attorney general and U.S. senator for New York. The Irish, however, were not the only immigrants to enter politics. Michael Dukakis, the son of Greek immigrants, was elected governor in 1974, becoming Democratic presidential candidate in 1988.

The late 20th century saw extensive immigration from the Caribbean, Southeast Asia, Pakistan, and India, adding new talents and cultural traditions to city life.

Spending leisure time in boats on the Charles River, evidence that Boston is prospering

1960 John F. Kennedy elected president

1988 Governor Michael Dukakis becomes Democratic presidential candidate

1993 John F. Kennedy Library and Museum (*see p102*) opens

2006 Deval Patrick elected as first African-American governor of Massachusetts

1950   1975   2000

1962 Edward Kennedy elected to U.S. Senate

1963 John F. Kennedy assassinated

Michael Dukakis, Democratic presidential candidate in 1988

2004 Red Sox win World Series

2010 Scheduled completion of the new American Wing Museum of Fine Arts (*see p104*)

BOSTON AT A GLANCE

Although it is a small, compact city, Boston offers a wealth of attractions that draw visitors from all over the world. Indeed the range of attractions can exceed that of much larger cities in the U.S. The sights in the center and a little way out of Boston are covered in the *Area by Area* section of the book. There are historic neighborhoods, such as Beacon Hill and Back Bay; examples of some of the best Federal architecture in the U.S., such as the Massachusetts State House; and beautiful examples of late 19th-century opulence such as Trinity Church. The treasures of the Museum of Fine Arts and the Harvard Museums are also shown. A selection of Boston's best is featured below.

BOSTON'S TOP TEN ATTRACTIONS

Beacon Hill
See pp42–5

Old State House
See pp60–61

Massachusetts State House
See pp50–51

Museum of Fine Arts *See pp104–7*

New England Aquarium
See pp76–7

John Hancock Tower
See p97

Trinity Church
See pp94–5

Old North Church
See p71

Harvard
See pp110–14

Boston Common
See pp46–7

◁ Trinity Church, reflected in the John Hancock Tower

Boston's Best: Museums

The city of Boston's Athenian self-image is manifested in dozens of museums, galleries, and archives. Wealthy 19th-century patrons stocked art museums that have now become world-class collections, the best example being the Museum of Fine Arts. Likewise, Boston's leadership in scientific inquiry has created first-rate natural history and science collections. Museums such as the John F. Kennedy Library and Museum provide insight into some of the city's most compelling and influential historical figures, while a strong architectural heritage means that some of the museum buildings are also very beautiful.

Museum of Science
A favorite family destination, this museum has more than 550 interactive exhibits, that explain the laws of nature and the science of computers.

Harvard University Museums
These museums house a diverse range of collections: European Art, archaeology, natural history, and Asian and Near Eastern Art. The Sackler Museum (right) displays highlights of the art collection.

Isabella Stewart Gardner Museum
This Venetian-style palazzo stands as Isabella Gardner left it – filled to the brim with fine old masters and modern paintings. Her taste in art was considered by many to be impeccable.

Museum of Fine Arts
One of the largest museums in North America, the MFA is famous for its Greek, Roman, and Egyptian art, and French Impressionist paintings.

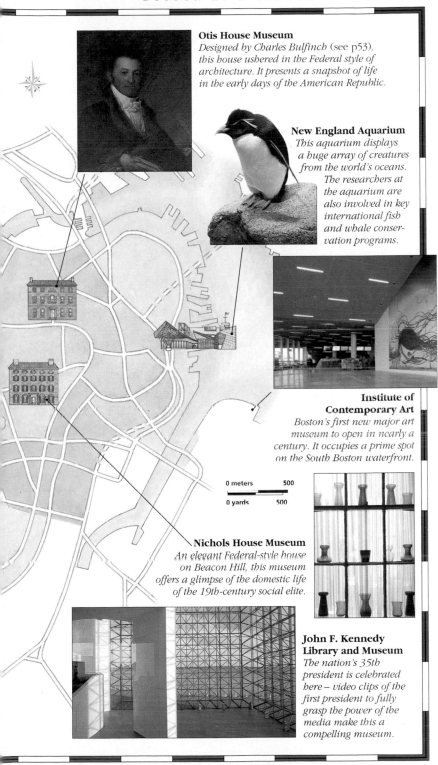

Otis House Museum
*Designed by Charles Bulfinch (see p53),
this house ushered in the Federal style of
architecture. It presents a snapshot of life
in the early days of the American Republic.*

New England Aquarium
*This aquarium displays
a huge array of creatures
from the world's oceans.
The researchers at
the aquarium are
also involved in key
international fish
and whale conser-
vation programs.*

**Institute of
Contemporary Art**
*Boston's first new major art
museum to open in nearly a
century. It occupies a prime spot
on the South Boston waterfront.*

0 meters   500
0 yards   500

Nichols House Museum
*An elegant Federal-style house
on Beacon Hill, this museum
offers a glimpse of the domestic life
of the 19th-century social elite.*

**John F. Kennedy
Library and Museum**
*The nation's 35th
president is celebrated
here – video clips of the
first president to fully
grasp the power of the
media make this a
compelling museum.*

Eminent Bostonians

Phillis Wheatley (1753–84)

Founded as a refuge for religious idealists, Boston has always been obsessed with ideas and learning. Mark Twain once observed that "In New York they ask what a man is worth. In Boston they ask, 'What does he know?'" This insistence on the power of ideas has made Boston a magnet for thinkers and doers, and a hotbed of reform movements and social revolution. Education has always been one of the city's leading industries. Consequently, Boston is disproportionately represented in the honor roll of American intellectual life. Bostonians are generally considered to be liberal minded, and tend to occupy the left flank of American political thought.

Malcolm X (1925–65), one of Boston's many famous residents

REFORMERS, RABBLE ROUSERS, AND REVOLUTIONARIES

Even while Boston was still in its infancy, Bostonians began to agitate to do things differently. Anne Hutchinson (1591–1643) was exiled for heresy in 1638 (she moved south to found Portsmouth, Rhode Island), while friend and fellow religious radical Mary Dyer died on the Boston Common gallows for Quakerism in 1660 *(see p19)* . Spokesman for the Sons of Liberty and part-time brewer Samuel Adams (1722–1803) incited Boston to revolution in the "Boston Tea Party" *(see p75)*. The city bubbled

Abolitionist William Lloyd Garrison (1805–79)

over with 19th-century reformers, including Dorothea Dix (1802–87), who championed the welfare of the mentally ill, and William Lloyd Garrison (1805–79), publisher of *The Liberator*, who was one of America's most strident voices calling for the abolition of slavery. Malcolm Little (1925–65) spent his adolescence in Boston before converting to Islam in prison and emerging as the charismatic Black Muslim leader Malcolm X. Like Malcolm X, Nguyen Tat Thanh (1890–1969) spent part of his youth in Boston, working for a time in the restaurant of the Omni Parker House Hotel *(see p58)*. Traveling much of the world in his 20s, he was later to assume the name Ho Chi Minh.

BOSTON BRAHMINS

In 1860 Oliver Wendell Holmes (1809–94) dubbed Boston's prosperous merchant class the "Boston Brahmins … a harmless, inoffensive, untitled aristocracy" *(see p45)*. Any suggestion that the Brahmins were unaccomplished, however, could not be farther from the truth. Julia Ward Howe (1819–1910) was a prominent abolitionist and later a crusader for women's rights. She also penned the Unionists' Civil War marching song, "The Battle Hymn of the Republic." Brahmin Colonel Robert Gould Shaw (1837–63) led the all-Black 54th Massachusetts Regiment in the Civil War, and Major Henry Lee Higginson (1834–1919) survived the war to found the Boston Symphony Orchestra in 1881.

Many famous authors were also Brahmins, notably the Lowell clan: James Russell Lowell (1819–91) was the leading literary critic of his day, Amy Lowell (1874–1925) championed "free verse" and founded *Poetry* magazine, and Robert Lowell (1917–77) broke the barriers between formal and informal verse in American poetry. The Brahmins' greatest chronicler was the noted historian Samuel Eliot Morison (1887–1976).

The Brahmins persist through business partnerships, family trusts, and intermarriage, as highlighted in their ditty: "And this is good old Boston, The home of the bean and the cod, Where the Lowells talk to the Cabots, And the Cabots talk only to God."

INVENTORS AND ENTREPRENEURS

Innovation has always been a way of life in Boston. Donald McKay's (1810–80) East Boston clipper ships revolutionized international sea trade in the 1850s. Working in his Cambridge

Edwin Land (1909–91), inventor of Polaroid instant photography

workshop, Elias Howe (1819–67) created the modern sewing machine, radically altering both the clothing trade and the shoe industry. Alexander Graham Bell (1847–1922) had offices in Cambridge and Boston, and later joined the faculty of Boston University. This was part of a trend of academic affiliation that became almost the rule for Boston's inventors. Edwin H. Land (1909–91) experimented with polarized light in his Harvard lab before inventing Polaroid instant photography. The innovators Bolt, Beranek, and Newman also made academic affiliations with the Massachusetts Institute of Technology, and they also sent the world's first electronic mail message in the 1970s.

THINKERS

In addition to showing the world how to do things, Bostonians have always been adept at explaining why. In his many essays and poems, Ralph Waldo Emerson (1803–82) first laid the philosophical groundwork for an American school of transcendental religious thought. Meanwhile, his friend and fellow Harvard graduate Henry David Thoreau (1817–62) wrote many seminal works of natural philosophy. A professor at Harvard, William James (1842–1910) not only taught psychology and physiology, but also promulgated philosophical pragmatism, the concept that the worth of an idea is based on its usefulness. His student, George Santayana (1863–1952) blossomed as the 20th-century's chief philosopher of aesthetics.

More pragmatically, the Harvard economist John Kenneth Galbraith (1908–2006) investigated the sources of societal affluence and advocated social policies to put that affluence to work for the common good.

POLITICAL LEADERS

Boston's most infamous politician was the "rascal king" James Michael Curley (1874–1958), who served many terms as mayor and U.S. Congressman, winning his last election from a jail cell. His life was to serve as the model for the novel *The Last Hurrah*. Boston also gave the country four presidents: John Adams (1735–1826) and his son John Quincy Adams (1767–1848); the tight-lipped ex-governor Calvin Coolidge (1872–1933), who rose to prominence by crushing the Boston police strike in 1919; and John F. Kennedy, infamously assassinated in Dallas in 1963. Kennedy's brothers were also prominent on the national stage: Robert F. Kennedy (1925–1968) served as attorney general and then as senator, when he, too, was assassinated. Edward M. Kennedy (born 1932) continues to serve as the senior warhorse for social justice in the U.S. Senate. His good friend, Thomas P. "Tip" O'Neill (1912–94), served as U.S. Speaker of the House.

John F. Kennedy campaign button

AUTHORS

America's first published author was Boston's Anne Bradstreet (1612–72). The first published African American author was Phillis Wheatley (1753–84), born in Africa, enslaved, then freed in Boston. Her 1778 volume, *Poems on Various Subjects, Religious and Moral*, echoed Boston authors' moral concerns. Henry Wadsworth Longfellow (1807–82) made his fortune from best-selling verse epics such as *Evangeline* and *Hiawatha*, but made his mark translating Dante. Although associated with nearby Concord, popular novelist Louisa May Alcott (1832–88) also lived on Beacon Hill and was active in Boston reform movements. New York-born Henry James (1843–1916) was educated at Harvard and often returned to Boston from his London home, spending a lifetime contrasting American and European culture. Nobel laureate poet and playwright Derek Walcott (born 1930) teaches at Boston University, as does the former U.S. poet laureate Robert Pinsky (born 1940). The popular Boston-based fictional detective Spenser is the creation of Robert Parker (born 1932), and when not hanging out with Clint Eastwood, novelist Dennis Lehane (born 1966) broods at Fort Point Channel.

Author Louisa May Alcott (1832–88), part of Boston's reform movement

Boston's Architecture

Buildings followed British styles through the 1790s, when the first American architect of note, Charles Bulfinch, defined the Federal style. In the 19th century, Bostonians evolved a local Victorian style, which first embraced Greek Classicism, then French and Italian styles. Two styles of the late 19th century, Renaissance Revival and Richardsonian Romanesque, remained influential through World War I. In the 20th century, Harvard University and Massachusetts Institute of Technology (M.I.T.) attracted many leading modern and post-modern architects, all of whom left their mark.

Renaissance Revival interior of the Boston Public Library

Freestanding Federal-style Harrison Gray Otis House

FEDERAL

Charles Bulfinch and his protégé Asher Benjamin adapted British Georgian styles to create Boston's first signature architectural style. Typical of this style are freestanding mansions and town houses, with symmetrical brick façades adorned by shuttered windows, and ground-floor windows set in recessed arches. Entrances are often cut from granite slabs, featuring gently fluted columns. The largest and most elegant rooms of Federal homes are usually found on the second floor.

Some of the grander examples of Federal domestic architecture, found mainly on Beacon Hill, feature ornamental ironwork and are often crowned with octagonal cupolas. Chestnut Street on Beacon Hill *(see pp42–3)* represents the greatest concentration of Federal-style row houses in Boston. Individual examples of the style include the Harrison Gray Otis House *(see p52)* and the Hepzibah Swan Houses *(see p45)*.

BOSTON GRANITE

The granite outcrops found around Boston Harbor provided stone for the city's waterfront development in the early 19th century. Technological advances had made it possible to cut entire columns from single blocks of granite. Freed from the constraints of soft limestone or sandstone, Alexander Parris and other architects adopted granite as a principal material for markets and warehouses, as can be seen for example at Charlestown Navy Yard *(see p115)* and Quincy Market *(see p64)*. Although the basic style is an adaptation of Greek Revival, it also includes modern innovations such as iron tension rods and laminated wooden ribs to support copper domes.

Granite Greek Revival façade of Quincy Market

Distinctive, multicolored, square tower of Trinity Church

RENAISSANCE REVIVAL

Charles McKim's 1887 design for the Boston Public Library *(see p96)*, conceived as a "palace of the people," established Renaissance Revival architecture as a favorite American style for monumental public structures. Evenly spaced windows and arches, adorned by inscriptions and sculptural details, define the style. Soaring, barrel vaulted interiors are also featured. Boston's Renaissance Revival structures make extensive use of New England and Italian marbles, carved stucco ceilings, and carved wood in staircases and walls. Many of the Italian artisans who were brought over to execute this work stayed in Boston, forming an elite group within the Italian immigrant community by around 1900.

RICHARDSONIAN ROMANESQUE

America is far too young to boast a true Romanesque style, but Henry Hobson Richardson effectively created one from European inspirations and American stone. By the 1870s, the wealthy city of Boston demanded more elaborate churches than the existing sparsely designed "boxes with a spire." Gothic styles, however, were associated with medieval Catholicism and were unacceptable to the Protestant heirs of the Puritans. Richardson's churches provided a pleasing alternative. Often, the building's main components were massed around a central tower, as can be seen in Boston's most important example of the style, Trinity Church (see pp94–5), as well as in the First Baptist Church (see p92). In sharp contrast to the Boston Granite style, which used many similar materials and sharp angles, Richardson used stones of contrasting colors and rounded off virtually every square edge.

Romanesque-style front portico of the First Baptist Church

VICTORIAN

Boston's Victorian style largely eschews the pointed Gothic lines of English Victorian in favor of French Academic, French Empire, and various Italianate influences. The variations are displayed in an almost chronological march of styles in the Back Bay and South End (see pp88–9), paralleling the decade-by-decade creation of filled land in those neighborhoods in the second half of the 19th century. Earlier buildings tend to reflect their stylistic influences more accurately; for example, the Italianate Gibson House Museum (see p92) on Beacon Street, which would have been among the first wave of Back Bay development. The later town houses of

Italianate interior detail of the Victorian Gibson House Museum

upper Newbury Street and Massachusetts Avenue reflect a more mature synthesis: raised granite entrances, slate-shingled mansard roofs, and dormer and bay windows. Nowhere is the transition from early to late Victorian styles so evident than on the walk westward, from the center of Boston, along Commonwealth Avenue (see p93).

ART DECO

Most of Boston's Art Deco buildings are clustered around Post Office Square in the Financial District, with the former Post Office (see p65) and the Verizon Building (see p65) being the finest examples. Essentially tall buildings of light gray granite, they are constructed with vertical strips and slit windows that elongate their forms. Elaborate geometric steps and surface ornament on the upper stories help

Art Deco exterior of the the Verizon Building, overlooking Post Office Square

relieve their mass. Boston Art Deco tends also to make great use of Greco-Roman geometric friezes and stylized, vegetable-inspired ornament. Some Financial District Art Deco buildings also feature bas-relief murals of historic and heroic themes. Back Bay was once the site of many Art Deco storefronts with stylized Parisian pilasters and grill-work, but only the former quarters of Shreve, Crump & Low Inc. on Boylston Street (see p96) remain intact.

Modernist interior of the Kresge Chapel, built in the 1950s

MODERNISM

The willing embrace of Modernism at Boston and Cambridge colleges has graced the Boston area with a wide range of outstanding 20th-century buildings where simplicity of form is favored over ornament, and expressive lines grow out of function. When Bauhaus director Walter Gropius fled the Nazis for the safety of Harvard University, he served as a magnet for some of the mid-century's great designers and architects. The range of styles in Boston's Modernist buildings is diverse: the poetic sculptural grace of Eero Saarinen's Kresge Auditorium and Chapel at M.I.T. (see p109); Le Corbusier's Carpenter Center for the Visual Arts (see p111); and Josep Lluis Sert's International-style Holyoke Center, both near Harvard Yard (see pp110–11).

BOSTON THROUGH THE YEAR

Perhaps more than in any other city in the U.S., Boston's cultural life tends to follow the academic calendar, with the "year" beginning when classes commence at its many colleges and universities in September, and winding down a little with the start of the summer recess in May and June. In between is so-called "ice cream" season, when the warm weather causes most activities to shift out of doors, and reading lists favor

fiction over more scholarly texts. Though the cultural life of the city tends to flourish from fall to spring, the summer months do feature many of Boston's major carnivals, festivals, parades, and free outdoor concerts at the Hatch Shell *(see p92)* . After the students' return to their studies in the fall, the busy performing arts season begins, with symphony concerts, theater, and ballet continuing into the following spring.

Model of a saint, North End Italian Feast Days

Springtime tulips in full bloom, Boston Public Garden

SPRING

When the weather warms, Boston bursts into bloom. Thousands of tulips explode in the Public Garden, and the magnolia trees of Commonwealth Avenue are sheathed in pink and white. Spring is a season of remembrance, with commemorations of events leading up to the American Revolution. It also marks the start of the season for the Boston Red Sox.

MARCH

Reenactment of Boston Massacre *(early Mar)*, Old State House. Marks watershed event that turned Bostonians against their British rulers.
New England Spring Flower Show *(mid-Mar)*, Bayside Expo Center. Oldest annual flower exhibition in the United States.
St. Patrick's Day Parade

(mid-Mar), South Boston. Annual parade also commemorates the British evacuation of Boston during the Revolutionary War.

APRIL

Baseball *(first week)*, Fenway Park. Major league season starts for Boston Red Sox.
Annual Lantern Celebration *(Patriots Day Eve)*, Old North Church. Commemorates hanging signal lanterns in the steeple to warn revolutionaries.
Patriots Day Parade *(third Mon)*, from City Hall Plaza to Paul Revere Mall, where the start of Paul Revere's Midnight Ride is reenacted.
Boston Marathon *(third Mon)*, Hopkinton to Back Bay. America's oldest marathon.

MAY

May Fair *(first Sat)*, Harvard Square. International street fair.
Walk for Hunger *(first Sun)*, 20-mile (32-km) walk, one of

the oldest and largest pledge walks in the country, raises funds for food banks.
Duckling Day Parade *(second Sun)*, Boston Common. Parade retracing the route of the ducklings in Robert McCloskey's classic children's storybook, *Make Way for Ducklings*.
Arts First *(early May)*, Cambridge. More than 200 free performances of music, theater, and dance – all on Harvard campus.
Hidden Gardens of Beacon Hill *(third Thu)*, Beacon Hill. Garden tours organized.
Lilac Sunday *(third Sun)*, Arnold Arboretum. More than 400 lilac bushes are in bloom.
Street Performers Festival *(late May)*, Faneuil Hall Marketplace. Street musicians, jugglers, acrobats and other performers.
Boston Pops *(May–Jun)*, Symphony Hall. Season features light Classical repertory and American popular music.

Runners at the finish of the annual Boston Marathon, held in April

AVERAGE DAILY HOURS OF SUNSHINE IN BOSTON

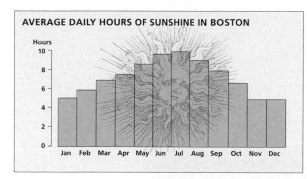

Hours

| 10 | 8 | 6 | 4 | 2 | 0 |

Jan Feb Mar Apr May Jun Jul Aug Sep Oct Nov Dec

Sunshine Chart
This chart shows the average daily number of hours of sunshine in Boston each month. The city enjoys long and light summer days from June to August, with July being the sunniest month. Fall has more sunshine than spring, but while spring is mild, fall becomes quite chilly. Winter days are shorter, but many are still clear and bright.

SUMMER

When summer's heat finally arrives, Bostonians head outdoors to relax on the grassy banks of the Charles River, along the harbor, and in the city's many parks. The Hatch Shell on the Esplanade becomes the scene of many free open-air concerts. The grandest celebration occurs on the Fourth of July, with one of the country's greatest fireworks displays, following an invariably rousing performance by the Boston Pops Orchestra.

Fourth of July fireworks lighting up the sky over the Charles River

Summer outdoor concert at Hatch Shell, Charles River Esplanade

JUNE

Performing Arts Series at the Hatch Shell *(Wed & Fri–Sun, Jun–Sep)*, Hatch Shell, Esplanade. Free outdoor movies, and pop, rock and classical concerts.
Boston International Film Festival *(early Jun)*. Nine days of film screenings, personal appearances, and awards.
Scooper Bowl *(early Jun)*, City Hall Plaza. One of the largest ice cream festivals in the U.S.
Bunker Hill Weekend *(weekend before Jun 17)*,

Charlestown. Costumed reenactments, demonstrations, a parade, and guided tours at Bunker Hill Monument.
Dragon Boat Festival *(mid-Jun)*, Charles River. Traditional, Asian dragon boat races.
Cambridge River Festival *(mid-Jun)*. Multicultural festival on the banks of the Charles River.

JULY

Italian Feast Days *(Jul–Aug)*, North End. Religious processions with music and food take place almost every weekend.
Boston Harborfest *(week of Jul 4)*. Features children's events, concerts, harbor cruises, and a Chowderfest on City Hall Plaza.
Boston Pops Annual Fourth of July Concert and Fireworks *(Jul 4)*, Esplanade. The largest of the free Boston Pops concerts in July.
Bastille Day *(Fri before Jul 14)*, Back Bay. Annual celebration sponsored by the French Library of Boston.

Annual Festival Betances *(late Jul)*, South End. Annual Puerto Rican festival with music, dance, and food.

AUGUST

August Moon Festival *(mid-Aug)*, Chinatown. Lion dance, martial arts, Chinese opera.
Boston Restaurant Week *(late Aug)*, Boston and Cambridge. More than 80 restaurants offer low fixed-price lunch and dinner menus.
Boston Caribbean Carnival *(third weekend)*, Franklin Park. Extravagant costumes, music, food, and dancing.

July 4th parade, Government Center

AVERAGE MONTHLY TEMPERATURE

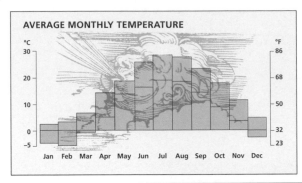

°C
30
20
10
0
-5

°F
86
68
50
32
23

Jan Feb Mar Apr May Jun Jul Aug Sep Oct Nov Dec

Temperature Chart
This chart shows the average minimum and maximum temperatures for each month in Boston. The highest temperatures of the year are in July and August, when it is hot and humid. Winters are cold, and while they can be clear and bright, they are also often stormy, resulting in wind-chill temperatures well below freezing point.

FALL

After Labor Day, Boston's massive student community returns. This time also sees the start of seasons for the performing arts and for basketball and hockey. The vivid colors of New England's deciduous fall trees attract thousands of people to Boston, on their way to backcountry tours. Mid-November brings cold weather and the beginning of the holiday season.

SEPTEMBER

Boston Fashion Week *(mid-Sep)*, city-wide. Variety of events showcase Boston's established couturiers and rising fashionistas.
Feast of Saints Cosma & Damiano *(second weekend)*, East Cambridge. Italian festival with parade.
Boston Blues Festival *(late Sep)*. Musicians emerge from cozy bars and nightclubs around the city to perform along the banks of the Charles River.
BeanTown Jazz Festival *(late Sep)*, South End event

Famous fiery colors of New England's fall foliage

features contemporary jazz, blues, and salsa.
Boston Open Studios *(Sep–early Dec)*. Art communities in Boston, including Fort Point and the South End, schedule studio tours.

OCTOBER

Boston Symphony Orchestra Season *(Oct–Apr)*. Orchestra performs in historic Symphony Hall.
Basketball *(Oct–Apr)*, TD BankNorth Garden. NBA (National Basketball Association) season begins for the Boston Celtics.
Hockey *(Oct–Apr)*, TD BankNorth Garden. NHL (National Hockey League) season begins for the Boston Bruins.
Columbus Day Parade *(early Oct)*, Parade alternates between East Boston (even years) and Downtown.
Boston Ballet Season *(mid-Oct–May)*, Opera House. Professional repertory company gives performances.

Head of the Charles Regatta *(second to last Weekend Oct)*, Cambridge. Rowing event featuring 1,400 boats and 3,000 athletes.
Ellis Memorial Antiques Show *(late Oct–early Nov)*, various locations.
Boston International Antiquarian Book Fair *(late Oct–early Nov)*, Hynes Convention Center. One of oldest and largest in the U.S.
Boston Jewish Film Festival *(late Oct–mid-Nov)*, contemporary films on Jewish themes, lectures, and discussions.

NOVEMBER

Ice Skating on Frog Pond *(mid-Nov–March)*, Boston Common.
Ski and Snowboard Expo *(mid-Nov)*, Bayside Expo. Sports enthusiasts prepare for the winter season.
Veterans Day Parade *(Nov 11)*, Downtown. Marching and high school bands, and veterans' groups honor all those who served in the armed forces.

Outdoor musical performance

AVERAGE MONTHLY PRECIPITATION

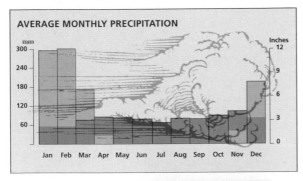

mm
300
240
180
120
60

Inches
12
9
6
3
0

Jan Feb Mar Apr May Jun Jul Aug Sep Oct Nov Dec

Rainfall Chart
This chart shows the average monthly rain and snowfall in Boston. Precipitation levels are fairly constant through- out the year, at around 3–4 inches (8–10 cm) per month. During the winter much of this falls as snow, which stays on the ground until March.

■ Rainfall (from baseline)

□ Snow (from baseline)

WINTER

Tree-lighting ceremonies and decorated store windows help make Boston's cityscape magical at Christmas. As the old year ends, the entire city, from downtown to the most remote neighborhoods, erupts with the joy of First Night, a worldwide institution launched in Boston. When the frigid weather arrives in mid-January, Bostonians get geared up to a busy season of performing arts and food and wine expositions.

DECEMBER

Crafts at the Castle *(first full weekend)*, Hynes Convention Center. Top-quality crafts exhibition rated by judges.
Reenactment of the Boston Tea Party *(mid-Dec)*. Begins at Old South Meeting House and proceeds to Boston Harbor, where this key historical event is replayed.

First Night ice sculpture

First Night *(Dec 31)*. The original city-wide New Year's Eve celebration, now an international phenomenon.

JANUARY

Chinese New Year *(late Jan to Mar depending on lunar calendar)*, China-town. Celebration includes parade, dragon dances, and firecrackers.
Boston Wine Expo *(late Jan–early Feb)*, World Trade Center. Two arduous days of international wine tastings and cooking demonstrations.

FEBRUARY

Beanpot Tournament *(mid-Feb)*, TD BankNorth Garden. Annual college hockey tourna-ment between Boston College, Boston University, North-eastern University, and Harvard University *(see pp110–11)*.
Longfellow Birthday Celebration, *(late Feb)*, Cambridge. Tours of Long-fellow House, poetry readings, and wreath-laying at the illustrious poet's grave.
Harvard's Hasty Pudding Club Parades *(variable)*, Cambridge. Outrageous Harvard theatrical club presents Man and Woman of the Year Awards to Hollywood celebri-ties after cross-dressing parades through Harvard Square.

PUBLIC HOLIDAYS

New Year's Day (Jan 1)
Martin Luther King Day (3rd Mon, Jan)
Presidents Day (mid-Feb)
Evacuation Day (Mar 17) (Boston only)
Patriots Day (3rd Mon, Apr) (Middlesex and Suffolk counties, including Boston and Cambridge)
Memorial Day (end May)
Bunker Hill Day (Jun 17) (Boston only)
Independence Day (Jul 4)
Labor Day (1st Mon, Sep)
Columbus Day (2nd Mon, Oct)
Veterans Day (Nov 11)
Thanksgiving (4th Thu, Nov)
Christmas Day (Dec 25)

Christmas lights on a snowy Boston Common in December

Aerial view of Boston and waterfront ▷

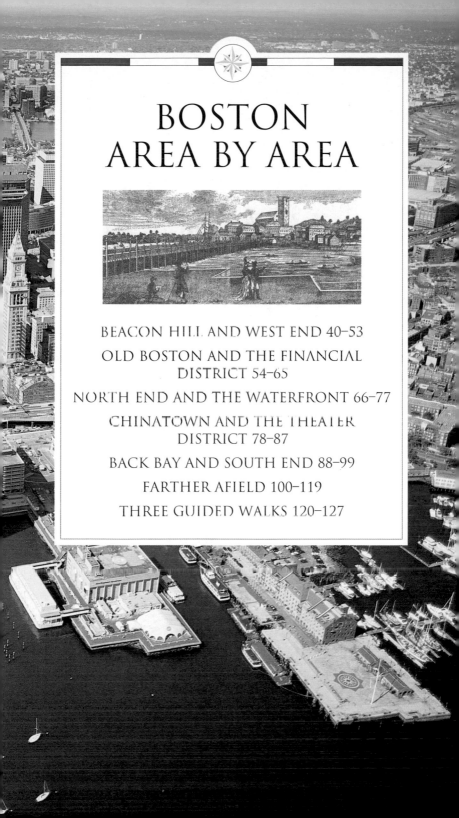

BOSTON
AREA BY AREA

BEACON HILL AND WEST END

Beacon Hill was developed from pastureland in the 1790s. The south slope, facing Boston Common, became the main seat of Boston wealth and power, while the north slope and the land rolling down to the mouth of the Charles River, known as the West End, became populated by tradesmen, servants, and free blacks. South-slope Beacon Hill

Stained glass, Massachusetts State House

retained its cachet into the late 19th century, while the north slope and West End degenerated. Urban renewal in the 1950s and 1960s cleared away the slums and coherent neighborhood of the West End, while gentrification of the north slope made even the most modest homes on Beacon Hill highly desirable, and this neighborhood one of Boston's most picturesque.

SIGHTS AT A GLANCE

Historic Streets and Squares
Beacon Street **6**
Charles Street **1**
Louisburg Square **2**
Mount Vernon Street **3**

Historic Buildings, Churches, and Museums
Boston Athenaeum **10**
Hepzibah Swan Houses **5**
Massachusetts General Hospital **15**
Massachusetts State House pp50–51 **11**
Museum of African American History **12**
Museum of Science and Science Park **16**
Nichols House Museum **4**
Old West Church **14**
Otis House Museum **13**
Park Street Church **8**

Parks and Cemeteries
Boston Common and Public Garden pp46–7 **7**
Old Granary Burying Ground **9**

GETTING THERE
This area is well served by public transportation. Park Street, Boylston, and Arlington "T" stations are closest to the main sights. The area is also served by Charles/ M.G.H. and Science Park. Buses 43 and 55 go to Boston Common.

0 meters   250
0 yards   250

KEY
▨ Street-by-street map *pp42–3*
Ⓣ "T" station
ℹ Tourist information

Street-by-Street: Beacon Hill

Lion door knocker, Beacon St.

From the 1790s to the 1870s, the south slope of Beacon Hill was Boston's most sought-after neighborhood – its wealthy elite decamped only when the more exclusive Back Bay *(see pp88–99)* was built. Many of the district's houses were designed by Charles Bulfinch *(see p53)* and his disciples, and the south slope evolved as a textbook example of Federal architecture. Elevation and view were all, and the finest homes are either on Boston Common or perched near the top of the hill. Early developers abided by a gentleman's agreement to set houses back from the street, but the economic depression of 1807–12 resulted in row houses being built right out to the street.

Cobbled street, once typical of Beacon Hill

PINCKNEY STREET

LOUISBURG SQUARE

MOUNT VERNON STREET

CEDAR STREET

CHARLES STREET

CHESTNUT STREET

Louisburg Square

The crowning glory of the Beacon Hill district, this square was developed in the 1830s. Today, it is still Boston's most desirable address ❷

Charles Street Meeting House was built in the early 19th century to house a congregation of Baptists.

KEY

– – – Suggested route

DE LUCA'S MARKET

"FRESHEST BY FAR SINCE 1905"

Back Bay and South End

★ Charles Street

This elegant street is the main shopping area for Beacon Hill. Lined with upscale grocers and antique stores, it also has some fine restaurants ❶

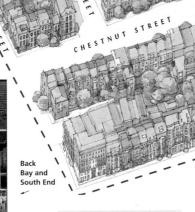

STAR SIGHTS

★ Charles Street

★ Nichols House Museum

★ **Nichols House Museum**
This modest museum offers an insight into the life of Beacon Hill resident Rose Nichols, who lived here from 1885 to 1960 ❹

LOCATOR MAP
See Street Finder map 1

| 0 meters | 50 |
| 0 yards | 50 |

Mount Vernon Street
Described in the 19th century as the "most civilized street in America," this is where the developers of Beacon Hill (the Mount Vernon Proprietors) chose to build their own homes ❸

WALNUT STREET

SPRUCE STREET

BEACON STREET

Massachusetts
State House

Boston
Common

Hepzibah Swan Houses
Elegant in their simplicity, these three Bulfinch-designed houses were wedding gifts for the daughters of a wealthy Beacon Hill proprietress ❺

Beacon Street
The finest houses on Beacon Hill were invariably built on Beacon Street. Elegant, Federal-style mansions, some with ornate reliefs, overlook the city's most beautiful green space, Boston Common ❻

Charles Street, lined with shops catering to the residents of Beacon Hill

Charles Street ❶

Map 1 B4. ⓉCharles/MGH.

This street originally ran along the bank of the Charles River, although subsequent landfill has removed it from the riverbank by several hundred feet. The main shopping and dining area of the Beacon Hill neighborhood, the curving line of Charles Street hugs the base of Beacon Hill, giving it a quaint, village-like air. Many of the houses remain residential on the upper stories, while street level and cellar levels were converted to commercial uses long ago. Though most of Charles Street dates from the 19th century, widening in the 1920s meant that some of the houses on the west side acquired new façades. The Charles Street Meeting House, designed by Asher Benjamin *(see p32)* in 1807, was built for a Baptist congregation that practiced immersion in the then adjacent river. It is now a commercial building. Two groups of striking Greek Revival row houses are situated at the top of

Charles Street, between Revere and Cambridge Streets. Charles Street was one of the birthplaces of the antique trade in the U.S. and now has some two dozen antique dealers.

Louisburg Square ❷

Map 1 B4. ⓉCharles/MGH, Park Street.

Home to millionaire politicians, best-selling authors, and corporate moguls, Louisburg Square is arguably Boston's most prestigious address. Developed in the 1830s as a shared private preserve on Beacon Hill, the square's tiny patch of greenery surrounded by a high iron fence sends a clear signal of the square's continued exclusivity. On the last private square in the city, the narrow Greek

Revival bow-fronted town houses sell for a premium over comparable homes elsewhere on Beacon Hill. Even the on-street parking spaces are deeded. The traditions of Christmas Eve carol singing and candlelit windows are said to have begun on Louisburg Square. A statue of Christopher Columbus, presented by a wealthy Greek merchant in 1850, stands at its center.

Mount Vernon Street ❸

Map 1 B4. ⓉCharles/MGH, Park Street.

In the 1890s the novelist Henry James *(see p31)* called Mount Vernon Street "the most civilized street in America," and it still retains that air of urbane culture. Most of the developers of Beacon Hill, who called themselves the Mount Vernon Proprietors, chose to build their private homes along this street. Architect Charles Bulfinch *(see p53)* envisioned Beacon Hill as a district of large freestanding mansions on spacious landscaped grounds, but building costs ultimately dictated much denser development. The sole remaining example of Bulfinch's vision is the second Harrison Gray Otis House, built in 1800 at No. 85. The current Greek Revival row houses next door (Nos. 59–83), graciously set back from the street by 30 ft (9 m), were built to replace the single mansion belonging to Otis's chief development partner, Jonathan Mason. The original mansion was torn down after Mason's death in 1836. The three Bulfinch-designed houses at Nos. 55, 57, and 59 Mount Vernon Street were built by Mason for his daughters. No. 55 was ultimately passed on to the Nichols family *(see p45)* in 1885.

Columbus Statue, Louisburg Square

OLIVER WENDELL HOLMES AND THE BOSTON BRAHMINS

In 1860, Oliver Wendell Holmes *(see p30)* wrote that Boston's wealthy merchant class of the time constituted a Brahmin caste, a "harmless, inoffensive, untitled aristocracy" with "their houses by Bulfinch, their monopoly on Beacon Street, their ancestral portraits and Chinese porcelains, humanitarianism, Unitarian faith in the march of the mind, Yankee shrewdness, and New England exclusiveness." So keenly did he skewer the social class that the term has persisted. In casual usage today, a Brahmin is someone with an old family name, whose finances derive largely from trust funds, and whose politics blend conservatism with *noblesse oblige* toward those less fortunate. Boston's Brahmins founded most of the hospitals, performing arts bodies and museums of the greater metropolitan area.

Oliver Wendell Holmes (1809–94)

Drawing room of the Bulfinch-designed Nichols House Museum

Nichols House Museum ❹

55 Mount Vernon St. **Map** 1 B4. ***Tel*** *(617) 227-6993.* [T] *Park Street.* 🕒 *Apr–Oct: noon–4pm Tue–Sat; Nov–Mar: noon–4pm Thu–Sat.* 💲 🚫📷 ♿
www.nicholshousemuseum.org

The Nichols House Museum was designed by Charles Bulfinch in 1804 and offers a rare glimpse into the tradition-bound lifestyle of Beacon Hill. Modernized in 1830 by the addition of a Greek Revival portico, the house is nevertheless a superb example of Bulfinch's domestic architecture. It also offers an insight into the life of a true Beacon Hill character. Rose Standish Nichols moved into the house aged 13 when her father purchased it in 1885. She left it as a museum in her will in 1960. A woman ahead of her time, strong-willed and famously hospitable, Nichols was, among other things, a self-styled landscape designer who traveled extensively around the world to write about gardens.

Hepzibah Swan Houses ❺

13, 15 & 17 Chestnut St. **Map** 1 B4. [T] *Park Street.* ● *to the public.*

The only woman who was ever a member of the Mount Vernon Proprietors *(see p44)*, Mrs. Swan had these houses built by Bulfinch as wedding presents for her daughters in 1806, 1807 and 1814. Some of the most elegant and distinguished houses on Chestnut Street, they are backed by Bulfinch-designed stables that face onto Mount Vernon Street. The deeds restrict the height of the stables to 13 ft (4 m) so that her daughters would still have a view over Mount Vernon Street. In 1863–65, No. 13 was home to Dr. Samuel Gridley Howe, abolitionist and educational pioneer who, in 1833, founded the first school for the blind in the U.S.

Beacon Street ❻

Map 1 B4. [T] *Park Street.*

Beacon Street is lined with urban mansions facing Boston Common. The 1808 **William Hickling Prescott House** at No. 55, designed by Asher Benjamin, offers tours of rooms decorated in Federal, Victorian, and Colonial Revival styles. The American Meteorological Society occupies No. 45, which was built as Harrison Gray Otis's last and finest house, with 11 bedrooms and an elliptical room behind the front parlor where the walls and doors are curved. The elite Somerset Club stands at Nos. 42–43 Beacon Street. In the 1920s to 1940s, Irish Catholic mayor James Michael Curley would lead election night victory marches to the State House, pausing at the Somerset to taunt the Boston Brahmins within. The Parkman House at No. 33 is now a city-owned meeting center. It was the home of Dr. George Parkman, who was murdered by Harvard professor and fellow socialite Dr. John Webster in 1849. Boston society was torn apart when Webster was sentenced to be hanged.

🏛 **William Hickling Prescott House**
55 Beacon St. ***Tel*** *(617) 742-3190.* 🕒 *May–Oct: noon–4pm Wed, Thu, Sat.* 💲 🚫📷 ♿

Elegant Federal-style houses on Beacon Street, overlooking Boston Common

Boston Common and Public Garden ❼

Acquired by Boston in 1634 from first settler William Blackstone, the 48-acre (19-ha) Boston Common served for two centuries as common pasture, military drill ground, and gallows site. British troops camped here during the 1775–76 military occupation. As Boston grew in the 19th century, the Boston Common became a center for open-air civic activity and remains so to this day. By contrast, the 24-acre (10-ha) Public Garden is more formal. When the Charles River mudflats were first filled in the 1830s, a succession of landscape plans were plotted for the Public Garden before the city chose the English-style garden scheme of George F. Meacham in 1869. The lagoon was added to the garden two years later.

The Public Garden, a popular green space in the heart of the city

Make Way for Ducklings
Based on the classic children's story by Robert McCloskey, this sculpture is of a duck and her brood of ducklings.

The Ether Monument memorializes the first use of anaesthesia in 1846.

★ George Washington Statue
Cast by Thomas Ball from bronze, with a solid granite base, this is one the finest memorial statues in Boston. It was dedicated in 1869.

Statue of Edward Everett Hale

Lagoon Bridge
This miniature, ornamental bridge over the Public Garden lagoon was designed by William G. Preston in 1869 in a moment of whimsy. The lagoon it "spans" was constructed in 1861.

Statue of Reverend William Ellery Channing

The Swan Boats, originally inspired by Wagner's *Lohengrin,* have been a feature of the Public Garden lake since 1877.

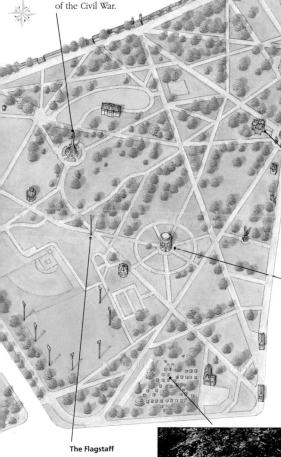

★ Shaw Memorial
This relief immortalizes the Civil War's 54th regiment of Massachusetts Infantry, the first free black regiment in the Union Army, and their white colonel Robert Shaw.

The Soldiers and Sailors Monument, erected in 1877, features prominent Bostonians from the time of the Civil War.

VISITORS' CHECKLIST

Map 1 B4. Ⓣ *Park Street, Boylston St, Arlington.* ○ *24 hrs.* **Visitors' Center** *148 Tremont St; (617) 426-3115.* ○ *8:30am–5pm Mon–Fri, 9am–5pm Sat & Sun. Times vary in winter.* **Swan Boats** *Boston Public Garden.* **Tel** *(617) 522-1966.* ○ *mid-Apr–mid-Sep: 10am–5pm daily. Times may vary.* 🖳 **www**.swanboats.com; **www**.bostonusa.com

Blackstone Memorial Tablet recalls the purchase of the common in 1634 and is cited as proof that it belongs to the people.

Park Street subway

Brewer Fountain was purchased at the 1867 Paris Expo

Visitors' Center

Parkman Bandstand
This bandstand was built in 1912 to memorialize George F. Parkman, who bequeathed $5 million for the care of Boston Common and other parks in the city.

The Flagstaff

0 meters	100
0 yards	100

Central Burying Ground
This graveyard, which dates from 1756, holds the remains of many British and American casualties from the Battle of Bunker Hill (see p20). The portraitist Gilbert Stuart is also buried here.

STAR FEATURES

- ★ Shaw Memorial
- ★ George Washington Statue

Park Street Church at the corner of Tremont and Park Streets, near Boston Common

Park Street Church **8**

1 Park St. **Map** 1 C4. *Tel (617) 523-3383.* Ⓣ *Park Street.* ◻ *Jul–Aug: 9am–3:30pm Tue–Sat; Sep–Jun: by appointment.* ✝ *Jul–Aug: 10:45am, 5:30pm Sun; Sep–Jun: 8:30am, 11am, 4pm, 6pm Sun.* 🚫 ♿ www.parkstreet.org

Park Street Church's 217-ft (65-m) steeple has punctuated the intersection of Park and Tremont Streets since its dedication in 1810. Designed by English architect Peter Banner, who adapted a design by the earlier English architect Christopher Wren, the church was commissioned by parishioners wanting to establish a Congregational church in the heart of Boston. The church was, and still remains, one of the city's most influential pulpits.

Contrary to popular belief, the sermons of Park Street ministers did not earn the intersection the nickname of "Brimstone Corner." Rather,

the name came about during the War of 1812 when the U.S. and Britain were in conflict over British restrictions on trade and freedom of the seas, as well as the U.S.'s ties with Napoleonic France. The U.S. militia, based in Boston, stored its gunpowder in the church basement as safekeeping against bombardment from the British navy, hence the nickname.

Park Street Church later became famous throughout the islands of the Pacific, when in 1819 the church sent a number of Congregational missionaries to carry the Gospel to Pacific islanders from a base in the Hawaiian Islands. In 1829, William Lloyd Garrison (1805–79), a firebrand of the movement to abolish slavery, gave his first abolition speech from the Park Street pulpit, while in 1849 a speech called *The War System of Nations* was addressed to the American Peace Society by Senator Charles Sumner. Much later, in 1893, the anthem *America the Beautiful* by Katharine Lee Bates debuted at a Sunday service. Today the church continues to be involved in religious, political, cultural, and humanitarian activities.

Old Granary Burying Ground **9**

Tremont Street. **Map** 1 C4. Ⓣ *Park Street.* ◻ *9am–5pm daily.*

Named after the early colonial grain storage facility that once stood on the adjacent site of Park Street Church, the Granary Burying Ground dates from 1660. Buried here were three important signatories to the Declaration of Independence *(see p21)* – John Hancock, Samuel Adams, and Robert Treat Paine, along with Benjamin Franklin's parents, merchant-philanthropist Peter Faneuil, and some victims of the Boston Massacre.

The orderly array of gravestones, often featured in films and television shows set in Boston, is the result of modern groundskeeping. Few stones, if any, mark the actual burial site of the person memorialized. In fact, John Hancock may not be here at all. On the night he was buried in 1793, grave robbers cut off the hand with which he had signed his name to the Declaration of Independence, and some scholars believe that the rest of the body was later spirited away during 19th-century construction work. Although many heroes of the Revolution are still known to be buried here, Paul Revere, one of Boston's most famous sons, was nearly denied the honor because the cemetery was technically full when he died in 1818. The city made an exception, and he was able to join his comrades in perpetuity.

Old Granary Burying Ground, final resting place for Revolutionary heroes

Stone frieze decoration on the 19th-century, Renaissance Revival style Athenaeum

Boston Athenaeum ⑩

10½ Beacon St. **Map** 1 C4. **Tel** (617) 227-0270. ⓣ Park Street. ☐ 8:30am–8pm Mon, 8:30am–5:30pm Tue–Fri; Sep–May: 9am–4pm Sat. ⬚ www.bostonathenaeum.org

Organized in 1807, the collection of the Boston Athenaeum quickly became one of the country's leading private libraries. Sheep farmer Edward Clarke Cabot won the 1846 design competition to house the library, with plans for a gray sandstone building based on Palladio's Palazzo da Porta Festa in Vicenza, a building Cabot knew from a book in the Athenaeum's collection. The building reopened in fall 2002 after extensive renovations. Among the Athenaeum's major holdings are the personal library that once belonged to George Washington and the theological library supplied by King William III of England to the King's Chapel (see p58). In its early years the Athenaeum was Boston's chief art museum; when the Museum of Fine Arts was proposed, the Athenaeum graciously donated much of its art, including unfinished portraits of George and Martha Washington purchased in 1831 from the widow of the painter Gilbert Stuart. Non-members of the Athenaeum may visit only the first floor of the building, an area that includes an art gallery (with changing exhibitions) and several reading rooms.

Massachusetts State House ⑪

See pp52–3.

Holmes Alley, once an escape route for slaves on the run

BLACK HERITAGE TRAIL

In the first U.S. census in 1790, Massachusetts was the only state to record no slaves. During the 19th century, Boston's substantial free African American community lived principally on the north slope of Beacon Hill and in the adjacent West End. The Black Heritage Trail links several key sites, ranging from the African Meeting House to private homes that are not open to visitors. Among them are the 1797 George Middleton House (Nos. 5–7 Pinckney Street), the oldest standing house built by African Americans on Beacon Hill, and the Lewis and Harriet Hayden House (No. 66 Phillips Street). Escaped slaves, the Haydens made their home a haven for runaways in the "Underground Railroad" of safe houses between the South and Canada. The walking tour also leads through mews and alleys, like Holmes Alley at the end of Smith Court, once used by fugitives to flee professional slave catchers.

Free tours of the Black Heritage Trail are led by National Park Service rangers – (617) 742-5415 – from Memorial Day weekend to Labor Day, 10am, noon, and 2pm Monday to Saturday, leaving from the Shaw Memorial. Tours are at 2pm Mon–Sat or by appointment the rest of the year.

Museum of African American History ⑫

46 Joy St. **Map** 1 C3. **Tel** (617) 725-0022. ⓣ Park Street. ☐ 10am–4pm Mon–Sat. ⬤ public hols. ⬚ donation. ⬚ www.afroammuseum.org

Built from town house plans by Asher Benjamin (see p32), using salvaged materials, the African Meeting House was dedicated in 1806 and is the centerpiece of the museum. The U.S.'s oldest black church building, it was the political and religious center of Boston's African American society. Cato Gardner, a native African, raised $1,500 toward the eventual $7,700 to build the church and is honored with an inscription above the entrance. The interior is plain and simple but rang with the oratory of some of the 19th century's most fiery abolitionists: from Sojourner Truth and Frederick Douglass to William Lloyd Garrison (see p30), who founded the New England Anti-Slavery Society in 1832. The meeting house basement was Boston's first school for African American children until the adjacent Abiel Smith School was built in 1831. When segregated education was barred in 1855, however, the Smith School closed. The meeting house became an Hasidic synagogue in the 1890s, as most of Boston's African American community moved to Roxbury and Dorchester. The synagogue closed in the 1960s, and in 1987 the building reopened as the linchpin site on the Black Heritage Trail.

Abiel Smith School, where Boston's free blacks received an education

Massachusetts State House ⑪

The cornerstone of the Massachusetts State
House was laid on July 4, 1795, by Samuel
Adams and Paul Revere. Completed on January
11, 1798, the Charles Bulfinch-designed center
of state government served as a model for the
U.S. Capitol Building in Washington and as
an inspiration for many of the state capitols
around the country. Later additions were made,
but the original building remains the archetype
of American government buildings. Its dome,
sheathed in copper and gold, serves as the
zero mile marker for Massachusetts, making
it, as Oliver Wendell Holmes *(see p45)*
remarked, "the hub of the universe."

The State House, from Boston Common

The Great Hall
is the latest addition to the State
House. Built in 1990, it is lined with
marble and topped by a glass dome,
and is used for state functions.

★ House of Representatives
*This elegant oval chamber was built for
the House of Representatives in 1895. The
Sacred Cod, which now hangs over the
gallery, came to the State House when it first
opened in 1798, and it has since hung over
any place where the representatives have met.*

Main Staircase
*Beautiful stained-glass
windows decorate the
main staircase. The win-
dows illustrate the many
varied state seals of
Massachusetts: from its
time as a colony through
to modern statehood.*

STAR SIGHTS

★ Nurses Hall

★ House of
   Representatives

The wings of the State
House, thought by many
to sit incongruously with
the rest of the structure,
were added in 1917.

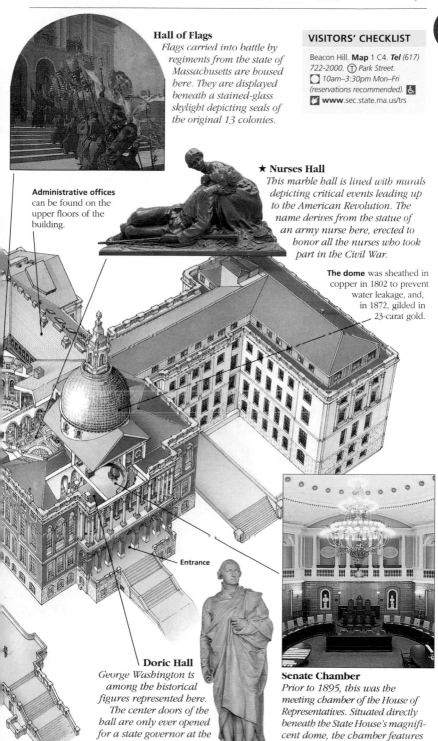

Hall of Flags
Flags carried into battle by regiments from the state of Massachusetts are housed here. They are displayed beneath a stained-glass skylight depicting seals of the original 13 colonies.

VISITORS' CHECKLIST

Beacon Hill. **Map** 1 C4. **Tel** (617) 722-2000. Ⓣ *Park Street.* ◯ *10am–3:30pm Mon–Fri (reservations recommended).* ♿ ✅ *www.sec.state.ma.us/trs*

Administrative offices can be found on the upper floors of the building.

★ Nurses Hall
This marble hall is lined with murals depicting critical events leading up to the American Revolution. The name derives from the statue of an army nurse here, erected to honor all the nurses who took part in the Civil War.

The dome was sheathed in copper in 1802 to prevent water leakage, and, in 1872, gilded in 23-carat gold.

Entrance

Doric Hall
George Washington is among the historical figures represented here. The center doors of the hall are only ever opened for a state governor at the end of his term or for a visiting head of state.

Senate Chamber
Prior to 1895, this was the meeting chamber of the House of Representatives. Situated directly beneath the State House's magnificent dome, the chamber features a beautiful sunburst ceiling, also designed by Charles Bulfinch.

Flamboyantly decorated dining room of the Otis House Museum

Otis House Museum ⑬

141 Cambridge St. **Map** 1 C3.
Tel (617) 227-3956. Ⓣ
Charles/MGH, Government Center.
⬜ *11am–4:30pm Wed–Sun.*
▨ ⊘ ◪ **www.**
historicnewengland.org

Designed by Charles Bulfinch for Harrison Gray Otis, co-developer of Beacon Hill *(see pp42–3)* and Boston's third mayor, this 1796 town mansion was built to serve the needs of a young man on the way up in Federal Boston. Descended from both British colonial administrators and Boston revolutionary patriots, Otis took a practical view of local government that paved the way for Boston's development as a powerhouse of international trade and finance. Having already made a fortune in the land development of Beacon Hill, Otis commissioned this home as a showpiece, where he could entertain. It was the first of three homes Bulfinch designed for him.

After Otis moved out, the house fell on hard times as the West End neighborhood around it absorbed successive waves of immigration, and tenements replaced single family homes. By the 1830s the Otis house was serving as a ladies' Turkish bath and later became a patent

medicine shop before ending up as a boarding house. Historic New England saved the building in 1916 and established its headquarters here. A new gallery in the house depicts the time when the building was a boarding house in the 1950s.

Visitors who tour the Otis house, now restored to the way it looked in around 1800, are often surprised by the bright, even gaudy, style of decoration. Although the rooms were initially decorated

in the muted Williams-burg Colonial style, subsequent art history detective work revealed that Bostonians had much more flamboyant taste than, for example, the wealthy Virginians. Thus, the house has been restored with touches typical of such upper-class aspirations. The wallpaper in the main entrance has a border of scenes from Pompeii and scores of lithographs showing views of European cities. The colors throughout the rest of the house are bright, and gilt detail flashes from moldings and furniture.

An architectural walking tour of Beacon Hill begins at the Otis House. It runs from May until the end of October.

Old West Church ⑭

131 Cambridge St. **Map** 1 C3.
Tel (617) 227-5088. Ⓣ *Charles/MGH, Bowdoin.* ⬜ *for Sunday worship.* ⬆ *11am Sun.* ⊘ ♿
www.oldwestchurch.org

A wood-frame church built on this site in 1737 was used as a barracks for British soldiers during the occupation of Boston *(see pp20–21)* in the period just prior to the American Revolution. The British later razed the original church in 1775, since they suspected revolutionary sym-pathizers of using the steeple to signal Continental Army troops across the Charles River. Many of the church's timbers were used to con-struct the African Meeting House *(see p49)*. Asher Benjamin *(see p32)*, a protégé of Charles Bulfinch, designed the current red-brick struc-ture, erected in 1806. The swag-ornamented clocks on the sides of the tower are distinctive landmarks, while inside there is a superb Fisk tracker-action pipe organ, This organ is often played in classical organ concerts and in recordings.

Red-brick façade of Asher Benjamin's Old West Church

Massachusetts General Hospital ⑮

Cambridge & Fruit Sts. **Map** 1 B2.
Tel (617) 726-8363. Ⓣ Charles/MGH.
◻ 24 hrs daily. **Bulfinch Pavilion
and Ether Dome** ◻ 9am–5pm
Mon–Fri. ♿ ▣ self-guided tour
brochure available at information
desk. **www**.massgeneral.org/vep

The sprawling complex of Massachusetts General Hospital covers the original site of Harvard Medical School, with which it remains affiliated as one of the world's leading teaching and research hospitals. The main hospital building, the George R. White Memorial Building, is a massive Art Deco structure from 1939, largely hidden from Cambridge Street by other buildings. The most interesting structure on the campus is the Bulfinch Pavilion and Ether Dome, which was Charles Bulfinch's last Boston commission (1818). Alexander Parris, who succeeded Bulfinch as the city's leading architect, was involved in preparing the drawings for this innovative "modern" hospital built of local Chelmsford granite. The operating theater, with seating for observers, is set beneath a skylit dome. In 1846, the use of ether as a surgical general anesthetic was first demonstrated here. A free tour of the hospital is offered at 12:30pm on the third Friday of each month (Jan–Nov, reservations are required).

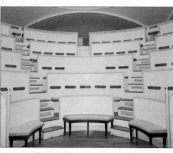

Charles Bulfinch's Ether Dome, part of the Massachusetts General Hospital

Museum of Science and Science Park ⑯

Science Park. **Map** 1 B2.
Tel (617) 723-2500. Ⓣ Science
Park. ◻ 9am–5pm Mon–Thu &
Sat–Sun (Jul–early Sep: 9am–7pm),
9am–9pm Fri. ● Thanksgiving,
Dec 25. 🎟 ♿ 🅿 **www**.mos.org

The Museum of Science straddles the Charles River atop the inactive flood control dam that sits at the mouth of the Charles River. The museum itself was built in 1951, but Science Park has taken shape around it since, virtually obscuring the dam structure with theater and planetarium buildings and a massive parking garage.

With more than 550 interactive exhibits covering natural history, medicine, astronomy, and the wonders of the physical sciences, the Science Museum is oriented to families with children. In 1999 the museum absorbed the holdings of Boston's Computer Museum, one of the first of its kind in the world.

The Mugar Omni Theater contains a five-story domed screen with multi-dimensional sound system with wraparound sound, and shows mostly educational films, usually with a natural science theme. The Charles Hayden Planetarium offers daily shows about stars, planets, and other celestial phenomena.

An extensive array of educational toys can be bought from the museum's shop, while the food court has a number of concessions catering to children's tastes.

CHARLES BULFINCH

Born in 1763 in Boston, Charles Bulfinch (see p32) was among America's first professional architects and one of the most influential. He rose to prominence with his 1795 plan for the Massachusetts State House (see pp50–51), and went on to design many of the neighboring mansions on Beacon Hill. His own forays into real estate development cast him into bankruptcy, but he continued to enjoy the steady patronage of Boston's wealthiest citizens for his elegant yet boldly confident house designs. These patrons also helped him secure many public commissions, including the renovation of St. Stephen's Church in the North End (see p72) and the enlargement of Faneuil Hall (see p63). His application of local granite building stone to the Massachusetts General Hospital surgical pavilion laid out principles later followed by Alexander Parris and others as they forged the Boston Granite style of architecture, exemplified by Quincy Market (see p64) and Charlestown Navy Yard (see p115). Bulfinch left Boston in 1818 to assume direction of the construction of the U.S. Capitol Building in Washington, DC.

19th-century view of Massachusetts State House from Boston Common

OLD BOSTON AND THE FINANCIAL DISTRICT

This is an area of Boston where old and new sit one on top of the other. Some of its sights, situated in the older part of the district closest to Boston Common, predate the American Revolution *(see pp20–21)*. Much of what can be seen today, though, was built more recently. The north of the district is home to Boston's late 20th-century, modernist-style City Hall and Government Center, while to the east is the city's bustling Financial District. This once formed part of Boston's harbor waterfront, a district built on mercantile wealth. Today, the wharves and warehouses have been replaced by skyscrapers belonging to banks, insurance companies, and high-tech industries.

British Lion, Old State House

SIGHTS AT A GLANCE

Historic Streets and Squares
Blackstone Block 10
Post Office Square 14

Historic Buildings and Churches
Center Plaza 7
Custom House 13
Faneuil Hall 11
Government Center 9
King's Chapel and Burying Ground 2
New City Hall 8
Old City Hall 3
Old Corner Bookstore 4
Old South Meeting House 5
Old State House pp60–61 6
Omni Parker House 1
Quincy Market 12

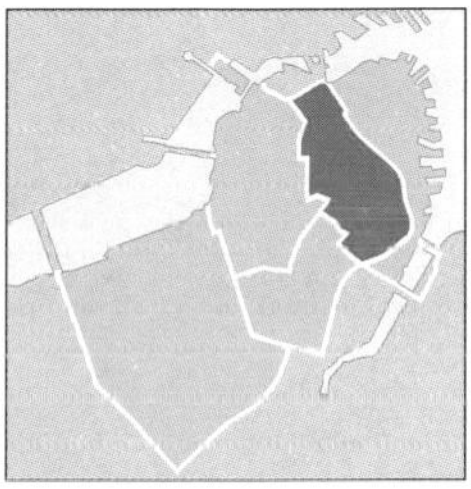

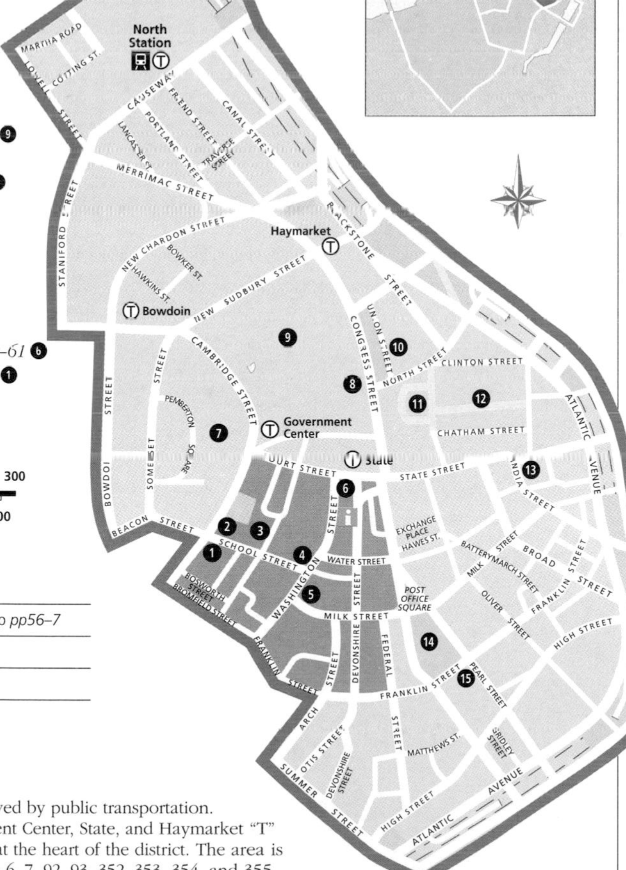

0 meters 300

0 yards 300

KEY

- Street-by-street map *pp56–7*
- Ⓣ "T" station
- Tourist information

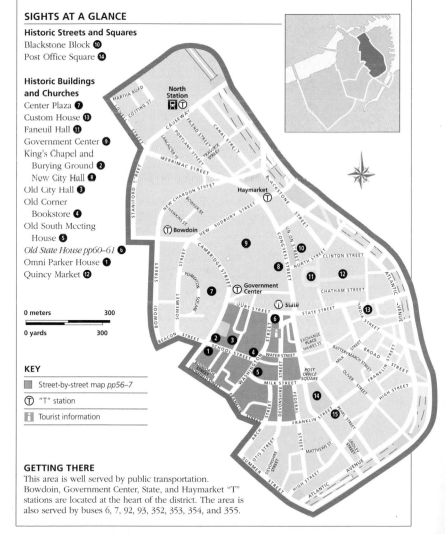

GETTING THERE

This area is well served by public transportation. Bowdoin, Government Center, State, and Haymarket "T" stations are located at the heart of the district. The area is also served by buses 6, 7, 92, 93, 352, 353, 354, and 355.

◁ **Custom House, Boston's original skyscraper and one of the most distinctive buildings on the city skyline**

Street-by-Street: Colonial Boston

An important part of Boston's Freedom Trail (*see pp124–7*) runs through this historic core of the city, the site of which predates American Independence. Naturally, the area is now dominated by more recent 19th- and 20th-century development, but glimpses of a colonial past are prevalent here and there in the Old State House, King's Chapel and its adjacent burying ground, and the Old South Meeting House. Newer buildings of interest include the Omni Parker House, as well as the towering skyscrapers of Boston's financial district, located on the northwest edges of this area.

Irish Famine memorial, Washington Street

Government Center

★ King's Chapel and Burying Ground
A church has stood here since 1688, though the current building dates from 1749. The adjacent cemetery is the resting place of some of the most important figures in U.S. history ❷

SCHOOL STREET

PROVINCE STREET

Omni Parker House
This hotel (see p133) first opened its doors in 1855, then underwent many renovations. Famed for its opulence, in the 19th century the hotel also gained a reputation as a meeting place for Boston intellectuals. The current building was erected in 1927 ❶

| 0 meters | 50 |
| 0 yards | 50 |

Old City Hall
This building served as Boston's City Hall from 1865 to 1969. Today it houses a steak house ❸

STAR SIGHTS

★ Old South Meeting House

★ Old State House

★ King's Chapel and Burying Ground

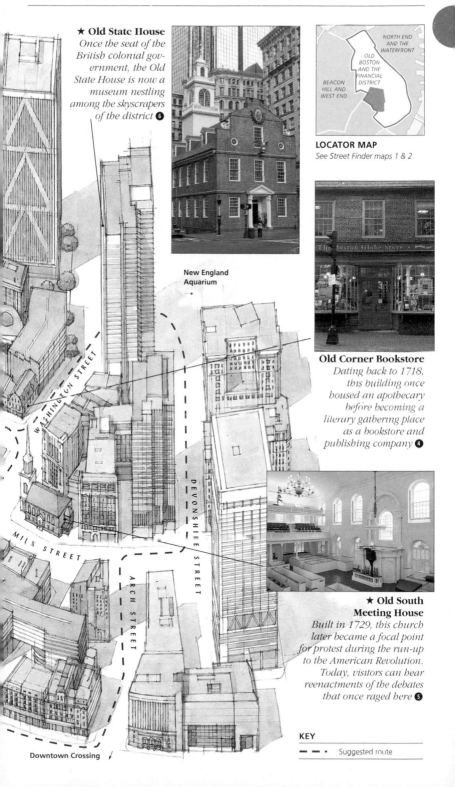

★ **Old State House**
Once the seat of the British colonial government, the Old State House is now a museum nestling among the skyscrapers of the district ❻

LOCATOR MAP
See Street Finder maps 1 & 2

NORTH END AND THE WATERFRONT

OLD BOSTON AND THE FINANCIAL DISTRICT

BEACON HILL AND WEST END

New England Aquarium

Old Corner Bookstore
Dating back to 1718, this building once housed an apothecary before becoming a literary gathering place as a bookstore and publishing company ❹

WASHINGTON STREET

DEVONSHIRE STREET

MILK STREET

ARCH STREET

★ **Old South Meeting House**
Built in 1729, this church later became a focal point for protest during the run-up to the American Revolution. Today, visitors can hear reenactments of the debates that once raged here ❺

KEY

— — · Suggested route

Downtown Crossing

Omni Parker House **1**

60 School St. **Map** 1 C4.
Tel (617) 227-8600. Ⓣ Park
Street, State, Government Center.
www.omnihotels.com

Harvey D. Parker, raised on a farm in Maine, became so successful as the proprietor of his Boston restaurant that he achieved his ambition of expanding the property into a first-class, grand hotel. His Parker House opened in 1855, with a façade clad in white marble, standing five stories high, and featuring the first passenger elevator ever seen in Boston. It underwent several, rapid transformations during its early years, with additions made to the main structure in the 1860s and a 10-story, French chateau-style annex completed later that century. The building saw many successive transformations, and its latest 14-story incarnation has stood across from King's Chapel on School Street since 1927.

This hotel attained an instant reputation for luxurious accommodations and fine, even lavish, dining, typified by 11-course menus prepared by a French chef.

Among Parker House's many claims to fame are its Boston Cream Pie, which was first created here, and the word "scrod," a uniquely Bostonian term for the day's freshest seafood, still in common usage. Two former Parker House employees later became recognized for quite different careers. Vietnamese revolutionary leader Ho Chi Minh worked in the hotel's kitchens around 1915, while black activist Malcolm X was a busboy in Parker's Restaurant in the 1940s.

Simply decorated, pure white interior of King's Chapel on Tremont Street

King's Chapel and Burying Ground **2**

58 Tremont St. **Map** 1 C4.
Tel (617) 523-1749. Ⓣ Park Street,
State, Government Center. ☐
late May–mid-Sep: 10am–4pm Mon,
Thu, Fri, Sat, 10am–11:15am &
1:30pm–4pm Tue & Wed, 1:30pm–
4pm Sun; mid-Sep–late May: call for
opening hours. Hours subject to
change during ongoing restoration.
Music Recitals 12:15pm Tue.
🔔 11am Sun, 12:15pm Wed.
www.kings-chapel.org

British crown officials were among those who attended Anglican services at the first chapel on this site, which was built in 1688. When New England's governor decided a larger church was needed, the present granite edifice – begun in 1749 – was constructed around the original wooden chapel, which was dismantled and heaved out the windows of its replacement. After the Revolution, the congregation's religious allegiance switched from Anglican to Unitarian. The sanctuary's raised pulpit – dating from 1717 and shaped like a wine glass – is one of the oldest in the U.S. High ceilings, open arches, and clear glass windows enhance the sense of spaciousness and light. The bell inside the King's Chapel is the largest ever cast by Paul Revere (see p21).

The adjacent cemetery is the oldest in Boston.

PARKER HOUSE GUESTS

Boston's reputation as the "Athens of America" was widely acknowledged when members of a distinguished social club began meeting for lengthy dinners and lively intellectual exchanges in 1857. Their get-togethers took place on the last Saturday of every month at Harvey Parker's fancy new hotel. Regular participants included New England's literary elite (see pp30–31): Henry Wadsworth Longfellow, Ralph Waldo Emerson, Nathaniel Hawthorne, and Henry David Thoreau, to name a few. Charles

John Wilkes Booth, infamous Parker House guest

Dickens participated while staying at the Parker House during his American speaking tours, and used his sitting-room mirror to rehearse the public readings he gave at Tremont Temple next door. The mirror now hangs on a mezzanine wall. In 1865, actor John Wilkes Booth, in town to see his brother, a fellow thespian, stayed at the hotel and took target practice at a nearby shooting gallery. Ten days later, at Ford's Theatre in Washington, he pulled a pistol and shot Abraham Lincoln.

Old City Hall ❸

45 School St. **Map** 2 D4.
ⓣ *Park Street, State, Government Center.*

A fine example of French Second Empire architectural gaudiness, this was Boston's City Hall from 1865 to 1969 – it was superseded by the rakishly modern New City Hall structure at nearby Government Center *(see p62)*. The renovated 19th-century building now features a steak house.

Previous occupants have included such flamboyant mayors as Honey "Fitz" Fitzgerald *(see p25)* and James Michael Curley. Statues here memorialize Josiah Quincy, Boston's second mayor and after whom Quincy Market is named, as well as Benjamin Franklin, who was born on nearby Milk Street.

19th-century French-style façade of Boston's Old City Hall

Old Corner Bookstore ❹

1 School St. **Map** 2 D4. ⓣ *Park Street, State, Government Center.*

A dormered gambrel roof crowns this brick landmark, which opened as Thomas Crease's apothecary shop in 1718 and was reestablished as the Old Corner Bookstore in 1829. Moving in 16 years later, the Ticknor & Fields publishing company became a gathering place for a notable roster of authors:

Emerson, Hawthorne, Longfellow, Thoreau, early feminist writer Margaret Fuller, and *Uncle Tom's Cabin* novelist Harriet Beecher Stowe. The firm is often credited with carving out the first distinctively American literature. The earliest editions of the erudite *Atlantic Monthly* periodical were also printed here under editor James Russell Lowell, before he handed the reins over to William Dean Howells. Julia Ward Howe's rousing tribute to American Civil War bravado, *The Battle Hymn of the Republic*, first appeared in the *Atlantic*'s February 1862 issue. Although no publishing activities take place here, the Old Corner Bookstore remains a touchstone of American literary history.

The Old Corner Bookstore, considered by some to be the cradle of American literature

Old South Meeting House ❺

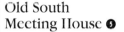
310 Washington St. **Map** 2 D4
Tel (617) 482-6439. ⓣ *Park Street, State, Government Center.* ⬜ *Apr–Oct. 9.30am–5pm daily, Nov–Mar. 10am–4pm daily.* ▨ ◪ ⬇ ⬛
www.oldsouthmeetinghouse.org

Built in 1729 for Puritan religious services, this edifice, with a tall octagonal steeple, had colonial Boston's biggest capacity for town meetings – a fact capitalized upon by a group of rebellious rabble-rousers calling themselves the Sons of Liberty *(see p20)*. Their outbursts against British taxation and other royal annoyances drew increasingly large and vociferous crowds to the pews and upstairs galleries.

During a candlelit protest rally on December 16 1773, fiery speechmaker Samuel Adams flashed the signal that led to the Boston Tea Party *(see p75)* down at Griffin's Wharf several hours later. The British retaliated by turning Old South into an officers' tavern and stable for General John Burgoyne's 17th Lighthorse Regiment of Dragoons. In 1877, the budding Historic Preservation Movement saved the building from destruction and created a museum. Displays, exhibits, and a multimedia presentation entitled *Voices of Protest* relive those raucous days as well as more recent occurrences well into the 20th century. The Meeting House offers a series of lectures covering a wide range of New England topics and also holds chamber music concerts and other musical performances.

There is a shop downstairs containing a broad selection of merchandise, which includes the ubiquitous tins of "Boston Tea Party" tea.

Directly across Washington Street, sculptor Robert Shure's memorial to the 1845–49 Irish Potato Famine was added to the small plaza here in 1998.

Old South Meeting House, in stark contrast to the modern city

Old State House 🟠

Dwarfed by the towers of the Financial District, this was the seat of British colonial government between 1713 and 1776. The royal lion and unicorn still decorate each corner of the eastern façade. After independence, the Massachusetts legislature took possession of the building, and it has had many uses since, including produce market, merchants' exchange, Masonic lodge, and Boston City Hall. Its wine cellars now function as a downtown subway station. The Old State House houses two floors of Bostonian Society memorabilia and a sound and light show about the Boston Massacre *(see p20)*.

Old State House amid the sky-scrapers of the Financial District

A gold sculpture of an eagle, symbol of America, can be seen on the west façade.

West Façade
A Latin inscription, relating to the first Massachusetts Bay colony, runs around the outside of this crest. The relief in the center depicts a local Native American.

Entrance

Keayne Hall
This is named after Robert Keayne who, in 1658, gave £300 to the city so that the Town House, predating the Old State House, could be built. Exhibits in the room depict events from the Revolution.

★ Central Staircase
A fine example of 18th-century workmanship, the central spiral staircase has two beautifully crafted wooden handrails. It is one of the few such staircases still in existence in the U.S.

SITE OF THE BOSTON MASSACRE

A circle of cobblestones below the balcony on the eastern façade of the Old State House marks the site of the Boston Massacre *(see pp20–21)*. After the Boston Tea Party *(see p75)*, this was one of the most inflammatory events leading up to the American Revolution. On March 5, 1770, an unruly mob of colonists taunted British guardsmen with insults, rocks, and snowballs. The soldiers opened fire, killing five colonists. A number of articles relating to the Boston Massacre are exhibited inside the Old State House, including a musket found near the site and a coroner's report detailing the incident.

Cobbled circle: site of the Boston Massacre

VISITORS' CHECKLIST

Washington & State Sts. **Map** 2 D4. *Tel* (617) 720-1713. Ⓣ *State.* ◖ *9am–5pm daily (to 4pm Jan, 6pm Jul–Aug).* ● *Jan 1, Thanksgiving, Dec 25.* 📷 ⌀ ♿ 🏪

The tower is a classic example of Colonial style. In 18th-century paintings and engravings it can be seen clearly above the Boston skyline.

British Unicorn and Lion
A royal symbol of Britain, the original lion and unicorn were pulled down when news of the Declaration of Independence reached Boston in 1776.

★ **East Façade**
This façade has seen many changes. An earlier clock from the 1820s was removed in 1957 and replaced with an 18th-century replica of the sundial that once hung here. The clock has now been reinstated.

Council Chamber
Once the chambers for the royal governors, and from 1780 chambers for the first governor of Massachusetts (John Hancock), this room has seen many key events. Among them were numerous impassioned speeches made by Boston patriots.

The Declaration of Independence was read from this balcony in 1776. In the 1830s, when the building was City Hall, the balcony was enlarged to two tiers.

STAR SIGHTS

★ East Façade

★ Central Staircase

Center Plaza ❼

Cambridge St. **Map** 1 C3.
Ⓣ *Government Center.*

Downtown's old, irregular
street pattern has given rise to
some unusual buildings,
including the Center Plaza,
which was designed
in the mid-1960s by Welton
Beckett & Associates. It was
designed specifically to follow
the long curve of the existing
Cambridge Street, and the
low-slung office complex
is often referred to as a
"skyscraper laid sideways."
Shops and restaurants run
at street level along Center
Plaza's sidewalk arcade, on
the Government Center side,
while the plaza behind
incorporates some much
older city center buildings.

**Curved, Modernist structure of
Center Plaza, on Cambridge Street**

New City Hall ❽

City Hall Plaza. **Map** 2 D3.
***Tel** (617) 635-4000.* Ⓣ *Government
Center.* ☐ *9am–5pm Mon–Fri.* ♿
www.ci.boston.ma.us

The firm of architects
Kallmann, McKinnell &
Knowles won a nationwide
design competition for their
striking city hall, a seemingly
top-heavy, cantilevered,
Modernist building. Com-
pleted in 1968, the concrete-
and-brick City Hall combines
the offices and services of
municipal government, with
ample space for holiday-
season concerts, school band
and glee-club performances,
and community art exhibits.
An outdoor stage on City
Hall's north side is often the
venue for evening rock and
pop concerts during the
summer months.

**Old-fashioned flower stall on the
sidewalk outside Center Plaza**

Government Center ❾

Cambridge, Court, New Sudbury &
Congress Sts. **Map** 2 D3.
Ⓣ *Government Center.*

This city center development
was built on the site of what
was once Scollay Square,
demolished as part
of the fad for local urban-
renewal that began in the
early 1960s. Some viewed the
development as controversial;
others did not lament what
was essentially a disreputable
cluster of saloons, burlesque
theaters, tattoo parlors, and
scruffy hotels. The overall
master plan for Government
Center was inspired by the
alfresco vitality and

spaciousness of Italian
piazzas. Architects I.M. Pei &
Partners re-created some of
this feeling by surrounding
Boston's new City Hall with a
vast terraced plaza covering
56 acres (23 ha), paved with
1,800,000 bricks. Its spaciousness makes it an ideal venue
for events such as skateboard
contests, political and sports
rallies, food fairs, patriotic
military marches, and concerts. The Cambridge Street
side accommodates a farmers'
market on Mondays and
Wednesdays from around
the middle of May to the
middle of November.
  A remnant of old Boston
hangs from the Sears Block
at City Hall Plaza's Court
Street perimeter. This gilded,
227-gallon *Steaming Tea
Kettle* was made for the
Oriental Tea Company by a
firm of coppersmiths in 1873.
Near New Sudbury Street,
the John F. Kennedy Federal
Office Building features two
pieces of abstract art: Dmitry
Hadzi's 15-ft (4.5-m) high
Thermopylae sculpture, and
Robert Motherwell's *New
England Elegy*, a mural
recalling the tragic assassination of President Kennedy
in Dallas in 1963. A memorial
standing in front of the
building marks the site of
Alexander Graham Bell's first
significant breakthrough
toward his invention of the
"electrical speech machine" in
1876 *(see p65)*.

New City Hall and Government Center, one of Boston's main focal points

Blackstone Block ⑩

Union, Hanover, North & Blackstone Sts. **Map** 2 D3. ⓣ *Government Center, Haymarket.*

Cobblestones pave Boston's only surviving web of 17th-century lanes and alleyways, a remnant of what was once the oldest neighborhood in Boston, with historical associations dating back to the colonial period. The district's most famous son, Benjamin Franklin, grew up near Union and Hanover Streets, where his father owned a candleworks. Prior to the landfill programs that expanded the city, the block was close to the water's edge, a fact suggested by the names of the streets in this small district: Marsh Lane, Creek Square, and Salt Lane.

The oldest surviving building in the Blackstone Block dates from 1714 – the Duke of Chartres, later to be crowned France's King Louis Philippe, was a guest here in 1798 and gave French lessons to support himself while waiting for funds. Since 1826 the building has housed the Union Oyster House *(see p143)*, renowned for its original mahogany raw oyster bar, its political clientele, including Congressman John F. Kennedy, and of course its oysters.

The Millennium Bostonian Hotel can also be found here, wedged among the Blackstone Block's twisting street pattern, while on afternoons on Fridays and all day on Saturdays vendors sell fruit, vegetables, and fish from stands along Blackstone, Hanover, and North Streets. Across Union Street is the New England Holocaust Memorial, dedicated in 1995 to the Jewish victims of World War II. Designed as a sculpture that the public can walk through, to do so is a surreal, justly disquieting experience.

Liberty and Union, Now and Forever by George Healy, Faneuil Hall

Faneuil Hall ⑪

Dock Sq. **Map** 2 D3.
Tel *No phone.* ⓣ *Government Center, Haymarket, State.* **Great Hall** ◯ *9am–5pm daily (may close for special events).* 🔱 ✔ ⋒
www.nps.gov/bost

A gift to Boston from the wealthy merchant Peter Faneuil in 1742, this Georgian, brick landmark has always functioned simultaneously as a public market and town meeting place. Master tinsmith Shem Drowne modeled the building's grasshopper weathervane after the one on top of the Royal Exchange in the City of London, England. Revolutionary gatherings packed the hall, and as early as 1763 Samuel Adams used the hall as a platform to suggest that the American colonies

The Union Oyster House, one of Boston's most famous restaurants, Blackstone Block

should unite against British oppression and fight to establish their independence *(see pp20–21)*; hence the building's nickname "Cradle of Liberty" and the bold posture of the statue of Sam Adams at the front of the building.

Toward the end of the 18th century it became apparent that the existing Faneuil Hall could no longer house the capacity crowds that it regularly attracted. The commission to expand the building was undertaken by Charles Bulfinch *(see p53)*, who completed the work from 1805 to 1806. The building then remained unchanged until 1898, when it was expanded still farther according to long-standing Bulfinch stipulations. Faneuil Hall was restored in the 1970s as part of the wider redevelopment of Quincy Market *(see p64)*.

Sam Adams statue, in front of Faneuil Hall

Among the paintings upstairs in the Neoclassical Great Hall is George Healy's enormous canvas, *Liberty and Union, Now and Forever*, showing Massachusetts Senator Daniel Webster in full oratorical passion. The uppermost floor contains the headquarters and armory of the Ancient and Honorable Artillery Company, chartered in 1638 for defense of the Massachusetts Bay Colony and an occupant of Faneuil Hall since 1746. Displays include weapons, commendations, and medals.

Gallery of the Greek Revival main dome in Quincy Market's central hall

Quincy Market ⑫

Between Chatham & Clinton Sts.
Map 2 D3. **Tel** (617) 523-1300. Ⓣ
Government Center, State. Ⓒ 10am–
10pm Mon–Sat, noon–6pm Sun. Ⓖ
www.faneuilhallmarketplace.com

This immensely popular
shopping and dining complex
attracts in the region of 14
million people every year,
and was developed from
the buildings of the former
Faneuil Hall produce and
meat market, or Quincy
Market. These buildings had
fallen into disrepair before
they underwent a widely
acclaimed restoration by the
architects Benjamin Thompson
& Associates in the 1970s.
The imposing centerpiece,
a granite Greek Revival
structure (see p32) dating

**Greek Revival Custom House tower,
one of Boston's most striking sights**

from 1825, was planned
as an extension to the first
Faneuil Hall Markets, which
had become overstretched by
Boston's rapid development.
Originally called the New
Faneuil Hall Market, the building came to be known as
Quincy Market after the mayor,
Josiah Quincy, whose original
vision was responsible for the
new market's creation. The
façade's four Doric columns
were, at the time of construction, the largest single pieces
of granite ever to be quarried
in the U.S. The 535-ft (163-m)
long colonnaded hall is now
filled with fast food stalls and
a comedy nightclub, located
in the spectacular Rotunda.
Completing the ensemble are
twin North and South Market
buildings – these individual
warehouses have been
refurbished to accommodate
boutiques, restaurants, pubs,
stores, and upstairs offices.

Custom House ⑬

3 McKinley Square. **Map** 2 E3.
Tel (617) 310-6300. Ⓣ Aquarium.
Museum Ⓒ 8am–9pm daily.
Tower Ⓒ 10am & 4pm Mon–Thu,
4pm Fri & Sat. **www**.marriott.com

Before landfill altered
downtown topography, early
Boston's Custom House
perched at the water's edge.
A temple-like Greek Revival
structure with fluted Doric
columns, the granite building
had a skylit dome upon
completion in 1847. Since
1915, however, it has supported an anachronistic tower

rising 495 ft (150 m), which
means that for the best part
of the 20th century, the
Custom House was Boston's
only bona fide skyscraper.
Four sculpted eagles and a
four-sided illuminated clock
add decorative flourishes.
The public has free access to
a small museum of maritime
history in the 19th-century
rotunda. It displays objects
on loan from the Peabody
Museum in Salem, including
maritime paintings, nautical
instruments, items that depict
Boston's trade with China,
and several pieces of decorative art. The observatory,
which offers panoramic
views, is also open to the
public. The rest of the building is occupied by a Marriott
hotel and timeshare apartments, not open to the public.

**Glass fountain on the Pearl Street
side of Post Office Square**

Post Office Square ⑭

Between Congress & Pearl Sts.
Map 2 D4. Ⓣ State, Aquarium.

This beautifully landscaped
park, a small island of green
situated amid the soaring
skyscrapers of the financial
district, replaced an ugly
concrete garage that once
stood here – it was
demolished and rebuilt as an
underground parking facility
in 1990. Vines climb a 143-ft
(44-m) long trellis along one
side of the park, and a fountain made of green glass
cascades on the square's
Pearl Street side. On Angell
Memorial Plaza across the
road, a fountain dating from
1912 commemorates George
Thorndike Angell, founder
of the Massachusetts' Society

ALEXANDER GRAHAM BELL (1847–1922)

A native of Edinburgh, Scotland, and son of a deaf mother, Bell moved to Boston in 1871 to embark on a career of teaching speech to the deaf. It led to his appointment, two years later, as professor of vocal physiology at Boston University. In a rented fifth-floor garret assisted by young repair mechanic and model maker Thomas Watson, Bell worked in his spare time on an apparatus for transmitting sound by electrical current. Initial success came on June 3, 1875, when the barely intelligible utterings of a human voice (his own) traveled over a laboratory wire. History was made on March 17, 1876, when Bell, while experimenting on voice transmission, upset a battery, spilling acid on his clothing. He called to another room: "Mr. Watson, come here. I want you." With each of those seven words reaching Watson clearly and distinctly, the "electrical speech machine" was invented. In August that year, Bell proved its practical value by sending messages over Canadian telegraph wires. By 1878, he had set up the first public telephone exchange in New Haven, Connecticut. Six years later, long-distance calls were being made between Boston and New York City.

for the Prevention of Cruelty to Animals. Some of the most important buildings overlooking the square and plaza include the Verizon Telephone Building and the John W. McCormack court house building, which formerly housed downtown's main post office. Other important buildings include the Langham Boston hotel *(see p133)* – this classic Renaissance Revival showpiece was completed in 1922 and was originally the Federal Reserve Bank – and One Post Office Square, which offers

great views over Boston Harbor and Downtown. These views can be seen from the atrium at the top of the building, which, not strictly open to the public, may be accessible through polite inquiry. A focal point for the whole district, the grassy space of the square comes into its own during the warmer months of the year, when office workers can be seen sprawling across its well-kept lawns – a great place for visitors to rest their weary feet and watch Bostonians take a few minutes out.

Distinctive, Art Deco-style Verizon Building, built in the 1940s

Verizon Building ⓯

185 Franklin St. **Map** 2 D4.
Tel (617) 743-9340. Ⓣ *State, Aquarium.* **Museum** ◻ *24 hours daily.* ♿

Dating from 1947 and overlooking the south side of Post Office Square, this Art Deco building is still in use today. Dean Cornwell's monumental 160-ft (49-m) long *Telephone Men and Women at Work* mural – populated by 197 life-size figures – has encircled the lobby since 1951 and is a truly remarkable work of art. The small museum at street level features an accurate restoration of Alexander Graham Bell's Court Street laboratory *(see p31)*, complete with his tools, books, actual workbench, and one of his garret window-frames overlooking a diorama of Scollay Square. The exhibit was constructed from parts of Bell's original workshop, put to one side and lovingly preserved when the house where he lived was demolished in the 1920s. It was opened on June 3, 1959, coincidentally the 84th anniversary of the invention of the telephone. The world's first commercial telephone and first telephone switchboard, both dating from May 1877, are also displayed in the museum.

Telephone Men and Women at Work, **Verizon Building**

NORTH END AND THE WATERFRONT

This was Boston's first neighborhood, and one that has been key to the city's fortunes. Fringed by numerous wharves, the area prospered initially through shipping and shipbuilding, with much of America's early trade passing through its warehouses. The more recent importance of finance and high-tech industries, however, has seen the waterfront evolve; its

Statue In Old North Church garden

old warehouses transformed into luxury apartment blocks and offices. Away from the waterfront, the narrow streets of the North End have historically been home to European immigrants, drawn by the availability of work. The area today is populated largely by those of Italian descent, whose many cafés, delis, and restaurants make it one of the city's most distinct communities.

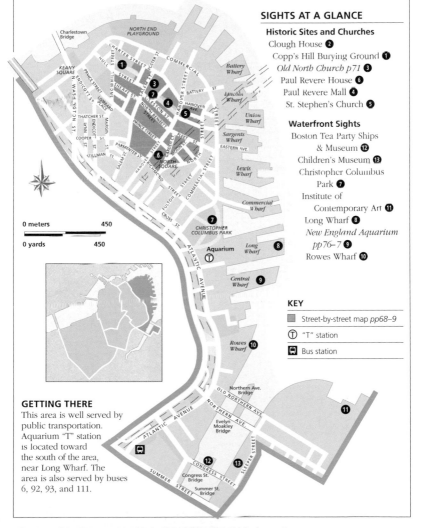

SIGHTS AT A GLANCE

Historic Sites and Churches
Clough House ❷
Copp's Hill Burying Ground ❶
Old North Church p71 ❸
Paul Revere House ❻
Paul Revere Mall ❹
St. Stephen's Church ❺

Waterfront Sights
Boston Tea Party Ships & Museum ⓬
Children's Museum ⓭
Christopher Columbus Park ❼
Institute of Contemporary Art ⓫
Long Wharf ❽
New England Aquarium pp76–7 ❾
Rowes Wharf ❿

KEY
▨ Street-by-street map *pp68–9*
Ⓣ "T" station
🚌 Bus station

GETTING THERE
This area is well served by public transportation. Aquarium "T" station is located toward the south of the area, near Long Wharf. The area is also served by buses 6, 92, 93, and 111.

◁ **Institute of Contemporary Art, with the Financial District in the background**

Street-by-Street: North End

Old North Church clock

The main arteries of this area are Hanover and Salem Streets. Topped by the Old North Church, Salem Street is indicative of this area's historical connections – indeed the Old North Church is one of Boston's premier Revolutionary sights. In general the area consists of narrow streets and alleys, with four- and five-story tenements, many of which are now expensive condominiums. Hanover Street, like much of the area, has a distinctly Italian feel, while just south of here is North Square, site of the famous Paul Revere House *(see p73)*.

Clough House
Period furnishings can be seen in this house by Ebenezer Clough, who also helped build the Old North Church ❷

Copp's Hill Burying Ground
During the American Revolution, the British used this low hilltop to fire cannon at American positions across Boston Harbor. Created in 1659 it is the city's second oldest graveyard ❶

★ Old North Church
Built in 1723 and famous for the part it played in Paul Revere's midnight ride (see p21), this is Boston's oldest religious building. On festive occasions, the North End still rings with the sound of its bells ❸

KEY

— — — Suggested route

STAR SIGHTS

★ Old North Church

★ Paul Revere House

★ Paul Revere Mall

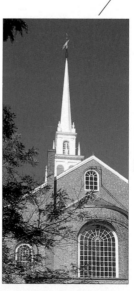

← Charlestown

HULL STREET

SHEAFE STREET

SALEM STREET

NORTH BENNET

PRINCE STREET

↓ Government Center

| 0 meters | | 50 |
| 0 yards | | 50 |

★ Paul Revere Mall
*Linking the Old North Church to
Hanover Street, this tree-lined mall
dates only from 1933. Its antique feel
is enhanced by a statue of Paul Revere,
which was modeled in 1885* ❹

LOCATOR MAP
See Street Finder map 2

St. Stephen's Church
*North End's Italian theme
continues in this church,
though only by chance.
Long before the first
Italians arrived, Charles
Bulfinch* (see p53) *incorporated Italian
Renaissance features
and a bell tower into
his refit of an earlier
church building* ❺

Hanover Street is the most Italian of all
Boston's streets, brought to life by Italian
restaurants and cafés, as well as the day-
to-day activities of its ethnic community.

↘ **The waterfront**

★ Paul Revere House
*This is the house where Paul Revere began
his midnight ride* (see p21). *Revere's home
from 1770 to 1800, it is now a museum* ❻

Slate tombstones of Boston's early settlers, **Copp's Hill Burying Ground**

Copp's Hill Burying Ground ❶

Entrances at Charter & Hull Sts.
Map 2 D2. Ⓣ *Government Center, North Station.* ◯ *9am–5pm daily.*

Existing since 1659, this is Boston's second-oldest cemetery after the one by King's Chapel *(see p58).* Nicknamed "Corpse Hill," the real name of the hill occupied by the cemetery derives from a local man by the name of William Copp. He owned a farm on its southeastern slope from 1643, and much of the cemetery's land was purchased from him. His children can be found buried here. Other more famous

Quiet, leafy street, typical of the area around Copp's Hill

people interred here include Robert Newman, the sexton who hung Paul Revere's signal lanterns in the belfry of Old North Church *(see p71),* and Edmund Hartt, builder of the *U.S.S. Constitution (see p115).* Increase, Cotton, and Samuel Mather, three generations of a family of highly influential colonial period Puritan ministers, are also buried here. Hundreds of Boston's Colonial-era black slaves and freedmen are also buried here, including Prince Hall, a free black man who founded the African Freemasonry Order in Massachusetts.

During the British occupation of Boston, the site was used by British commanders who had an artillery position here. They would later exploit the prominent hilltop location during the Revolution, when they directed cannon fire from here across Boston harbor toward American positions in Charlestown. King George III's troops were said to have used the slate headstones for target practice, and pockmarks from their musket balls are still visible on some of them.

Copp's Hill Terrace, directly across Charter Street, is a prime observation point for

Decorative column, Copp's Hill

views over to Charlestown and Bunker Hill. It is also the site where, in 1919, a 2.3-million-gallon molasses tank exploded, creating a huge, syrupy tidal wave that killed 21 people.

Clough House ❷

21 Unity St. **Map** 2 E2. **Tel** *(617) 523-6676.* Ⓣ *Haymarket, Aquarium.* ◯ *Jun: Wed (call for opening hours).*

Ebenezer Clough was a master mason and one of the Sons of Liberty who participated in the Boston Tea Party *(see p75).* One of two masons who helped to build the neighboring Old North Church *(see p71),* he was also the head of a syndicate that laid out Unity Street in 1710 and built a series of six town houses here. The only building to survive is the one at No. 21 Unity Street, which was built in 1712, and was the house in which Ebenezer Clough himself lived. In a bad state of decay for many years, and in danger of demolition, the house was only saved when the Reverend P. Kellet, vicar of Christ Church, launched a fund-raising campaign in 1962. A rather austere three-story building, it is typical of much of Boston's colonial architecture. Now fully restored to its former condition, the house has finely executed window and door lintels, decorated with raised brick panels over the first-floor windows and simple, carved-brick detailing over the door. The Heritage Room on the second floor features typical period furnishings and household accessories.

Clough House once stood alongside an identical brick residence, which was acquired by Benjamin Franklin in 1748. He bought the house for his two widowed sisters but never lived here himself. It was demolished in the 1930s to make way for the Paul Revere Mall *(see p72).*

Old North Church™ ❸

Christ Episcopal Church is the official name of this, Boston's oldest surviving religious edifice, which dates from 1723. It was built of brick in the Georgian style similar to that of St. Andrew's-by-the-Wardrobe in Blackfriars, London, designed by Sir Christopher Wren. The church was made famous on April 18, 1775, when sexton Robert Newman, aiding Paul Revere (*see p21*), hung a pair of signal lanterns in the belfry. These were to warn the patriots in Charlestown of the westward departure of British troops, on their way to engage the revolutionaries.

VISITORS' CHECKLIST

193 Salem St. **Map** 2 E2. *Tel* *(617) 523-6676.* Ⓣ *Haymarket, Aquarium, North Station.* ◯ *9am–5pm daily (Jan, Feb until 4pm; Jun–Oct until 6pm).* ◻ *9am, 11am.* ✍ ♿ 📷 ✔ *call for details.* **www**.oldnorth.com

Box Pews
The unusual, high-sided box pews in the church were designed to enclose footwarmers, which were filled with hot coals or bricks during wintry weather.

Tower
The tower of the Old North Church contains the first set of church bells in North America cast in 1745.

Chandeliers
The distinctive chandeliers were brought from England in January 1724 for the first Christmas season.

Entrance

STAR SIGHTS

★ Bust of George Washington

★ Box Pews

★ **Bust of George Washington**
This marble bust of the first U.S. president, modeled on an earlier one by Christian Gullager, was presented to the church in 1815.

Paul Revere Mall ❹

Hanover St. **Map** 2 E2.
Ⓣ *Haymarket, Aquarium.* ♿

This brick-paved plaza gives
the crowded neighborhood of
the North End a precious
stretch of open space
between Hanover and Unity
Streets. A well-utilized
municipal resource, the Mall
is always full of local people:
children, teenagers, young
mothers, and older residents
chatting in Italian and playing
cards or checkers. Laid out in
1933, and originally called the
Prado, its focal point is Cyrus
Dallin's equestrian statue of
local hero Paul Revere, which
was originally modeled in
1885. However, it was only
sculpted and
placed here in
1940. Bronze bas-
relief plaques on
the mall's side
walls commem-
orate a number
of North End
residents who
have played
an important

**Equestrian statue by Cyrus
Dallin, Paul Revere Mall**

role in the history of Boston.
Benches, a fountain, and twin
rows of linden trees complete
the space, which has a
distinctly European feel.

St. Stephen's Church ❺

401 Hanover St. **Map** 2 E2.
***Tel** (617) 523-1230.* Ⓣ *Haymarket,
Aquarium.* ◯ *8:30am–4:30pm
Mon–Sat.* ✝ *11am Sun, 4:30pm
Sat, 7:30am Tue–Fri.*

Opened in 1714 as a
humble Congregationalist
meeting house, St. Stephen's
Church was extensively
enlarged and embellished by
the architect Charles Bulfinch
(see p53) in 1802–04.
Bulfinch incorporated
a range of harmonious
Italian Renaissance
motifs in his re-
design, adding a
number of decor-
ative pediments
and pedestals,
tall arched
windows,
as well as

**St. Stephen's Church, with its
Renaissance-style bell tower**

an ornate bell tower that is
topped by a gilded cap. One
year after that project's completion, the first-ever bell
cast by the famous revolutionary and master metalworker,
Paul Revere *(see p21)*, was
hung in the belfry.

The church's present name
dates from 1862, when it
became Roman Catholic to
accommodate the North End's
increasing numbers of Irish
immigrants. When Hanover
Street was widened in 1869,
the entire structure was
moved back 16 ft (5 m) and,
a year later, it was raised 6 ft
(2 m) to accommodate a
basement chapel. Damaged
by fires in 1897 and 1929,
and redecorated each time,
the church was restored to
its Bulfinch design in 1965.

The church's interior features
include a gracefully curved
ceiling, original white-painted
pine columns, and a pair of
pewter chandeliers, which are
copies of those hanging in the
Doric Hall of the Massachusetts
State House. The church's
pews were donated in honor
of the numerous Irish, Italian,
and Portuguese parishioners
who live in the neighborhood,
while the Italian mahogany
Stations of the Cross are part
of the 1965 refit. St. Stephen's
is listed on the National
Register of Historic Places.

THE GREAT BRINKS ROBBERY

Masterminded by Tony Pino, this infamous event took
place on the night of January 17, 1950 on North End's
Commercial Street. Disguised as Brinks guards, seven of
Pino's men made off with $2,775,395.12 in payroll money –
including cash totaling $1,218,211.29 – from the head-
quarters of the Brinks Armored Car Company. Nationwide
headlines trumpeted the robbery as the biggest heist in U.S.
history. Even though all members of the Brinks gang were
eventually caught and imprisoned, only $60,000 of the loot
has been recovered more than half a century after the event.

Members of the infamous Brinks gang, in police custody

Paul Revere House ❻

19 North Sq. **Map** 2 E2. *Tel (617) 523-2338.* ⓣ *Haymarket, Aquarium.* ▢ *mid-Apr–Oct: 9:30am–5:15pm daily; Nov–mid-Apr: 9:30am–4:15pm daily (Pierce-Hichborn House call for tour hours).* ● *Jan–Mar: Mon.* ♿ 🛈 📷 www.paulreverehouse.org

The city's oldest surviving clapboard frame house is historically significant, for it was here in 1775 that Paul Revere began his legendary horseback ride to warn his compatriots in Lexington of the impending arrival of British troops *(see p21)*. This historic event was later immortalized in a boldly patriotic, epic poem by Henry Wadsworth Longfellow *(see p108)*. It begins "Listen, my children, and you shall hear of the midnight ride of Paul Revere."

Revere, a Huguenot descendent, was by trade a versatile gold- and silversmith, copper engraver, and maker of church bells, cannons, and false teeth. He and his second wife Rachel, mother of eight of his 16 children, owned the house from 1770 to 1800. Small leaded casement windows, an overhanging upper story, and nail-studded front door all contribute to make it a fine example of 17th-century Early American architecture. In the courtyard along one side of the house is a large bronze bell, cast by Paul Revere for a church in 1804 – Revere made nearly 200 church bells. Three rooms in the house contain period artifacts, including original pieces of family furniture, items made in Revere's workshop, and colonial banknotes. The house, which by the mid-19th century had become a decrepit tenement fronted by stores, was saved from demolition by preservationists' efforts led by a great-grandson of Revere.

Colonial banknotes, exhibited in the Paul Revere House

Next door, the early 18th-century Pierce-Hichborn House is the earliest brick town house remaining in New England. It features Georgian English motifs such as shallow arches over the doors and windows, and twin chimneys. Admission is via the Paul Revere House.

Paul Revere House kitchen, as it was in the 17th century

Christopher Columbus Park ❼

Atlantic Avenue, between Long & Commercial Wharves. **Map** 2 E3. ⓣ *Aquarium.*

Extensive urban renewal along the Inner Harbor resulted in the completion of this handsome park in 1976. It covers 4.5 acres (2 ha) with wisteria clinging to a 340 ft (104-m) long arched trellis, and is a superlative spot for views of the waterfront and the Financial District. The commemorative Rose Fitzgerald Kennedy Garden was added to the park's layout in 1987.

View toward the Custom House and the Financial District, across Christopher Columbus Park

Rowes Wharf development, typical of Boston's waterfront regeneration

Institute of Contemporary Art ⓫

Northern Avenue. **Map** 2 F5.
Tel (617) 478-3100. Ⓣ Courthouse.
🔲 10am–5pm Tue, Wed, Sat, Sun,
10am–9pm Thu, Fri. 🔲 🔲

In 2006 the Institute of Contemporary Art moved to a dramatic new wood, steel, and glass landmark building on Fan Pier. Light-flooded galleries, a performance space open to harbor views, and a cutting-edge media center mean that the ICA can extend its seven-decade history of innovation well into the 21st century. Its exhibitions typically break the mold of convention and it is building its first permanent collection of avant-garde work.

Long Wharf ❽

Atlantic Avenue. **Map** 2 E3.
Ⓣ Aquarium.

The nation's oldest continuously operated wharf was built in 1710 to accommodate the boom in early maritime commerce. The following century was to be Boston's international maritime heyday; it was the busiest port in North America and one of the most important in the colonies, surpassed only by London and Bristol in the amount of cargo that it handled. Once extending 2000 ft (610 m) into Boston harbor, and lined with shops and warehouses, Long Wharf provided secure mooring for the largest ships of the time.

Today, Long Wharf is used by boat services to Provincetown, Charlestown Navy Yard, and the Harbor Islands. The attractive esplanade at the end also offers good views across the city's waterfront. Running along the waterfront, Harbor Walk connects Long Wharf with other adjacent wharves, such as Union, Lewis, and Commercial wharves. Dating from the early 1800s, most are now converted to fashionable harborside apartments and condominiums.

New England Aquarium ❾

See pp76–7.

Rowes Wharf ❿

Atlantic Avenue. **Map** 2 E4.
Ⓣ Aquarium.

Completed in 1987, this fine example of waterfront revitalization replaced the two-part India wharf dating from the 1760s. Built of Bostonian red brick and designed by Skidmore, Owings & Merrill, the complex houses the luxury Boston Harbor Hotel (see p133), condominiums, offices, and a marina. A large archway links the city to the harbor.

Boston Tea Party Ships & Museum ⓬

Congress St. Bridge. **Map** 2 E5. **Tel**
(617) 338-1773. Ⓣ South Station.
🔲 at least until summer 2009. 🔲
www.historictours.com/boston

Griffin's Wharf, where the Boston Tea Party took place on December 16, 1773 (see p75), was buried beneath landfill many years ago. Beginning in 2009, replicas of three British East India Company ships involved in the Tea Party will anchor in Fort Point Channel. Today, modern-day patriots toss imitation bales of tea overboard, recreating one of the acts of American defiance that

View down Long Wharf toward the waterfront and Custom House

prompted Britain to close Boston Harbor in 1773 and put the Massachusetts Bay Colony under martial law.

On an adjacent pier, ship models, Tea Party memorabilia, and other educational exhibits are displayed in a museum.

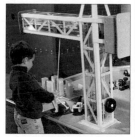

Playing on the mini-construction site at Boston's Children's Museum

Children's Museum ⑬

300 Congress St. **Map** 2 E5. *Tel (617) 426-6500.* Ⓣ *South Station.* ◯ *10am–5pm daily, 10am–9pm Fri.* 🈳 🅱 **www**.bostonchildrens museum.org

Overlooking Fort Point Channel, a pair of rejuvenated 19th-century wool warehouses contain one of the country's best children's museums, which underwent an extensive expansion in 2007. There are many interesting exhibits, and youngsters are able to participate in games and learning activities, and hoist themselves up a climbing structure in the New Balance Center.

The Art Studio provides a hands-on recycling area with barrels of materials that children can use in self-instructive creative projects, while the new KidPower exhibition is designed to encourage active, healthy lifestyles. An international flavor is injected into the proceedings by a visit to the silk merchant's house, which has been transplanted from the city of Kyoto in Japan (Boston's sister city).

A towering milk bottle from a local dairy stands outside in front of the museum building and is used as an ice-cream stand in summer. A new outdoor park features mazes, giant boulders, and spaces for outdoor performances.

THE BOSTON TEA PARTY

In 1767, when Britain decided to tax its American colonies, there was outrage. Boycotts were placed on British goods, and protesters took to the streets. One such protest in 1773 culminated in the Boston Massacre *(see p20).*

Despite a subsequent reduction in taxation, tax on tea remained. Parliament then granted the British East India Company sole rights to sell tea in the colonies, which caused prices to rise further. In November 1773, ships arrived in Boston Harbor loaded with tea, and merchants, who refused to buy the tea, came under pressure from Thomas Hutchinson, the Monarchist governor. On the night of December 16, however, around 7,000 rebels, gathered by Samuel Adams, marched to the wharf declaring "Tonight Boston Harbor is a teapot!" Fifty men, dressed as Mohawks, boarded the ships and dumped their cargoes into the water.

Britain reacted strongly, closing the port and putting Massachusetts under martial law. This retribution unified patriots across America, and the "Boston Tea Party," as the protest was soon known, became the spark that ignited the Revolutionary War.

Thomas Hutchinson
Governor of Boston and staunch monarchist, Thomas Hutchinson tried to force the rebels to comply with British colonial law.

Many of the rebels were dressed as Mohawks.

342 bales of tea were thrown into the sea.

A crowd of about 7,000 watched the events from the quayside.

The Boston Tea Party, depicted in a 19th-century engraving

New England Aquarium ⑨

The waterfront's prime attraction dominates Central Wharf. Designed by a consortium of architects in 1969, the aquarium's core encloses a vast four-story ocean tank, which contains a wide array of marine animals. A curving walkway runs around the outside of the tank from top to bottom and provides viewpoints of the interior of the tank from different levels. Also resident are colonies of penguins, playful harbor and fur seals, anacondas, rays, and mesmerizing seadragons. An IMAX® Theatre rounds out the facility.

Edge of the Sea Tidepool
A fiberglass shore recreates a world where the land meets the sea. It is home to animals such as horseshoe crabs and sea urchins.

★ **Penguin Pool**
One of the main attractions of the aquarium, the penguin pool runs around the base of the giant tank. It contains African, rockhopper, and blue penguins.

★ **Whale Watch**
A naturalist aboard the Aquarium boat explains marine ecology on trips to Stellwagen Bank, 75 minutes away. You can see whales, sea birds, and other marine life.

Main entrance

Ticket booth

Harbor Seals
An outdoor tank covered by a steel canopy, is home to a lively colony of harbor seals.

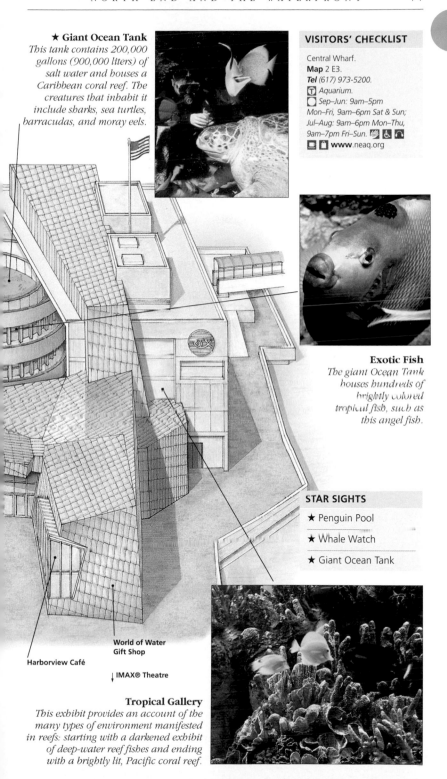

★ **Giant Ocean Tank**
*This tank contains 200,000
gallons (900,000 litters) of
salt water and houses a
Caribbean coral reef. The
creatures that inhabit it
include sharks, sea turtles,
barracudas, and moray eels.*

VISITORS' CHECKLIST

Central Wharf.
Map 2 E3.
Tel (617) 973-5200.
T Aquarium.
Sep–Jun: 9am–5pm
Mon–Fri, 9am–6pm Sat & Sun;
Jul–Aug: 9am–6pm Mon–Thu,
9am–7pm Fri–Sun.
www.neaq.org

Exotic Fish
*The giant Ocean Tank
houses hundreds of
brightly colored
tropical fish, such as
this angel fish.*

STAR SIGHTS

★ Penguin Pool

★ Whale Watch

★ Giant Ocean Tank

**World of Water
Gift Shop**

Harborview Café

IMAX® Theatre

Tropical Gallery
*This exhibit provides an account of the
many types of environment manifested
in reefs: starting with a darkened exhibit
of deep-water reef fishes and ending
with a brightly lit, Pacific coral reef.*

CHINATOWN AND THE THEATER DISTRICT

ocated south of Boston Common *(see pp46–7)* and west of the Financial District, this part of town has a noticeably gritty, more down-to-earth ambience. The area around Washington Street, with Downtown Crossing at its center *(see pp80–81)*, is the city's main shopping district. South of here is Chinatown, one of the most populous in the United States – only the Chinatowns in San Francisco and New York are larger. West of Chinatown is the Theater District, featuring touring Broadway shows and local productions. A long time red-light district, the "Combat Zone" grew up at the lower end of Washington Street, between Chinatown and the Theater District. Today, it is being gentrified and, though an area where caution should be exercised, is moving increasingly upscale.

Gilt cherub, the Colonial Theater

SIGHTS AT A GLANCE

Historic Streets, Buildings, and Churches
Bay Village ⑩
Brattle Book Shop ④
Chinatown ⑧
Downtown Crossing ②
Ladder District ③
Jacob Wirth ⑨
Massachusetts State
    Transportation Building ⑥
St. Paul's Cathedral ①

Theaters
Colonial Theatre ⑦
Opera House ⑤
Shubert Theatre ⑪
Wang Theatre ⑫

KEY
Street-by-street map *pp80–81*
Ⓣ "T" station

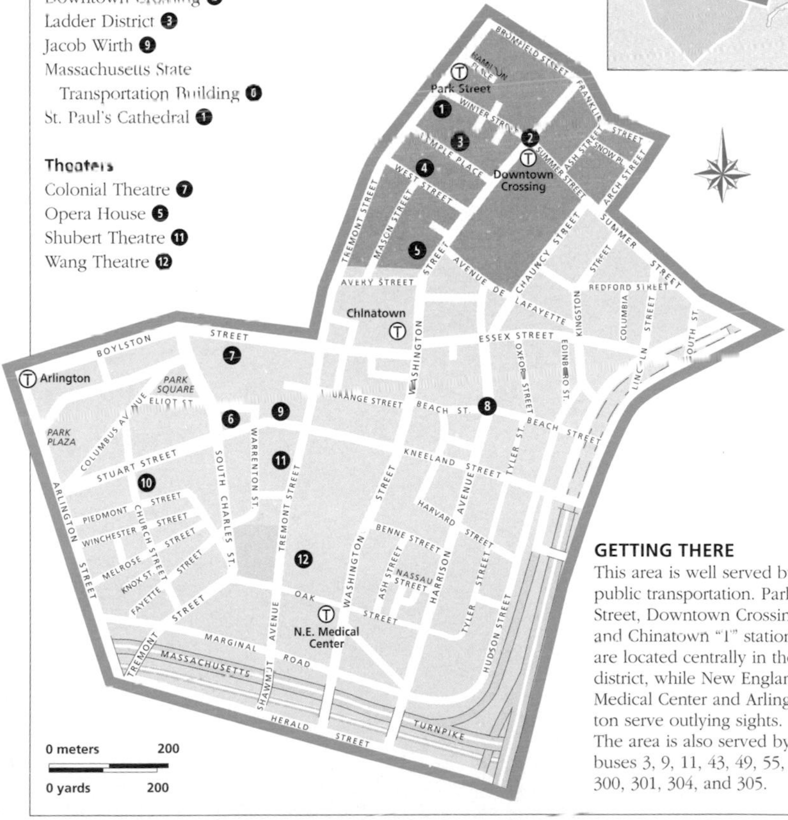

GETTING THERE
This area is well served by public transportation. Park Street, Downtown Crossing, and Chinatown "T" stations are located centrally in the district, while New England Medical Center and Arlington serve outlying sights. The area is also served by buses 3, 9, 11, 43, 49, 55, 300, 301, 304, and 305.

0 meters 200
0 yards 200

◁ Colorful August Moon Festival, held in Boston's Chinatown

Street-by-Street: Around Washington Street

Running northeast from the Theater District, Washington Street lies at the heart of Boston's main shopping area. Its main focal point, Downtown Crossing, lies at its intersection with Winter and Summer Streets. Saturday afternoons here, in particular, offer visitors a glimpse of Boston's sophisticated, and often multi-ethnic population, as they go about their shopping. Macy's is the main department store, though Washington Street and the streets

Decoration, Downtown Crossing

off it offer a range of outlets such as bookstores, camera stores, and jewelers. Just to the south, the Theater District and Chinatown are only a few minutes away on foot. Visitors should note that incidences of petty crime sometimes occur in this crowded area.

Sidewalk café on Summer Street

Boston Common

St. Paul's Cathedral
Dating from around 1820, this was one of the first Greek Revival granite buildings to go up in Boston. Today it is still used to broadcast Sunday morning religious programs ❶

★ Brattle Book Shop
At first glance, there is not a lot to recommend a second look at this Boston literary landmark. Inside, however, are more than 250,000 rare books and magazines, a treat for any lover of the printed word ❹

Theater District and Chinatown

★ Opera House
This building was opened as a theater in 1928. Closed in 1991, it was completely restored and reopened in 2004, making it the focus of a newly revitalized lower Washington Street ❺

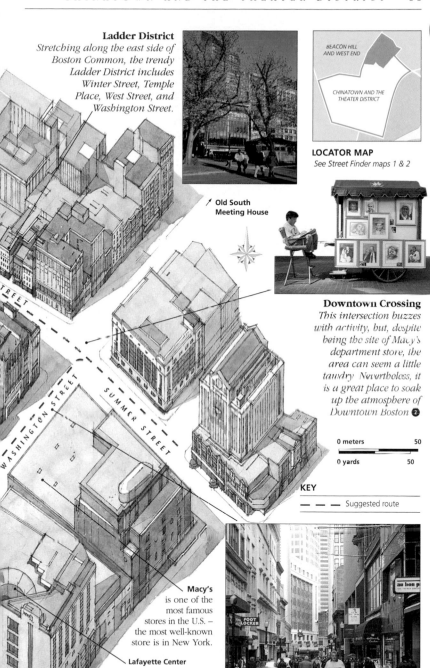

Ladder District
Stretching along the east side of Boston Common, the trendy Ladder District includes Winter Street, Temple Place, West Street, and Washington Street.

LOCATOR MAP
See Street Finder maps 1 & 2

BEACON HILL AND WEST END

CHINATOWN AND THE THEATER DISTRICT

↗ **Old South Meeting House**

Downtown Crossing
This intersection buzzes with activity, but, despite being the site of Macy's department store, the area can seem a little tawdry. Nevertheless, it is a great place to soak up the atmosphere of Downtown Boston ❷

0 meters   50
0 yards   50

KEY
– – – Suggested route

Macy's
is one of the most famous stores in the U.S. – the most well-known store is in New York.

Lafayette Center

STAR SIGHTS

★ Opera House

★ Brattle Bookshop

↘ **Boston Tea Party Ship**

Washington Street
The main street of this district, Washington Street has many stores. New developments, such as the Lafayette Center, make it increasingly upscale.

Classical chancel and box pews of the interior of St. Paul's Cathedral, typically austere in style

St. Paul's Cathedral **①**

138 Tremont St. **Map** 4 E1.
Tel (617) 482-5800. ⓣ *Park Street.*
🕀 *8am, 10am & 12:30pm Sun;*
1pm Mon, 12:15pm Tue, Fri. ♿
www.stpaulboston.org

Consecrated in 1820, Boston's second example of Greek Revival architecture was designed by Alexander Parris, five years before the completion of his Quincy Market hall *(see p64)*, which also has the outward appear-

ance of a Greek temple. The first Greek Revival Church in Boston came about with Charles Bulfinch's design for the façade of the original New South Church, which was subsequently demolished.

The stone work on St. Paul's Cathedral is by Solomon Willard, who gave the church a portico of six unfluted stone columns with Ionic capitals. The building's pediment was initially intended to feature a frieze depicting St. Paul preaching before King Agrippa, but this was never constructed due to considerations of the cost involved.

The interior of the church, dominated by a classical chancel, curved apse, and box pews, is spacious and austere, typical of a style found in New England churches.

In 1908 the church became the cathedral of Massachusetts' Episcopal diocese, the largest in the U.S. The United States' longest-running religious radio program has been broadcast from the cathedral each Sunday since the 1920s.

Downtown Crossing **②**

Washington, Winter & Summer Sts.
Map 4 F1. ⓣ *Downtown Crossing.*

As an antidote to heavy traffic congestion, this shopping-district crossroads was laid out as a pedestrian zone between 1975 and 1978. The area is anchored by the Beaux Arts building, which was formerly Filene's, and Modernist Macy's. Smaller retail outlets, some in restored buildings with terracotta and cast-iron façades, are plentiful in the streets radiating from Downtown Crossing and Washington Street. Lively push cart vendors and sparkling diamonds in the jeweler's district can also be found here. South of Downtown Crossing, the area retains an atmosphere of an earlier era when this inner city district went by the name of the Combat Zone.

Ladder District **③**

Connecting streets and rear alleys between Washington & Tremont Sts.
Map 4 E1–F2. ⓣ *Downtown Crossing & Chinatown.*

Once a rather rundown part of Downtown, the web of small streets connecting Washington and Tremont Streets, along the east side of Boston Common, came into its own at the start of the new millennium. Soaring new buildings were erected on vacant parking lots and old architectural treasures on the dark streets were refurbished and brought back to life. Today they house restaurants, bars, and nightclubs.

Along with new upmarket condos came the Ritz-Carlton Boston Common hotel *(see p134)*, housed in a building that stretches the length of Avery Street. This building played a central role in the renaissance of what used to be a no man's land between the Theater District and Downtown Crossing. In addition to the luxury hotel, a cutting-edge restaurant, and a fashionable gym, the Sports

Beaux Arts façade of former Filene's department store, Downtown Crossing

Club/LA, the structure also houses the Loews Boston Common (see p161). Boston's first premier cinema has 19 screens, stadium seating, an upmarket bar, and multiple dining concessions.

The nightclubs and restaurants of the Ladder District are often indistinguishable, although if a long line is standing outside, the establishment probably serves more liquor than food. Club names also tend to change frequently as owners tweak the themes to attract different crowds. Many maps do not show all the small streets in the district, such as Pi Alley, so it is best to take a leisurely stroll and discover the area for yourself.

Vintage magazines displayed at the Brattle Book Shop

Brattle Book Shop ❹

9 West St. **Map** 4 E1.
Tel (617) 542-0210.
Ⓣ *Park Street, Downtown Crossing.*
🕐 *9am–5:30pm Mon -Sat.* ♿
www.brattlebookshop.com

Founded in 1825 and located at various sites around Boston since, this bibliophiles' treasure house is packed with more than 250,000 used, rare, and out-of-print books. Proprietor Kenneth Gloss also stocks back issues of periodicals, *Life, Look,* and *Collier's* magazines among them, along with antiquarian ephemera such as maps, prints, postcards, greeting cards, and autographed manuscripts. In front of and alongside the three-story building, passersby browse through bins and carts full of discounted bargain books priced in the range of $1 to $5.

Spanish Baroque, terracotta ornamentation on the façade of the Opera House

Opera House ❺

539 Washington St. **Map** 4 E1.
Tel (617) 931-2787. Ⓣ *Downtown Crossing, Chinatown, Boylston.* ♿
www.broadwayinboston.com

The building that is now the Opera House has been known by many names. Built on the site of the original Boston Theater, and designed by Thomas Lamb, it opened in 1928 as the B. F. Keith Memorial Theater, named after the late 19th-century showman who added the term "vaudeville" to show business vocabulary. It was renamed the Savoy Theater in the 1940s and served as home for the Opera Company of Boston from the late 1950s until 1991. The venue became internationally recognized for Sarah Caldwell's daringly innovative productions.

With its white Spanish Baroque, terracotta façade, high ceilings, and three-tier horseshoe balconies, the theater represents the apogee of early 20th century hall design. A$38 million renovation completed in 2004 restored the theater's original opulence with gilded surfaces and exquisite ceiling murals, while installing modern climate control, technical systems, and seating. Primarily used for large touring Broadway musicals, the Opera House is again the jewel of lower Washington Street.

LIBERTY TREE

At the corner of Washington Street and Boylston Street, a low relief of a tree marks the exact site of the famous Liberty Tree, where the Sons of Liberty would meet during the prelude to the American Revolution. The tree's fame first became widespread when it became a focal point for opposition to the Stamp Act (see p20). The British stamp master, Andrew Oliver, was hung in effigy from its branches, an incident that caused people from all over the region to gather around it. The tree was also a meeting place in the days running up to the Boston Tea Party (see p75). In August 1775, during the early part of the Revolution when Boston was still occupied by the British, a mob of Redcoats vented their anger on the tree and chopped it down.

Bostonians protest the Stamp Act of 1765, around the Liberty Tree

Massachusetts State Transportation Building ⑥

8–10 Park Plaza, Stuart & Charles Sts. **Map** 4 E2. ⓣ *Boylston.*
Atrium restaurants ⬜ *11am–8pm Mon–Fri, noon–6pm Sat.* ♿

The main feature of the Massachusetts State Transportation Building, constructed in 1983, is its seven-story-high, skylit City Place atrium, which is directly accessible to the public. Covering most of a sizeable city block, this red-brick and glass cantilevered building has won several prestigious design awards. It incorporates offices and public-service facilities, maintained by the state's transportation administrators, around a central mall of wide-ranging shops and restaurants

Lunchtime concerts, pop or light-classical music, are frequently scheduled in the central mall, while gallery showings are often held on the upper levels overlooking the atrium. Other facilities in the building include a bank, newsstand, and several fast-food eateries.

The City Place atrium in the Massachusetts State Transportation Building

Gilt ornamentation from the lavishly decorated interior of the Colonial Theater

Colonial Theatre ⑦

106 Boylston St. **Map** 4 E2.
Tel *(617) 426-9366.* ⓣ *Boylston.*
⬜ *phone to check.* ♿
www.broadwayacrossamerica.com

Clarence H. Blackall designed 14 Boston theaters during his architectural career, among them the Colonial, which is the city's oldest theater to have been in continuous operation under the same name. A two-story loggia sits atop Blackall's structure, which is otherwise quite plain. The interior, on the other hand, is an impressively opulent show-piece by H.B. Pennell: his Rococo lobby boasts gilded trim, chandeliers, and lofty arched ceilings. The 1,658-seat auditorium is decorated with allegorical figures, frescoes, and friezes.

The theater opened on December 20, 1900 with a suitably extravagant perfor-mance of the melodrama *Ben Hur*, featuring a cast of 350 and an on-stage chariot race involving a dozen horses pulling Roman chariots on treadmills. Today the theater is best remembered for premiering lavish shows. In particular it was the venue for productions by directors such as Irving Berlin, Sigmund Romberg, and Rodgers and Hammerstein, and is where Ziegfeld premi-ered his Follies *(see p87)*.

Chinatown ⑧

Bounded by Kingston, Kneeland, Washington & Essex Sts. **Map** 4 E2.
ⓣ *Chinatown.*

This area is the third largest Chinatown in the U.S. after those in San Francisco and New York. It covers blocks of filled land that had been the South Cove tidal backwater until the early 19th century. Pagoda-topped telephone booths, as well as a three-story gateway guarded by four marble lions, set the neighborhood's Asian tone.

The first 200 Chinese to settle in New England came by ship from San Francisco in 1870. Mostly unskilled, they were recruited to break a labor strike at a shoe factory in Massachusetts, but were jobless by 1874. At this time, some drifted to Boston, at first pitching their tents on Oliver Place, which they renamed

Colorful, contemporary city mural in Chinatown

Ping On Alley – "the Street of Peace and Security." In the 1880s another wave of Chinese immigration from California was prompted by an economic boom that led to job openings in construction, on the railroad, and the laying of telephone lines. Boston's Chinese colony was fully established by the turn of the 19th century, and with it came ubiquitous new garment and textile industries.

Political turmoil in China immediately following World War II, and more recent arrivals from Vietnam, Laos, Korea, Thailand, and Cambodia, have swelled Chinatown's population, which now stands at around 8,000. Restaurants, bakeries, food markets, curio shops, and dispensers of Chinese medicine are especially numerous along the main thoroughfare of Beach Street, as well as on Tyler, Oxford, and Harrison Streets.

Typical store and restaurant façades in Boston's Chinatown

Jacob Wirth ❾

31–37 Stuart St. **Map** 4 E2. **Tel** (617) 338-8586. Ⓣ Boylston, Chinatown. ⬛ 11:30am–8pm Sun & Mon (to 10pm Tue Thu, to midnight Fri, to 11pm Sat). ♿ **www**.jacobwirth.com

Occupying a 19th-century row house, Jacob Wirth has been in business since 1868. It is Boston's second oldest restaurant after the Union Oyster House (see p143). Restaurateur Jacob Wirth had the majestic mahogany restaurant bar shipped in small pieces from Russia. Overall, the old-fashioned beer-hall, with its globe lighting, ceiling fans, dark paneling, bare wood floors, and brass railings, has barely changed since the time that it opened. Sausage-and-sauerkraut menu staples, combined with draft beers and Rhine wines, make this the only authentic German restaurant in a city that is far more famous for its Irish and Italian heritage. Friday night piano sing-alongs are very popular.

Bay Village ❿

Bounded by Tremont, Arlington & South Charles Sts. **Map** 4 D2. Ⓣ New England Medical Center, Boylston.

Originally an expanse of mud flats, the Bay Village area was drained in the early 1800s and initially became habitable with the construction of a dam in 1825. Many carpenters, cabinetmakers, artisans, and house painters involved in the construction of Beacon Hill's pricier town houses built their own modest but well-crafted residences here. As a result there are many similarities between the two neighborhoods, including plenty of red brick, arched doorways, window boxes and shutters, courtyards, tidy gardens, and antique gas lamps. Fayette Street was laid out in 1824 to coincide with the triumphant U.S. visit of the Marquis de Lafayette, the French general who allied himself with George Washington for some of the campaigns of the Revolutionary War.

Bay Street, located just off Fayette Street, features a single dwelling and is generally regarded as the city's

Bay Village doorway, similar to those of Beacon Hill

shortest street. In 1809, poet and short-story writer Edgar Allen Poe was born in a boarding house on Carver Street, where his thespian parents were staying while in Boston on tour with a traveling theatrical company.

In the 1920s, at the height of the Prohibition era, clandestine speakeasies gave Bay Village its still-prevalent bohemian ambience. More recently, the neighborhood has become a center for Boston's gay community.

Bay Village's Piedmont Street is noteworthy for two very different reasons. The W. S. Haynes Company at No. 12 has been hand-crafting flutes and piccolos since 1888, and has acquired a worldwide reputation for its instruments among soloists and symphony orchestra performers alike.

The street's other claim to fame is less auspicious. The Coconut Grove nightclub fire of 1942, when 491 of the club's patrons died, remains one of the United States' highest fire death tolls. This devastating occurrence resulted in infamy for the area but, ultimately, to more stringent fire-safety codes throughout the United States.

The vast Grand Lobby of the Wang Theatre

Shubert Theatre ⓫

265 Tremont St. **Map** 4 E2.
Tel *(617) 482-9393*. Ⓣ *Boylston,*
New England Medical Center.
◯ *phone for details.* ♿
www.citicenter.org

The 1,650-seat Shubert
Theater rivals the Colonial
Theater *(see p84)* for its
long history of staging
major pre-Broadway musical
productions. Designed by
the architects Charles Bond

**Palladian-style window over the
entrance to the Shubert Theater**

and Thomas James, the
theater first opened its doors
in 1910, and during its
heyday many famous stars
walked the boards here.
Among them were Sarah
Bernhardt, W.C. Fields,
Cary Grant, Mae
West, Humphrey
Bogart, Ingrid
Bergman, Henry
Ford, and Rex
Harrison.
   The Shubert Theater
is listed on the National
Register of Historic
Places, and features
a white, Neoclassical façade
with a pair of Ionic columns
flanking a monumental,
Palladian-style window that
sits over the entrance. The
entrance also boasts an ornate, wrought-iron canopy.
   The theater closed for a
number of years but in 1997
it reopened to premiere
the pre-Broadway hit *Rent*.
Local companies also stage
performances here.
   A plaque to the side of
the main entrance recounts
the history of the theater.

**Ornate, gilt
decoration at
the Wang**

Wang Theatre ⓬

270 Tremont St. **Map** 4 E2.
Tel *(617) 482-9393*. Ⓣ *Boylston,*
New England Medical Center.
◯ *phone for details.* ♿
www.citicenter.org

Opened in 1925 as the
Metropolitan Theater and
later named the Music Hall,
New England's most ornate
variety theater was inspired
by the Paris Opera House,
and was originally intended
to be a movie theater. Like
the nearby Colonial Theater,
the Metropolitan was de-
signed by Clarence Blackall.
When it was first built the
auditorium had over 4,000
seats, which made it one
of the largest in the world.
It was so big that at its
opening, which over
20,000 people attended,
one Hollywood magnate
described it as a theater
of "mountainous splendour,
a movie palace of fabulous
grandeur and stupendous
stage presentations." Another
observer described it as a
"cathedral of the movies."
   The theater was restored
and renamed in 1983.
The five-story Grand
Lobby and seven-story
auditorium are designed
in a magnificent and ornate
Renaissance Revival style:
gold-plated chandeliers,
bronze detailing,
stained glass,
florid ceiling
murals, rose
jasper pillars,
and marble-framed
doorways. There are
also three sumptuous
lobbies, which visitors
must pass through
before finally arriving at the
awesome Grand Lobby.
   Today, the theater hosts
a wide variety of events,
including Broadway road
shows, touring national
and international dance
and opera productions,
celebrity concert appearances,
and motion-picture revivals. It
is also a popular performance
venue for local dance and
theater companies. Both
the Wang and Shubert
theaters are operated by
Citi Performing Arts Center.

The History of Boston's Theater District

Boston's first theater opened in 1793 on Federal Street. Fifty years later Boston had become a major tryout town and boasted a number of lavish theaters. The U.S. premiere of Handel's *Messiah* opened in 1839, the U.S. premiere of Gilbert and Sullivan's *H.M.S. Pinafore* in 1877, and the world premiere of Tchaikovsky's *First Piano Concerto* in 1875. In

South Pacific, Rodgers and Hammerstein

the late 19th century theaters came under fire from the censorious Watch and Ward Society. In the 20th century, dramas such as Tennessee Williams' *A Streetcar Named Desire* and Eugene O'Neill's *Long Day's Journey into Night* debuted here. Premieres included *Ziegfeld Follies*, Gershwin's *Porgy and Bess*, and musicals by Rodgers and Hammerstein.

Theatergoers *in 19th-century Boston came primarily from the city's social elite, who were often patrons of the arts. In this way Boston's theaters flourished.*

The planned new theater remained in use until 1835. It became the Academy of Music from 1835 to 1846.

Old theater

Athena

Cupids

The Federal Street Theater, *designed by Charles Bulfinch, burned down in 1798. The old and new theaters are depicted in this allegorical painting, possibly a set design, which also shows characters from Greek mythology. Other Bulfinch buildings are also shown.*

Tennessee Williams' A Streetcar Named Desire *premiered at Boston's Wilbur Theater. It starred a young Marlon Brando and Jessica Tandy.*

Ziegfeld Follies, *produced in the 1920s, had eight pre-Broadway "tryouts" at the Colonial Theater (see p84).*

The Rodgers and Hammerstein *musical* Oklahoma! *premiered in Boston as a production entitled* Away We Go! *It was refined in Boston before hitting Broadway.*

BACK BAY AND SOUTH END

Until the 19th century Boston was situated on a narrow peninsula surrounded by tidal marshes. Projects to fill Back Bay began in the 1850s and were made possible by new inventions such as the steam shovel. The Back Bay was filled by 1880 and developers soon moved in. Planned along French lines, with elegant boulevards, Back Bay is now one of Boston's most exclusive neighborhoods. The more bohemian South End, laid out on an English model of town houses clustered around squares, is home to many artists and Boston's gay community.

Sargent mural, Boston Public Library

SIGHTS AT A GLANCE

Historic Streets and Squares
Boylston Street **8**
Commonwealth Avenue **4**
Copley Place **14**
Copley Square **7**
The Esplanade **1**
Newbury Street **5**
Union Park **16**

Historic Buildings, Churches, and Museums
Boston Center for the Arts **15**

Boston Public Library **9**
Christian Science Center **13**
First Baptist Church **3**
Gibson House Museum **2**
Berklee Performance Center **11**
John Hancock Tower **10**
Prudential Center **12**
Trinity Church pp94–5 **6**

KEY
Street-by-street map *pp90–91*
"T" station
Railroad station
Bus station
Tourist information

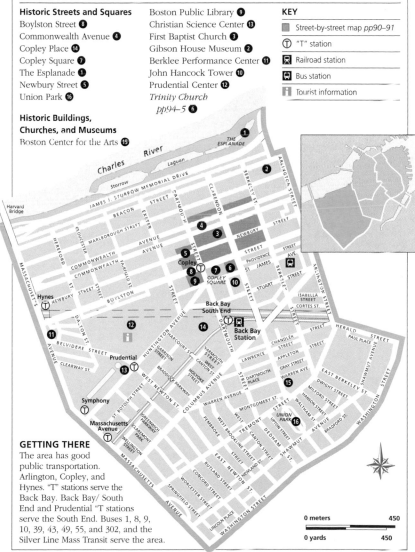

GETTING THERE
The area has good public transportation. Arlington, Copley, and Hynes. "T" stations serve the Back Bay. Back Bay/ South End and Prudential "T stations serve the South End. Buses 1, 8, 9, 10, 39, 43, 49, 55, and 302, and the Silver Line Mass Transit serve the area.

| 0 meters | 450 |
| 0 yards | 450 |

◁ **View of Back Bay's characteristic row houses, from the top of the Prudential Center Skywalk observatory**

Street-by-Street: Back Bay

This fashionable district unfolds westward from the Public Garden *(see pp46–7)* in a grid that departs radically from the twisting streets found elsewhere in Boston. Commonwealth Avenue, with its grand 19th-century mansions and parkland, and Newbury and Boylston Streets are its main arteries. Newbury Street is a magnet for all of Boston wanting to indulge in some upscale shopping, whereas the more somber Boylston Street bustles with office workers. Copley Square anchors the entire area and is the site of Henry Hobson Richardson's magnificent Trinity Church *(see pp94–5)* and the 60-story John Hancock Tower *(see p97)*, the tallest building in New England.

Weekly summer and fall farmers' market, Copley Square

Copley Square
This square was a marsh until 1870. It took on its present form only in the late 20th century as buildings around its edges were completed. A farmers' market, concerts, and folk-dancing feature regularly **7**

COMMONWEALTH AVENUE

NEWBUR

Fenway Park ←

DARTMOUTH STREET

Boylston Street
The site of the Prudential Center (see p98) and the Boston Public Library (see p96), Boylston Street is also the location of the fabulous New Old South Church (see p96) **8**

BOYLSTON STREET

★ Boston Public Library
One of the first free public libraries in the world, this building was designed by Charles McKim. Inside are murals by John Singer Sargent **9**

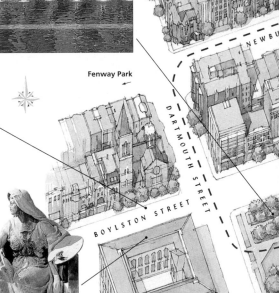

South End ↓

First Baptist Church
By Henry Hobson Richardson (see p92), this church is a fine example of his Romanesque Revival style ❸

Beacon Hill

COMMONWEALTH AVENUE

CLARENDON STREET

SIREET

Public Garden

LOCATOR MAP
See Street Finder map 3

BEACON HILL AND WEST END

BACK BAY AND SOUTH END

Commonwealth Avenue
Envisioned as Boston's Champs-Elysées, this avenue boasts beautiful town houses and a tree-lined central mall ❹

★ **Newbury Street**
High fashion outlets, galleries, and restaurants characterize this street – Boston's most fashionable, and a great place for people-watching ❺

★ **Trinity Church**
Acknowledged as Henry Hobson Richardson's Romanesque Revival masterpiece, this is one of the most important churches in the U.S. ❻

KEY

– – – Suggested route

STAR SIGHTS

★ Newbury Street

★ Trinity Church

★ Boston Public Library

0 meters 50
0 yards 50

The Esplanade ❶

Map 1 A4. ⓣ *Charles/MGH.*
◯ *24 hrs daily.* ♿

Running along the Boston side of the Charles River, between Longfellow Bridge and Dartmouth Street, are the parkland, lagoons, and islands known collectively as the Esplanade. The park is used extensively for in-line skating, cycling, and strolling and it is also the access point for boating on the river, including gondola rides. It is also the site of the city's leading outdoor concert venue.

In 1929, Arthur Fiedler, then the young conductor of the Boston Pops Orchestra, chose the Esplanade for a summer concert series that became a tradition. The Hatch Memorial Shell was constructed in 1939, and its stage is widely used by musical ensembles and other musical groups throughout the summer. Fourth of July concerts by the Boston Pops, which are followed by fireworks, can attract upward of 500,000 spectators *(see p35)*.

Fountains at the Esplanade, next to the Charles River

Gibson House Museum ❷

137 Beacon St. **Map** 1 A4.
Tel *(617) 267-6338.* ⓣ *Arlington.*
◯ *obligatory tours at 1pm, 2pm, 3pm Wed–Sun.* 🎦 🚫 📷
www.thegibsonhouse.org

Among the first houses built in the Back Bay, the Gibson House preserves its original Victorian decor and furnishings throughout all six stories. The 1860 brownstone and red-brick structure was

The original Victorian-style library of the Gibson House Museum

designed in the popular Italian Renaissance Revival style for the widow Catherine Hammond Gibson, who was one of the few women to own property in this part of the city. Her grandson Charles Hammond Gibson, Jr., a noted eccentric, poet, travel writer, horticulturalist, and bon vivant, arranged for the house to become a museum after his death in 1954. As a prelude to this, Gibson began to rope off the furniture in the 1930s, instead inviting his guests to sit on the stairs to drink martinis made with his own bathtub gin.

One of the most modern houses of its day, the Gibson House boasted such technical advancements as gas lighting, indoor plumbing in the basement, and coal-fired central heating. Visitors can see a full dinner setting in the dining room or admire the whimsical Turkish pet pavilion. But it is Gibson's preservation of the 1860s decor (with some modifications in 1888) that makes the museum a true time capsule of Victorian life in Boston.

Detail of Bartholdi's frieze atop the distinctive square tower of the First Baptist Church

First Baptist Church ❸

110 Commonwealth Ave.
Map 3 C2. ***Tel*** *(617) 267-3148.*
ⓣ *Arlington.* ◯ *for Sunday worship.* 🕇 *11am Sun.* 🚫 ♿

The Romanesque-style First Baptist Church on the corner of Commonwealth Avenue and Clarendon Street was Henry Hobson Richardson's *(see p32)* first major architectural commission and became an instant landmark when it was finished in 1872. Viewed from Commonwealth Avenue, it is one of the most distinctive buildings of the city skyline.

Richardson considered the nearly freestanding bell tower, which he modeled roughly on Italian campaniles, to be the church's most innovative structure. The square tower is topped with a decorative frieze and arches protected by an overhanging roof. The frieze was modeled in Paris by Bartholdi, the sculptor who created the Statue of Liberty, and was carved in place by Italian artisans after the stones were set. The faces in the frieze, which depict the sacraments, are likenesses of prominent Bostonians of that time, among them Henry Wadsworth Longfellow and Ralph Waldo Emerson *(see p31)*. The trumpeting angels at the corners of the tower gave the building its nickname, "Church of the Holy Bean Blowers."

Four years after the church was completed, the Unitarian congregation dissolved because it was unable to bear the expense of the building. The church stood vacant until 1881, when the First Baptist congregation from the South End took it over.

Commonwealth Avenue ❹

Map 3 B2. ⓣ *Arlington, Copley, Hynes Convention Center/ICA.*

Back Bay was Boston's first fully planned neighborhood, and architect Arthur Gilman made Commonwealth Avenue, modeled on the elegant boulevards of Paris, the centerpiece of the design. At 200 ft (61 m) wide, with a 10 ft (3 m) setback from the sidewalks to encourage small gardens in front of the buildings, Commonwealth became an arena for America's leading domestic architects in the second half of the 19th century. A walk from the Public Garden to Massachusetts Avenue is like flicking through a catalog of architectural styles.

Few of the grand buildings on either side of the avenue are open to the public, but

strollers on the central mall of the avenue encounter a number of historic figures in the form of bronze statues. Some have only tangential relationships to the city, like Alexander Hamilton, the first secretary of the U.S. Treasury. The end of the mall features an heroic bronze of Leif Erikson, erected as a historically unsupported flight of fancy that the Norse explorer landed at Boston. The patrician statue of abolitionist William Garrison is said to capture exactly the man's air of moral superiority. The best-loved memorial depicts sailor and historian Samuel Eliot Morison dangling his feet from a rock.

Newbury Street ❺

Map 3 C2. ⓣ *Arlington, Copley, Hynes Convention Center/ICA.*

Newbury Street is a Boston synonym for "stylish." The Taj Boston, formerly the Ritz-Carlton Hotel, at Arlington Street sets an elegant tone for the street that continues with a mix of prestigious and often

William Garrison statue on Commonwealth Avenue

well-hidden art galleries, stylish boutiques, and some of the city's most *au courant* restaurants.

Churches provide vestiges of a more decorous era. The Church of the Covenant at No. 67 Newbury contains the world's largest collection of Louis Comfort Tiffany stained-glass windows and an elaborate Tiffany lantern. A chorus and orchestra perform a Bach cantata each Sunday at Emmanuel Church on the corner of Newbury and Berkeley Streets.

Most of Newbury Street was constructed as town-house residences, but the desirability of these spaces for retail operations has pushed residents to the upper floors, while ground and underground levels are devoted to chic boutiques and eateries. Modern-day aspiring celebrities may be spotted at the sidewalk tables of Newbury's "hottest" restaurants, such as Sonsie *(see p146).*

⌂ Church of the Covenant
67 Newbury St. **Tel** (617) 266-7480. ◯ *10:30am Sun for church service.* ◙ ♿ ▣ ◹
www.churchofthecovenant.org

Stylish Newbury Street, with its elegant shops, galleries, and restaurants, the epitome of Boston style

Trinity Church ⑥

Routinely voted one of America's 10 finest buildings, this masterpiece by Henry Hobson Richardson dates from 1877. Trinity Church was founded in 1733 near Downtown Crossing, but the congregation moved the church to this site in 1871. The church is a granite and sandstone Romanesque structure standing on wooden piles driven through mud into bedrock, surmounted with granite pyramids. John LaFarge designed the interior, while some of the windows are designed by Edward Burne-Jones and executed by William Morris.

The bell tower was inspired by the Renaissance cathedral at Salamanca, central Spain.

Bas-relief in Chancel
On the wall of the chancel, behind the altar, are a series of gold bas-reliefs. This one shows St. Paul before King Agrippas.

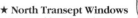

★ **North Transept Windows**
Designed by Edward Burne-Jones and executed by William Morris, the three stained-glass windows above the choir relate the story of Christmas.

Parish House

The pulpit is covered with carved scenes from the life of Christ, as well as portraits of great preachers through the ages.

Chancel
Designed by Charles Maginnis, the present-day chancel was not dedicated until 1938. The seven windows by Clayton & Bell, of London, show the life of Christ.

David's Charge to Solomon
Located in the baptistry, to the right of the chancel, this beautiful window is also the result of a partnership between Edward Burne-Jones and William Morris. The story shown is one of the few in the church from the Old Testament.

VISITORS' CHECKLIST

Copley Sq. **Map** 3 C2. **Tel** (617) 536-0944. Ⓣ Copley. ⬤ 9am–5:30pm Mon–Sat, 1–5pm Sun. ✝ 7:45am, 9am, 11:15am, 6pm Sun. **Concerts** Sep–Jun: 12:15pm Fri. 📷 📶 call for tour times. ♿ **www**.trinitychurchboston.org

John LaFarge's lancet windows show Christ in the act of blessing. They were designed at the request of Phillips Brooks – he wanted LaFarge to create an inspirational design for the west nave, which he could look at while preaching.

★ **West Portico**
Richardson disliked the original flat façade of Trinity Church, and so modeled the deeply sculpted west portico after St. Trophime in Arles, France. It was added after his death.

Carving of Phillips Brooks and Christ

PHILLIPS BROOKS

Born in Boston in 1835 and educated at Harvard, Brooks was a towering charismatic figure. Rector of Trinity Church from 1869, he gained a reputation for powerful sermons. From 1872 Brooks worked closely with Henry Hobson Richardson on the design of the new Trinity Church – at least five sculpted likenesses of him can be seen in and around the building.

STAR SIGHTS

★ West Portico

★ North Transept Windows

Main entrance

The New Old South Church, which looks across Copley Square

Copley Square ❼

Map 3 C2. ⓣ *Copley.*

Named after John Singleton Copley, the great Boston painter born nearby in 1737, Copley Square is a hive of civic activity surrounded by some of Boston's most striking architecture. Summer activities include weekly farmers' markets, concerts, and even folk-dancing.

The inviting green plaza took years to develop; when Copley was born it was just a marshy riverbank, which remained unfilled until 1870. Construction of the John Hancock Tower in 1975 anchored the southeastern side of Copley Square, and Copley Place (see p99) completed the square on the southwestern corner in 1984. Today's Copley Square, a wide open space of trees, grass, and fountains, took shape in the heart of the city in the 1990s, after various plans to utilize this hitherto wasted space were tendered.

A large plaque honoring the Boston Marathon, which ends at the Boston Public Library, was set in the sidewalk in 1996 to coincide with the 100th race. As well as pushcart vendors, the plaza has a booth for discounted theater, music, and dance tickets.

Boylston Street ❽

Map 3 C2. ⓣ *Boylston, Arlington, Copley, Hynes Convention Center/ICA.*

The corners of Boylston and Berkeley streets represent Boston architecture at its most diverse. The stately French Academic-style structure on the west side was erected for the Museum of Natural History, a forerunner of the Museum of Science (see p53). Its present occupant is the upscale clothier Louis. The east side spouts a Robert A.M. Stern tower and a Philip Johnson office building that resembles a table radio. Boston's finest jeweler Shreve, Crump & Low occupied the Art Deco building at the corner of Arlington Street until relocating to 440 Boylston Street in 2005.

Some notable office buildings stand on Boylston Street. The lobby of the New England building at No. 501 features large historical murals and dioramas depicting the process of filling Back Bay during the late 19th century. The towers of the Prudential Center (see p98) dominate the skyline on upper Boylston Street. Adjoining the Prudential

is the Hynes Convention Center. It was enlarged in 1988 to accommodate the city's burgeoning convention business.

The Italian Gothic-style **New Old South Church**, at the corner of Dartmouth and Boylston Streets, was built in 1874–5 by the congregation that had met previously at the Old South Meeting House (see p59).

> ⓘ **New Old South Church**
> 645 Boylston St. **Map** 3 C2.
> **Tel** (617) 536-1970. ⬤ 9am–7pm
> Mon–Fri, 10am–4pm Sat, 9am–4pm
> Sun. ✝ 9am, 11am Sun, 6pm Thu.
> ✗ ♿ 🎧 🛈 www.oldsouth.org

Boston Public Library ❾

Copley Square. **Map** 3 C2. **Tel** (617) 536-5400. ⓣ *Copley.* **General Library** ⬤ 9am–9pm Mon–Thu, 9am–5pm Fri–Sat, 1–5pm Sun. ⬤ public hols; Jun–Sep: Sun. 🎧 2:30pm Mon, 6pm Tue & Thu, 11am Fri & Sat, 2pm Sun. ♿ 🛈 www.bpl.org

Founded in 1848, the Boston Public Library was America's first metropolitan library for the public. It quickly outgrew its original building, hence the construction of the Italian *palazzo*-style Copley Square building in 1887–95, with "Free to All" emblazoned above the entrance. The architect Charles McKim drew on the highly skilled force of mostly Italian construction workers and artisans who had come to Boston to build mansions in the Back Bay and South End. Sculptor Daniel Chester French fashioned the huge bronze doors that represent Music and Poetry, Knowledge and Wisdom, and Truth and Romance. French painter Puvis de Chavannes executed the murals that wind up the staircase and along the second-floor corridor. Edward Abbey's

The vast Bates Hall in the Boston Public Library, noted for its high barrel-vaulted ceiling

Pre-Raphaelite murals of the Quest for the Holy Grail line the book request room, and John Singer Sargent's murals of Judaism and Christianity cover a third-floor gallery.

The McKim building, largely restored for its 1995 centennial, is a marvel of wood and marble. Bates Hall, on the second floor, is particularly noted for the soaring barrel-vaulted ceiling. A café and restaurant offer breakfast, lunch, and afternoon tea.

The library's circulating collection is housed in the 1971 Boylston Street addition, a modernist structure by architect Philip Johnson.

John Hancock Tower ⑩

200 Clarendon St. **Map** 3 C2.
Ⓣ *Copley* 🚫 *to the public.*

The tallest building in New England, the 740-ft (226 m) rhomboid that is the John Hancock Tower cuts into Copley Square with its slimmest edge, its mirrored façade reflecting the surroundings and sky. The innovative design has created a 60-story office building that shares the square with its neighbors, the Romanesque Trinity Church and the Italian Renaissance Revival Copley Plaza Hotel, without dwarfing them. When the tower was under construction, 65 windows, each weighing 500lb (1,100 kg), came crashing to the ground. All 10,344 panes were replaced at a cost of almost $7 million before the building could be occupied in 1975.

Designed by Henry Cobb of I.M. Pei & Partners, the magnificent building inspired Massachusetts author John Updike to observe: "All art, all beauty, is reflection." From one angle viewers can see the reflections of Trinity Church and the original (1947) Hancock Building, topped by a weather beacon.

The observatory on the 60th floor of the tower closed for safety reasons following the tragic events in September 2001 at the World Trade Center in New York.

View over Back Bay and the Charles River

Berklee Performance Center ⑪

136 Massachusetts Ave.
Map 3 A3. **Tel** *(617) 266-7455.*
Ⓣ *Hynes.* **www**.berkleebpc.com

Acquired by the Berklee College of Music in 1972, the Berklee Performance Center has since undergone extensive renovations to transform it into one of the city's entertainment and cultural highlights.

The largest independent music college in the world, Berklee was founded in 1945 and has produced a number of stars in jazz, rock, and pop music. Included in the list of well-known talents are the likes of producer and arranger Quincy Jones, the singer and songwriter Melissa Etheridge, and jazz saxophonist and composer Branford Marsalis. The school's students and distinguished faculty enliven the Boston music scene, performing primarily at the on-site Berklee Performance Center. The center boasts extraordinary acoustics and a state-of-the art light and sound system. It frequently hosts a wide range of events, including legendary music recitals, operas, plays, and comedy nights. Mainstream and emerging artists perform here and there are also faculty and student concerts. There is a full program of special events, including film screenings and business conferences, available. The center's website gives up-to-date and informative listings of all upcoming events.

Musicians playing at the state-of-the-art Berklee Performance Center

Prudential Center ⑫

800 Boylston St. **Map** 3 B3. **Tel** (617) 859-0648. ⓣ Prudential, Hynes Convention Center/ICA. **Skywalk**
◯ Mar–Oct: 10am–9:30pm daily; Nov–Feb: 10am–8pm daily. ◐ Thanksgiving, Dec 25. ▦ ⑇ ⌂

When it was erected in 1965, the Prudential Tower was the first skyscraper in the Back Bay, rising 52 floors. Office buildings and a shopping center now girdle its base, and the "Pru" is linked through indoor walkways with the Hynes Convention Center and the Sheraton Back Bay Hotel in one unified complex. An enclosed walkway even links its shops to the more

Prudential Tower viewed across the Christian Science reflecting pool

Inside the beautiful, stained-glass Mapparium, Christian Science Center

glamorous Copley Place across busy Huntington Avenue. Apart from the shops and food courts, the principal attraction of the "Pru" is the Skywalk on the 50th floor. The Skywalk is the only 360-degree aerial observatory in Boston, and its location near the top of Boylston Street hill provides striking views of the Emerald Necklace (see p103) as well as downtown and the waterfront. Signs on the windows assist in identifying the landmarks below. A similar view, which visitors do not need to pay for, is available at the Top of the Hub restaurant on the 52nd floor. Some of the bar windows here face west, so those having a drink can enjoy spectacular sunset views over Boston.

Christian Science Center ⑬

175 Huntington Ave. **Map** 3 B3. ⓣ Symphony. **Mother Church Tel** (617) 450-2000. ◯ noon–4pm Thu–Sat. ⑇ 11am Sun. **Library Tel** (617) 450-7000. ◯ 10am–4pm Tue–Sun (last entry to Mapparium 3:40pm). ✝ 10am & 7pm Sun, noon & 7:30pm Wed (no evening service Jul–Aug). ⑇ ⌨ www.marybakereddylibrary.org

The world headquarters of the First Church of Christ, Scientist, occupies 14 acres on the corner of Huntington and Massachusetts Avenues. Known also as the Christian Science Church, this religious body was formed in 1879 by Mary Baker Eddy. The granite, Romanesque-style Mother Church dates from 1894, but it serves only as a chapel at the rear of a grander basilica, which was built in 1906 to seat 5,000 worshipers. The basilica houses the western hemisphere's largest pipe organ, manufactured in Boston by the Aeolian-Skinner Company. Between 1968 and 1973 the Christian Science complex expanded to its present design, which includes an elegant office tower, a reflecting pool, and a monumental plaza.

 The Mary Baker Eddy Library for the Betterment of Humanity, on the Massachusetts Ave side of the complex, emphasizes Eddy's inspiration rather than church doctrine. Visitors can peer through a glass wall into the newsroom of the Christian Science Monitor. The most

MARY BAKER EDDY

Born in Concord, New Hampshire in 1821, Mary Baker was plagued with poor health for much of her early life. Fearing death after a severe fall in 1866, she sought comfort in her Bible, where she found an account of how Jesus had healed a palsied man. Her own miraculous recovery led her to the principle of Christian Science, a doctrine which emphasizes spiritual regeneration and healing through prayer alone. In 1875 she published her ideas in Science and Health with Key to the Scriptures, the textbook of Christian Science, and gathered students around her, including Asa Gilbert Eddy, whom she married in 1877. Two years later she organized the First Church of Christ, Scientist, in Boston, from which Christian Science churches spread across the world. Mrs. Eddy remained the active leader of the Christian Science movement until her death in 1910. She is buried at Mount Auburn Cemetery in Cambridge.

popular exhibit is the recently restored Mapparium, where visitors literally walk through the globe viewing the planet from the inside. The different colors represent the world's political boundaries of 1935.

Copley Place  14

Huntington Ave & Dartmouth St. **Map** 3 C3. **Tel** (617) 369-5000. ⓣ Back Bay/South End, Copley. ◯ 10am–9pm Mon–Sat, 11am–6pm Sun. ♿

Copley Place is a creature of late 20th-century urban development, with hotels, an upscale shopping center, and restaurants. Offices and luxury apartments are also part of the development, which rises on land created above the Massachusetts Turnpike. Copley Place bears little relation to Copley Square, but the shopping mall was a success from the day it opened in 1984 and still ranks as Boston's most luxurious indoor shopping mall. Its stores include the jeweler Tiffany's and the status-conscious department store Neiman-Marcus (see p153).

Boston Center for the Arts 15

539 Tremont St. **Map** 4 D3. **Tel** (617) 426-5000. ⓣ Back Bay/South End. **Cyclorama** ◯ 9am–5pm Mon–Fri. **Mills Gallery** ◯ noon–5pm Wed, Thu, Sun, noon–9pm Fri, Sat. ● public hols. ♫ for performances. 💵 ♿ www.bcaonline.org

The centerpiece of a resurgent South End, the BCA complex includes four stages, an art gallery, and artists' studios as well as the Boston Ballet Building, home to the company's educational programs, rehearsal space, and administrative offices.

The Tremont Estates Building at the corner of Tremont Street, an organ factory in the years after the Civil War, now houses artists' studios, rehearsal space, and an art gallery.

The largest of the BCA buildings is the circular, domed

Bow-fronted, red-brick houses, typical of South End's Union Park

Cyclorama, which opened in 1884 to exhibit the 50-ft (15-m) by 400-ft (121-m) painting *The Battle of Gettysburg* by the French artist Paul Philippoteaux. The painting was removed in 1889 and is now displayed at Gettysburg National Historic Park. It now serves as a performance and exhibition space.

The Stanford Calderwood Pavilion, with a 360-seat and a 200-seat theater, opened in 2004 as the first new theater built in Boston in 75 years.

The Mills Gallery houses exhibitions focusing on emerging contemporary artists, with the emphasis on multimedia installations and shows with confrontational, often provocative, themes.

Red-brick façade of the Boston Center for the Arts, site of theaters and exhibition spaces

Union Park 16

Tremont & Shawmut Sts. **Map** 4 D4. ⓣ Back Bay/South End. ♿

Union Park is the green gem of the South End, built from 1857 to 1859 when the neighborhood was still fashionable. South End property values crashed in the Panic of 1873, and the entire district, Union Park included, became tenement housing for immigrants arriving from eastern Europe and the Middle East. The South End remains broadly mixed by ethnicity, race, and sexual orientation. The handsome town houses along Union Park led the South End's economic resurgence in the 1970s, and it has become, once again, a coveted address. A pair of fountains, an iron fence, and large shade trees present a truly parklike setting for the beautifully restored brick row houses. The 19th-century ornamental ironwork on and around these houses is particularly prized by architecture buffs. Union Park is strictly residential, although there are a few small shops, and restaurants which have become very popular for Saturday and Sunday brunch.

FARTHER AFIELD

The late 19th and 20th centuries saw Boston expand out of the central colonial and Victorian city into the surrounding area. The old marshlands of the Fenway now house two of Boston's most important art museums, the Museum of Fine Arts and the Isabella Stewart Gardner Museum. Southeast of the city center, Columbia Point was developed in the mid-20th century and is home to the John F. Kennedy Library and Museum. West of central Boston, across the Charles River, lies Cambridge, sometimes referred to as the "Socialist Democratic Republic of Cambridge," a reference to the politics of Harvard and the Massachusetts Institute of Technology, its two major colleges. Harvard Square is a lively area of bookstores, cafés, and street entertainers. Charlestown is the site of the Bunker Hill Monument and the Charlestown Navy Yard, where the U.S.'s most famous warship, the *U.S.S. Constitution*, is moored. Farther northwest lie historic Concord and Lexington, where the first major battles of the Revolutionary War took place in 1775.

Statue of William Prescott, Bunker Hill Monument

SIGHTS AT A GLANCE

Towns
Cambridge ❼
Charlestown ❽
Concord ❾
Lexington ❿

Museums and Historic Sites
Isabella Stewart Gardner Museum ❺

John F Kennedy Library and Museum ❶
John F. Kennedy National Historic Site ❹
Museum of Fine Arts pp104–7 ❻

Gardens and Zoos
Arnold Arboretum ❸
Franklin Park Zoo ❷

KEY

▨	Main sightseeing area
☐	Urban area
✈	Airport
▣	Railroad station
▬	Highway
▬	Major road
═	Minor road
—	Railroad

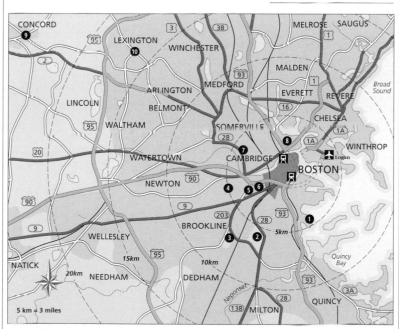

◁ Central courtyard of the *palazzo*-style Isabella Stewart Gardner Museum

John F. Kennedy Library and Museum ❶

Columbia Point, Dorchester.
Tel (617) 514-1600. Ⓣ JFK/U Mass.
◯ 9am–5pm daily. ● Jan 1,
Thanksgiving, Dec 25.
▨ ⬛ ⬛ ⬛ www.jfklibrary.org

The soaring white concrete and glass building housing the John F. Kennedy Library stands sentinel on Columbia Point near the mouth of the Boston Harbor. This striking white and black modern building by the architect I. M. Pei is equally dramatic from the interior, with a 50-ft (15-m) wall of glass looking out over the sea. Exhibitions extensively chronicle the 1,000 days of the Kennedy presidency with an immediacy uncommon in many other historical museums. Kennedy was among the first politicians to grasp the power of media. The museum takes full advantage of film and video footage to use the president's own words and image to tell his story: his campaign for the

Democratic Party nomination, landmark television debates with Republican opponent Richard M. Nixon (who later became infamous for the Watergate Scandal), and his many addresses to the nation.

Several rooms recreate key chambers of the White House during the Kennedy administration, including the Oval Office, and gripping film clips capture the anxiety of nuclear brinksmanship during the Cuban missile crisis as well as the inspirational spirit of the space program and the founding of the Peace Corps. Recently expanded exhibits on Robert F. Kennedy's role as Attorney General touch on both his deft handling of race relations and his key advisory role to his brother. The combination of artifacts, displays, and television footage evoke both the euphoria of "Camelot" and the numb horror of the assassination.

Lowland gorilla with her baby in the simulated natural environment of Franklin Park Zoo

Franklin Park Zoo ❷

1 Franklin Park Rd. **Tel** (617) 541-5466. Ⓣ Forest Hills. ▦ 16 from Forest Hills subway. ◯ Apr–Sep: 10am–5pm Mon–Fri, 10am–6pm Sat–Sun; Oct–Mar: 10am–4pm daily.
● Jan 1, Thanksgiving, Dec 25. ▨
⬛ www.zoonewengland.com

The zoo, originally planned as a small menagerie, has expanded dramatically over the past century and long ago discarded caged enclosures in favor of simulated natural environments. Lowland gorillas roam a forest edge with caves for privacy, lions lounge around a rocky kingdom while zebras, ostriches, and giraffes are free to graze on open grassland. The Butterfly Landing is a dense garden within a large hooped enclosure where as many as 1,000 butterflies flit from flower to flower. New Age and light classical music augment the sense of fantasy. In the small petting zoo youngsters can meet farm animals.

Arnold Arboretum ❸

125 Arborway, Jamaica Plain.
Tel (617) 524-1718. Ⓣ Forest Hills.
▦ 39. ◯ sunrise–sunset daily.
Visitors Center ◯ 9am–4pm
Mon–Fri, 10am–4pm Sat, noon–
4pm Sun. ● public hols. ⬛
www.arboretum.harvard.edu

Founded by Harvard University in 1872 as a living catalog of all the indigenous and exotic trees and shrubs adaptable to New England's climate, the Arboretum is planted with

Dramatic, modern structure of the John F. Kennedy Library and Museum

more than 15,000 labeled specimens. It is the oldest arboretum in the U.S. and a key resource for botanical and horticultural research. The Arboretum also serves as a park where people jog, stroll, read, and paint.

The park's busiest time is on the third Sunday in May – Lilac Sunday – when tens of thousands come to revel in the sight and fragrance of the lilac collection, one of the largest in the world. The range of the Arboretum's collections guarantees flowers from late March into November, beginning with cornelian cherry and forsythia. Blooms shift in late May to azalea, magnolia, and wisteria, then to mountain laurel and roses in June. Sweet autumn clematis bursts forth in September, and native witch hazel blooms in October and November. The Arboretum also has fine fall foliage in September and October.

A large scale model of the Arboretum can be seen in the Visitors' Information Center just inside the main gate.

John F. Kennedy National Historic Site ❹

83 Beals St, Brookline. **Tel** (617) 566-7937. Ⓣ Coolidge Corner. ◯ late May–Sep: 10:30am–4:30pm Wed–Sun. ◗ Thanksgiving. ▨ ∅ ♿ ▣ ▥ www.nps.gov/jofi

The first home of the late president's parents, this Brookline house saw the birth of four of nine Kennedy children, including J.F.K. on May 29, 1917. Although the Kennedys moved to a larger house in 1921, the Beals Street residence held special memories for the family, who repurchased the house in 1966 and furnished it with their belongings circa 1917 as a memorial to John F. Kennedy. The guided tour includes a taped interview of J.F.K.'s mother Rose. A walking tour takes in other neighborhood sites relevant to the Kennedy family's early years.

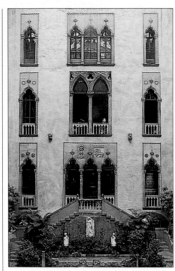

Central courtyard of the *palazzo-*style **Isabella Stewart Gardner Museum**

Isabella Stewart Gardner Museum ❺

280 The Fenway. **Tel** (617) 566-1401. Ⓣ MFA. ◯ 11am–5pm Tue–Sun. ◗ Jan 1, Thanksgiving, Dec 25. ▨ ∅ ▣ call for concert schedule. www.gardnermuseum.org

The only thing more surprising than a Venetian *palazzo* on The Fenway is the collection of more than 2,500 works of art inside. Advised by scholar Bernard Berenson, the strong-willed Isabella Stewart Gardner turned her wealth to collecting art in the late 19th century, acquiring a notable collection of Old Masters and Italian Renaissance pieces. Titian's *Rape of Europa,* for example, is considered his best painting in a U.S. museum. The eccentric "Mrs. Jack" had an eye for her contemporaries as well. She purchased the first Matisse to enter an American collection and was an ardent patron of James McNeill Whistler and John Singer Sargent. The paintings, sculptures, and tapestries are displayed on three levels around a stunning skylit courtyard. Mrs. Gardner's will, which was instrumental in the setting up of the museum, stipulates the collection should remain assembled in the manner that she originally intended. Unfortunately, her intentions could not be upheld; in 1990 thieves made off with 13 of these priceless works, including a rare Rembrandt seascape, *Storm on the Sea of Galilee,* then conservatively valued in the region of $200 million.

THE EMERALD NECKLACE

Best known as designer of New York's Central Park, Frederick Law Olmsted based himself in Boston, where he created parks to solve environmental problems and provide a green refuge for inhabitants of the 19th-century industrial city. The Emerald Necklace includes the green spaces of Boston Common and the Public Garden *(see pp46–7)* and Commonwealth Avenue *(see p93).* To create a ring of parks, Olmsted added the Back Bay Fens

Jamaica Pond, part of Boston's fine parklands

(site of beautiful rose gardens and gateway to the Museum of Fine Arts and the Isabella Stewart Gardner Museum), the rustic Riverway, Jamaica Pond (sailing and picnicking), Arnold Arboretum, and Franklin Park (a golf course, zoo, and cross-country ski trails). The 5-mile (8-km) swath of parkland makes an excellent bicycle tour or ambitious walk.

The Museum of Fine Arts ❻

This is the largest art museum in New England and one of the five largest in the United States. Its collection includes around 450,000 items, ranging from Egyptian artifacts to paintings by John Singer Sargent. The original 1909 Classical-style building was augmented in 1981 by the addition of the West Wing, designed by I.M. Pei. The north and east sides are currently being expanded to create a new American Wing; as a result, galleries are subject to change.

★ Japanese Temple Room
This room was created in 1909 to provide a space in which to contemplate Buddhist art. The M.F.A. has one of the finest Japanese collections outside Japan.

American Silver
The revolutionary Paul Revere (see p21) was also a noted silversmith and produced many beautiful objects, such as this ornate teapot.

First floor

Fenway entrance

★ Egyptian Mummies
Among the museum's Egyptian and Nubian art is this tomb group of Nes-mut-aat-neru (767–656 BC) of Thebes.

Huntington entrance

★ Copley Portraits
John Singleton Copley (1738–1815) painted the celebrities of his day, hence this portrait of a dandyish John Hancock (see p21).

★ **Impressionist Paintings**
Boston collectors were among the first to appreciate French Impressionism. Dance at Bougival (1883) by Renoir is typical of the M.F.A. collection.

VISITORS' CHECKLIST

Avenue of the Arts,
465 Huntington Ave.
Tel *(617) 267-9300.* Ⓣ *MFA.*
◯ *10am–4:45pm Mon–Tue,*
10am–9:45pm Wed–Fri, 10am–
4:45 Sat–Sun. ● *most public*
hols. 🖼 ♿ 🖊 🎥
Lectures, concerts, and films.
🍴 ♿ 🛗 www.mfa.org

KEY

☐ Court level

☐ First floor

☐ Second floor

Sargent Murals
John Singer Sargent spent the last years of his life creating artwork for the M.F.A. Originally commissioned to produce three paintings, Sargent instead constructed these elaborate murals, which were unveiled in 1921 and can still be seen today. He went on to create the works of art in the adjacent colonnade until his death in 1925.

Second floor

Court level

Head of Aphrodite
This rare example of Ancient Greek sculpture dates from about 330–300 BC.

GALLERY GUIDE
The museum is undergoing complete renovation with the addition of a new American Wing designed by Norman Foster. Until its scheduled completion in late 2010 galleries are subject to change – call ahead for the latest information.

STAR EXHIBITS

★ Copley Portraits

★ Impressionist Paintings

★ Egyptian Mummies

★ Japanese Temple Room

Exploring the Museum of Fine Arts

In addition to the major collections noted below, the Museum of Fine Arts has important holdings in the arts of Africa, Oceania, and the ancient Americas. The museum also houses collections of works on paper, contemporary art, and musical instruments. Several galleries are devoted to temporary thematic exhibitions. Other features of the museum include a seminar room, lecture hall, and well-stocked bookstore. The museum is currently undergoing major renovation and exhibits are subject to change. Call ahead for the latest information.

11th-century, silver Korean ewer

Boston Harbor by the Luminist painter Fitz Hugh Lane (1804–65)

AMERICAN PAINTINGS, DECORATIVE ARTS, AND SCULPTURE

The M.F.A. displays a wealth of American art, which includes over 1,600 paintings. The earliest works on show are anonymous portraits painted in the late 17th century. The Colonial period is well-represented with more than 60 portraits by John Singleton Copley, perhaps America's most talented 18th-century painter, as well as works by Charles Wilson Peale. Other works on display are 19th-century landscapes, including harbor scenes by Fitz Hugh Lane, an early Luminist painter, lush society portraits of John Singer Sargent, and those of other late 19th-century artists who constituted the "Boston School." There are also notable seascapes by Winslow Homer on show, who often painted on the Massachusetts coast, as well as the muscular

figure portraiture of Thomas Eakins. The M.F.A. also houses a sampling of works by 20th-century masters including Stuart Davis, Jackson Pollock, Georgia O'Keeffe, and Arthur Dove.

The museum's holdings of American silver are superb. As well as works by John Coney, there are two cases containing tea services and other pieces by Paul Revere *(see p73)*. It also traces the development of the Boston style of 18th-century furniture through a definitive collection of desks, high chests, and tall clocks. Its famed period rooms, displaying decorative arts in a historical context, will be re-installed in the new American wing, currently under const-ruction. Until the new wing is complete, many objects from these rooms, along with the museum's contemporary crafts, will be housed in temporary galleries.

EUROPEAN PAINTINGS, DECORATIVE ARTS, AND SCULPTURE

This collection of European paintings and sculpture ranges from the 7th to the late 20th century. It showcases numerous masterpieces by English, Dutch, French, Italian and Spanish artists, including various portraits by the 17th-century Dutch painter, Rembrandt. The collection of works from 1550 to 1700 is impressive both for the quality of art and for its size, which includes Francisco de Zurbarán, El Greco, Paolo Veronese, Titian, and Peter Paul Rubens.

Boston's 19th-century collectors enriched the M.F.A. with wonderful French painting: the museum features several paintings by Pierre François Millet (the M.F.A. has, in fact, the largest collection of his work in the world) as well as by other well-known 19th-century French artists, such as Edouard Manet, Pierre-Auguste Renoir, and Edgar Degas. Among this collection are the hugely popular and infamous *Waterlilies* (1905) by Claude Monet and *Dance at Bougival* (1883) by Renoir. The M.F.A.'s Monet holdings are among the world's largest, and there is also a good collection of paintings by the Dutch artist Vincent van Gogh. Early 20th-century

La Berceuse by the Dutch painter Vincent van Gogh (1853–90)

Part of the Processional Way of Ancient Babylonia (6th century BC)

European art is also exhibited.

The M.F.A. is well-known for its extensive collection of European decorative arts. Tableware, ceramics, and glass clustered by period from the early 17th to early 20th centuries are some examples of the works exhibited.

The construction of the new wing at the museum has temporarily reduced available gallery space. Some prized decorative arts collections have been put into storage as a result. These include the opulent displays of 18th-century French silver normally housed in the Louis XVI style gallery, and the striking holdings of Chinese export porcelain.

ANCIENT EGYPTIAN, NUBIAN, AND NEAR EASTERN ART

The M.F.A.'s collection of Egyptian and Nubian materials is unparalleled outside of Africa, and derives primarily from M.F.A.-Harvard University excavations along the Nile, which began in 1905. One of the highlights is a 1998 installation showing Egyptian Funerary Arts, which uses the M.F.A.'s superb collection of mummies from nearly three millennia to illustrate the technical and art historical aspects of Egyptian burial practices. Also on display are some exceptional Babylonian, Assyrian, and Sumerian reliefs. Works from ancient Nubia, the cultural region around the Nile stretching

roughly between the modern African cities of Aswan and Khartoum, encompass gold and silver artefacts, ceramics, and jewels.

Other highlights from the Egyptian and Nubian collections include two monumental sculptures of Nubian kings from the Great Temple of Amen at Napata (620–586 BC and 600–580 BC). A few of the galleries are set up to re-create Nubian burial chambers, which allows cuneiform wall carvings to be displayed in something akin to an original setting; a superb example is the offering chapel of Sekhem-ankh-Ptah from Sakkara (2450–2350 BC).

CLASSICAL ART

The M.F.A. boasts one of America's top collections of Greek ceramics. In particular the red- and black-figured vases dating from the 6th and 5th centuries BC are exceptional. The Classical

Roman fresco, excavated from a Pompeian villa (1st century AD)

galleries of the museum are intended to thematically highlight the influence of Greek arts on both Etruscan and Roman art. The Etruscan collection has several carved sarcophagi, gold jewelry, bronze mirrors, and colorful terracottas, while the Roman collection features grave markers, portrait busts, and a series of wall panel paintings unearthed in Pompeii on an M.F.A. expedition in 1900–01.

ASIAN ART

The Asian collection is one of the most extensive that can be found under one roof. A range of works from India, the Near East and Central Asian art are exhibited. Among the highlights are Indian sculpture and changing exhibitions of Islamic miniature paintings and Indian narrative paintings. Elsewhere, works from Korea feature some Buddhist paintings and sculptures, jewelry, and ornaments.

Tang Dynasty Chinese Horse (8th century)

The museum also boasts calligraphy, ceramics, and stone sculptures from China and the largest collection of Japanese prints outside Japan. Extensive holdings and limited display space mean that specific exhibitions change often, but the M.F.A.'s exhibitions of Japanese and Chinese scroll and screen paintings are, nevertheless, unmatched in the West. The strength of the M.F.A.'s Japanese art collection is largely due to the efforts of collectors such as Ernest Fenollosa and William Bigelow Sturgis. In the 19th century they encouraged the Japanese to maintain their traditions, and salvaged Buddhist temple art when the Japanese imperial government had withdrawn subsidies from these institutions. This collection is considered to contain some of the finest examples of Asian temple art in the world.

Cambridge ❼

Part of the greater Boston metropolitan area, Cambridge is, nonetheless, a town in its own right, and has the mood and feel of such. Principally a college town, it is dominated by Harvard University and other college campuses. It also boasts a number of important historic sights, such as Christ Church and Cambridge Common, which have associations back to the American Revolution. Harvard Square is the area's main entertainment and shopping district.

Site of the Washington Elm, on Cambridge Common

🏛 Longfellow National Historic Site

105 Brattle St. **Tel** *(617) 876-4491.*
🕐 *May–Oct: 10am–4:30pm Wed–Sun.* ⬤ *Wed & Sun in Jun.*
🔲 ⬚ ♿ 🎫 www.nps.gov/long
This house on Brattle Street, like many around it, was built by Colonial-era merchants loyal to the British Crown during the Revolution. It was seized by American revolutionaries and served as George Washington's head-quarters during the Siege of Boston.

The poet Henry Wadsworth Longfellow boarded here in 1837, was given the house as a wedding present in 1843, and lived here until his death in 1888. He wrote his most famous poems here, including *Tales of a Wayside Inn and The Song of Hiawatha.* Longfellow's status as literary dean of Boston meant that Nathaniel Hawthorne and Charles Sumner, among others, were regular visitors.

Street musician, Harvard Square

🏛 Harvard Square

ℹ *(617) 491-3434.* ♿
www.harvardsquare.com
Even Bostonians think of Harvard Square as a stand-in for Cambridge – the square was the original site of Cambridge from around 1630. Dominating the square is the Harvard Cooperative Society ("the Coop"), a Harvard institution, that sells inexpensive clothes, posters, and books.

Harvard's large student population is very much in evidence here, adding color to the character of the square. Many trendy boutiques, inexpensive restaurants, and numerous cafés cater to their needs. Street performers abound, especially on the weekends, and the square has long been a place where pop trends begin. Club Passim *(see p162),* for example, has incubated many successful singer-song-writers since Joan Baez first debuted here in 1959.

🏛 Cambridge Common

Set aside as common pasture and military drill ground in 1631, Cambridge Common has served as a center for religious, social, and political activity ever since. George Washington took command of the Conti-nental Army here on July 3, 1775, beneath the Washington Elm, now marked by a stone. The common served as the army's encampment from 1775 to 1776. Today the ball fields and playgrounds are popular with families. In 1997 the first monument in the U.S. to the victims of the Irish Famine was unveiled on the common.

⛪ Christ Church

Garden St. **Tel** *(617) 876-0200.*
🕐 *8am–6pm Mon–Fri & Sun, 8am–3pm Sat.* ✝ *7:45am, 10:15am, 5:30pm Sun; 12:10pm Wed.*
⬚ ♿ www.cccambridge.org
With its square bell tower and plain, gray shingled edifice, Christ Church is a restrained example of an Anglican church. Designed in 1761 by Peter Harrison, the architect of Boston's King's Chapel *(see p58),* Christ Church came in for rough treatment as a barracks for Continental Army troops in 1775 – British loyalists had almost all fled Cambridge by this time. The army even melted down the organ pipes to cast musket balls. The church was restored on New Year's Eve, 1775, when George Washington and his wife Martha were among the worshipers. Anti-Anglican sentiment remained strong in Cambridge, and Christ Church did not have its own rector again until the 19th century.

Simple interior of Christ Church, designed prior to the Revolution in 1761

🏛 Radcliffe Institute for Advanced Study

Brattle St. ***Tel*** *(617) 495-8601.* ♿ **www**.radcliffe.edu

Radcliffe College was founded in 1879 as the Collegiate Institution for Women, when 27 women began to study by private arrangement with Harvard professors. By 1943, members of Harvard's faculty no longer taught separate undergraduate courses to the women of Radcliffe, and in 1999 Radcliffe ceased its official existence as an independent college. It is now an institute for advanced study promoting scholarship of women's culture. The first Radcliffe building was the 1806 Federal-style mansion, Fay House, on the northern corner of what became Radcliffe Yard. Schlesinger Library, on the west side of the yard, is considered a significant example of Colonial Revival architecture. The library's most famous holdings are an extensive collection of cookbooks and reference works on gastronomy.

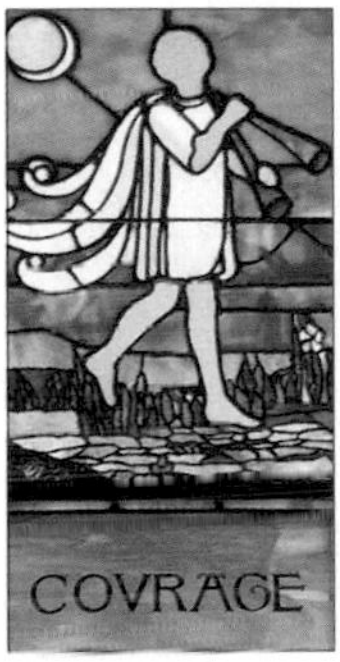
COVRAGE

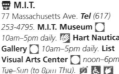

Stained glass, Radcliffe Institute

🏛 M.I.T.

77 Massachusetts Ave. ***Tel*** *(617) 253-4795.* **M.I.T. Museum** ○ *10am–5pm daily.* 🎟 **Hart Nautical Gallery** ○ *10am–5pm daily.* **List Visual Arts Center** ○ *noon–6pm Tue–Sun (to 8pm Thu).* 📷 ♿ 🛍 **www**.mit.edu

Chartered in 1861 to teach students "exactly and thoroughly the fundamental principles of positive science with application to the industrial arts," the Massachusetts Institute of Technology has evolved into one of the world's leading universities in engineering and the sciences. Several architectural masterpieces dot M.I.T.'s 135-acre (55-ha) campus along the Charles River. Finnish Modernism is represented by Alvar Aalto's seminal Baker House dormitory (1949). Eero Saarinen's compressed arches make Kresge Auditorium (1955) seem poised for flight. The spare lines of Kresge Chapel (1955) embody ascetic faith. The Wiesner building houses the **List Visual Arts Center**, noted for its avant garde art.

The **Hart Nautical Gallery** in the Rogers Building focuses on marine engineering, with models of ships and exhibits of the latest advances in underwater research. The **M.I.T. Museum** blends art and science, with exhibits such as Harold Edgerton's ground-breaking stroboscopic flash photographs, and the latest holographic art.

VISITORS' CHECKLIST

[T] *Harvard.* 🚌 *1, 69.* ℹ **Harvard Square Information Booth** *(617) 497-1630,* **Cambridge Office of Tourism** *(800) 862-5678, (617) 441-2884.* 🚫 *Sun.* 🎪 *River Festival (mid-June.)* **www**.harvard.edu **or** **www**.cambridge-usa.org

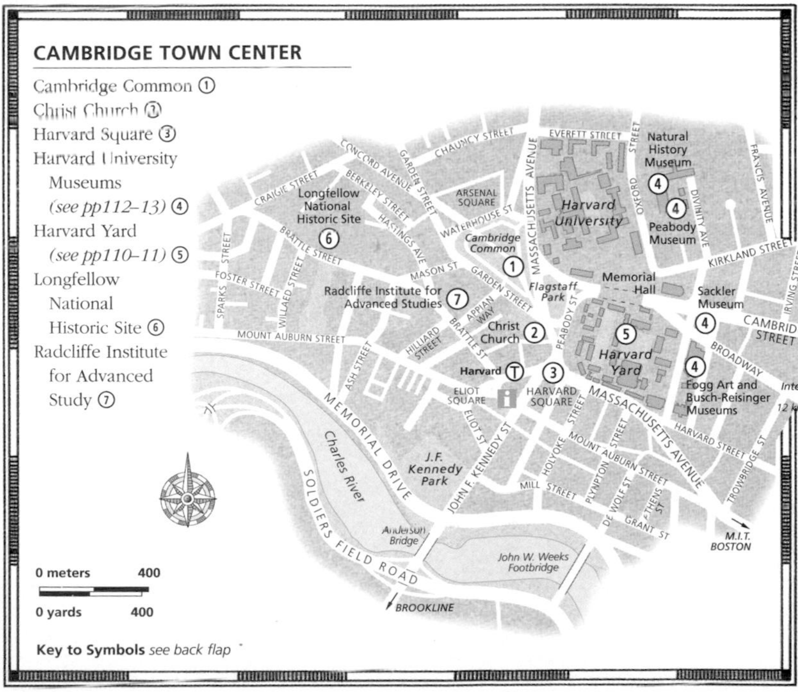
CAMBRIDGE TOWN CENTER
Cambridge Common 1
Christ Church 2
Harvard Square 3
Harvard University Museums (see pp112–13) 4
Harvard Yard (see pp110–11) 5
Longfellow National Historic Site 6
Radcliffe Institute for Advanced Study 7
Longfellow National Historic Site
Radcliffe Institute for Advanced Studies
Cambridge Common
Christ Church
Harvard
Harvard University
Harvard Yard
Natural History Museum
Peabody Museum
Memorial Hall
Sackler Museum
Fogg Art and Busch-Reisinger Museums
Flagstaff Park
ELIOT SQUARE
HARVARD SQUARE
ARSENAL SQUARE
J.F. Kennedy Park
Charles River
Anderson Bridge
John W. Weeks Footbridge
CHAUNCY STREET
EVERETT STREET
OXFORD STREET
DIVINITY AVE
FRANCIS AVENUE
KIRKLAND STREET
IRVING STREET
CAMBRIDGE STREET
BROADWAY
HARVARD STREET
TROWBRIDGE ST
MASSACHUSETTS AVENUE
CONCORD AVENUE
GARDEN STREET
BERKELEY STREET
HASTINGS AVE
CRAIGIE STREET
BRATTLE STREET
WATERHOUSE ST
MASON ST
APPIAN WAY
HILLIARD STREET
FOSTER STREET
SPARKS STREET
WILLARD STREET
MOUNT AUBURN STREET
ASH STREET
MEMORIAL DRIVE
SOLDIERS FIELD ROAD
ELIOT ST
JOHN F. KENNEDY ST
PEABODY ST
HOLYOKE STREET
PLYMPTON STREET
DE WOLF ST
ATHENS ST
GRANT ST
MILL STREET
Logan International Airport 12 km (7 miles)
M.I.T. BOSTON
BROOKLINE
0 meters 400
0 yards 400
Key to Symbols see back flap

Harvard Yard

In 1636 Boston's well-educated Puritan leaders founded a college in Newtowne. Two years later cleric John Harvard died and bequeathed half his estate and all his books to the fledgling college. The colony's leaders bestowed his name on the school and rechristened the surrounding community Cambridge after the English city where they had been educated. The oldest university in the U.S., Harvard is now one of the world's most prestigious centers of learning. The university has expanded to encompass more than 400 buildings, but Harvard Yard is still at its heart.

Holden Chapel
Built in 1742, the chapel was the scene of revolutionary speeches and was later used as a demonstration hall for human dissections.

Hollis Hall was used as barracks by George Washington's troops during the American Revolution.

Massachusetts Hall, built in 1720, is Harvard's oldest building.

★ **Old Harvard Yard**
This leafy yard dates from the founding of the college in 1636. Freshman dormitories dot the yard, and throughout the year it is a focal point for students.

Harvard University Information Center

★ **John Harvard Statue**
This statue celebrates Harvard's most famous benefactor. Almost a place of pilgrimage, graduates and visitors invariably pose for photographs here.

University Hall, designed by Charles Bulfinch, was built in 1816.

★ **Widener Library**
This library memorializes Harry Elkins Widener who died on the Titanic *in 1912. With more than 3 million volumes, it is the third largest library in the U.S.*

★ **Memorial Church**
This church was built in 1931 and copies earlier styles. For example, the steeple is modeled on that of the Old North Church (see p71) in Boston's North End.

VISITORS' CHECKLIST

Massachusetts Ave. ⓣ *Harvard.*
◯ *24 hrs.* ◉ *2nd Thu in Jun (Commencement).* ♿ ◯
☐ *Mon–Sat (call for details.)*
Harvard Information Center
Tel (617) 495-1573.
Harvard Box Office
Tel (617) 496-2222.
Harvard Film Archive *Tel (617) 495 4700.* **www**.harvard.edu

Memorial Hall, a Ruskin Gothic building, memorializes Harvard's Union casualties from the Civil War.

⸕ **Sackler and Peabody Museums, and Harvard Museum of Natural History** *(see pp114–15)*

Sever Hall
One of the most distinctive of Harvard's Halls, this Romanesque style-building was designed by Henry Hobson Richardson (see p32).

Fogg Art and Busch-Reisinger Museums *(see pp112–13)*

Tercentenary Theater

STAR SIGHTS

★ Old Harvard Yard

★ John Harvard Statue

★ Widener Library

★ Memorial Church

0 meters   50

0 yards   50

Carpenter Center for Visual Arts
Opened in 1963, the Carpenter Center is the only building in the U.S. designed by the avant-garde Swiss architect Le Corbusier.

The Harvard University Museums

Harvard's museums were originally conceived to revolutionize the process of education; students were to be taught by allowing them access to artifacts from around the world. Today, this tradition continues, with the museums housing some of the world's finest university collections: art from Europe and America in the Fogg Art and Busch-Reisinger Museums; archaeological finds in the Peabody Museum; Asian, Islamic and Indian art in the Sackler Museum, and a vast collection of artifacts in the Harvard Museum of Natural History.

Main entrance to the Fogg Art and Busch-Reisinger Museums

Fogg Art and Busch-Reisinger Museums

32 Quincy St. **Tel** (617) 495-9400.
for renovation until 2013.
www.artmuseums.harvard.edu

The Fogg Art and Busch-Reisinger museums are closed for renovation until 2013. Select items are currently on display at the Sackler Museum (see p114.) The Fogg Art Museum was created in 1891 when Harvard began to build its own art collection in order to teach art history more effectively. Both the Fogg and the Busch-Reisinger, which was grafted onto the Fogg in 1991, have select collections of art from Europe and America.

The collections, which focus on Western art from the late Middle Ages to the present, are organized around a central courtyard modeled on a 16th-century church in Montepulciano, Italy. The ground-floor corridors surrounding the courtyard feature 12th-century capitals from Moutiers St-Jean in Burgundy, France.

Two small galleries near the entrance, and the two-story Warburg Hall, display the Fogg's collections that prefigure the Italian Renaissance. The massive altarpieces and suspended crucifix in the Warburg are particularly impressive.

The ground floor galleries on the left side of the entrance are devoted to 17th-century Dutch, Flemish, French, and Italian paintings, including four studies for Francesco Trevisiani's *Massacre of the Innocents*, a masterpiece destroyed in Dresden during World War II. Another room details Gian Lorenzo Bernini's use of clay models for his large-scale marbles and bronzes.

The museum's second level features the emergence of landscape as a subject in French 19th-century painting.

Galleries along the front of the building change exhibitions frequently, often focusing on drawings and graphic arts. The highlight of the second level is the Maurice Wertheim collection of Impressionist and Post-Inpressionist art, most of it collected in the late 1930s.

With a number of important paintings by Renoir, Manet, and Degas, the Wertheim gallery is the Fogg's most popular.

Surprises lurk in an adjacent gallery of art made in France 1885-1960, often by expatriate artists. Edvard Munch's 1891 painting of *Rue de Rivoli*, for example, is both bright and impressionistic, in contrast with his bleak Expressionism.

The museum also houses rotating displays from its collection of 19th- and 20th-century African art.

Werner Otto Hall, which contains the Busch-Reisinger Museum, is entered through the second level of the Fogg. The museum's collections focus on Germanic art and

Bernini Model (1674–75) *Gian Lorenzo Bernini crafted this clay model of a kneeling angel to guide the artisans casting his larger bronze.*

First floor

Main entrance

GUIDE TO THE FOGG ART AND BUSCH-REISINGER MUSEUMS

Western art from the Middle Ages to the present is on the first floor of the Fogg Art Museum. French and American art from the 19th and 20th centuries and 20th-century American art are on the second floor. The Busch-Reisinger Museum focuses on Germanic art.

Light-Space Modulator (1923–30) by the Hungarian Moholy-Nagy

design from after 1880, with an emphasis on German Expressionism. Harvard was a safe haven for many Bauhaus artists, architects, and designers who fled Nazi Germany, and both Walter Gropius and Lyonel Feininger chose the Busch-Reisinger as the depository of their personal papers and drawings.

Periodic exhibitions explore aspects of the work and philosophy of the Bauhaus movement. Although small, the museum owns major paintings and sculptures by 20th-century masters such as Max Beckmann, Wassily Kandinsky, Moholy-Nagy, Paul Klee, Oskar Kokoschka, Emil Nolde, and Franz Marc.

Calderwood Courtyard of the Fogg Art Museum

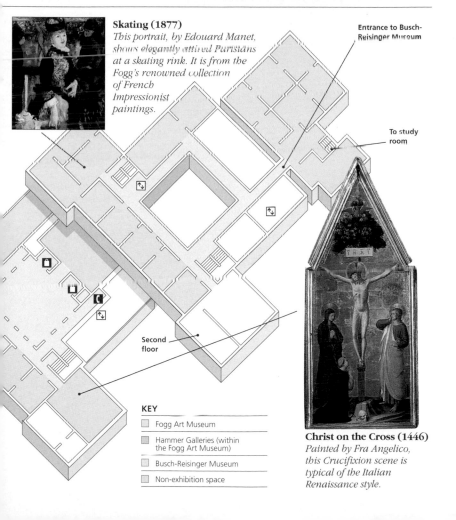

Skating (1877)
This portrait, by Edouard Manet, shows elegantly attired Parisians at a skating rink. It is from the Fogg's renowned collection of French Impressionist paintings.

Entrance to Busch-Reisinger Museum

To study room

Second floor

KEY

- ☐ Fogg Art Museum
- ☐ Hammer Galleries (within the Fogg Art Museum)
- ☐ Busch-Reisinger Museum
- ☐ Non-exhibition space

Christ on the Cross (1446)
Painted by Fra Angelico, this Crucifixion scene is typical of the Italian Renaissance style.

Peabody Museum of Archaeology and Ethnology

11 Divinity Ave. **Tel** (617) 496-1027. ◐ 9am–5pm daily. ● Jan 1, Jul 4, Thanksgiving, Dec 24, 25. 📷 ♿ 💳 www.peabody.harvard.edu

The Peabody Museum of Archaeology and Ethnology was founded in 1866 as the first museum in the Americas devoted solely to anthropology. The many collections, which include several million artifacts and more than 500,000 photographic images, come from all around the world. The Peabody's pioneering investigations began with excavations of Mayan sites in Central America, research on the precontact Anasazi people of the American Southwest, and on the cultural history of the later Pueblo tribes of the same region. Joint expeditions sponsored by the Peabody Museum and the Museum of Fine Arts *(see pp104–7)* also uncovered some of the richest finds of dynastic and predynastic Egypt. Later research embraced the cultures of the islands of the South Pacific.

The Native American tribes of the Northern Plains are interpreted

largely through an exhibition detailing the 1804–6 expedition, from the east to the west coast, by Lewis and Clark, who collected innumerable artifacts on the way. Other outstanding exhibits include totem carvings by Pacific Northwest tribes and a wide range of historic and contemporary Navajo weavings. The third floor is devoted to Central American anthropology, with casts of some of the ruins uncovered at Copán in Honduras and Chichen Itza in Mexico. The fourth floor concentrates on Polynesia, Micronesia, and other islands of the Pacific.

Native American totem pole, Peabody Museum

Harvard Museum of Natural History

26 Oxford St. **Tel** (617) 495-3045. ◐ 9am–5pm daily. ● Jul 4, Thanksgiving, Dec 24, 25. 📷 ♿ 💳 www.hmnh.harvard.edu

The Harvard Museum of Natural History is actually three museums rolled into one, with collections from the Mineralogical and Geological Museum, the Museum of Comparative Zoology, and the Botanical Museum.

The mineralogical galleries include some of Harvard University's oldest specimen collections. Virtually every New England mineral, rock, and gem type is represented, including rough and cut gemstones and one of the world's premier meteorite collections.

The zoological galleries owe their inception to the great 19th-century biologist Louis Agassiz and include his personal arachnid collection. The collection of taxidermied bird, mammal, and reptile specimens is comprehensive, and there is also a collection of dinosaur skeletons.

The collections in the botanical galleries include the Ware Collection of Blaschka Glass Models of Plants, popularly known as the "glass flowers." Between 1887 and 1936, father and son artisans Leopold and Rudolph Blaschka created these 3,000 exacting models of 850 plant species. Each species is illustrated with a scientifically accurate lifesize model and magnified parts.

Sackler Museum

485 Broadway, Cambridge. **Tel** (617) 495-9400. ◐ 10am–5pm Mon–Sat, 1–5pm Sun. ● public hols. 📷 ♿ 💳 www.artmuseums.harvard.edu

Named after a famous philanthropist, physician, and art collector, the Arthur M. Sackler Museum is normally

Triceratops skull in the Harvard Museum of Natural History

home to Harvard's collection of ancient, Asian, Islamic, and later Indian art. During renovations to the Fogg and Busch-Reisinger Museums, lasting through 2013, the Sackler will display select items from the collections of all three museums. Be sure to pick up a gallery map and flyers on the configuration of current exhibitions.

Opened in 1985, the Sackler is housed in a modern building designed by James Stirling and is itself a bold artistic statement, while the starkly modern interior galleries provide optimal display space. The 30-ft (10-m) entrance lobby features a 1997 wall painting by Conceptual artist Sol Lewitt, whose trademark colorful geometric shapes appear to float in space.

The best way to tour the Sackler is to start on the fourth floor and work back to the lobby. The head of the stairwell ends at gallery 10 at the back of the building, which during normal times is devoted to changing exhibitions highlighting ancient Greek art.

The second-floor galleries are equally spacious, but less suffused with natural light. The first-floor gallery, which is behind the ticket booth, is notably smaller than those on the other floors.

Southeast Asian Buddha head, Sackler Museum

Charlestown ❽

Situated on the north bank of the Charles River, directly opposite the North End, Charlestown exudes history. The site of the infamous Battle of Bunker Hill, when American troops suffered huge losses in their fight for independence, today the district forms a major part of Boston's Freedom Trail (*see pp124–7*).

VISITORS' CHECKLIST

🚇 Community College.
🚌 93. ⛴ from Long Wharf.
🕐 Wed. 🎉 June 24.

Granite obelisk of the Bunker Hill Monument, erected in 1843

🏛 Bunker Hill Monument
Monument Square. **Tel** (617) 242-5641. ☐ 9am–5pm daily (last climb: 4:30pm). ⬤ Jan 1, Thanksgiving, Dec 25. **www**.nps.gov/bost

In the Revolution's first pitched battle between British and colonial troops, the British won but failed to escape from Boston. Following the June 17, 1775 battle, American irregulars were joined by other militia to keep British forces penned up until George Washington forced their evacuation by sea the following March. A Tuscan-style pillar was erected in 1794 in honor of Dr. Joseph Warren, a Boston revolutionary leader who died in the battle, but Charlestown citizens felt something grander was in order. Accordingly, they began raising funds for the Bunker Hill Monument in 1823, laid the cornerstone in 1825, and dedicated the 221-ft (67-m) granite obelisk in 1843. The building has no elevator, but 294 steps lead to the top and give spectacular views of Boston harbor. Exhibitions recount the significance and drama of the bloody battle.

🏛 John Harvard Mall
Ten families founded Charlestown in 1629, a year before the rest of Boston was settled. They built their homes and a palisaded fort on Town Hill, a spot now marked by John Harvard Mall. A small monument within the enclosed park pays homage to John Harvard, the young cleric who ministered to the settlers (*see p110*).

When John Winthrop arrived with three shiploads of Puritan refugees in 1630 (*see p18*), they settled nearby in the marshes at the base of Town Hill, now City Square.

🏛 Charlestown Navy Yard
Tel (617) 242-5601. ☐ 9am–5pm daily. ♿ ✉
Established in 1800 as one of the country's first military shipyards, for 174 years Charlestown Navy Yard played a key role in supporting the U.S. Atlantic fleet, as the Navy moved from wooden sailing ships to steel giants. The men and women working at the yard built more than 200 warships and carried out maintenance repairs on thousands of others. The yard was designed by Alexander Parris, architect of Quincy Market (*see p64*), and was one of the first examples of industrial architecture in Boston.

On decommissioning, 30 acres of the Navy Yard were transferred to the National Park Service, and rangers now give tours of the facility on a daily basis, including the Chain Forge (where die-lock anchor chain was first made), the Rope Walk, and Dry Dock 1 (one of the first dry docks in the U.S.). A Visitor Center is located at Building 5.

Municipal art in City Square

🏛 U.S.S. Constitution
Charlestown Navy Yard. **Tel** (617) 242-5671. ☐ Apr–Oct: 10am–3:50pm Tue–Sun; Nov–Mar: 10am–3:50pm Thu–Sun. ♿ ✉ **www**.ussconstitution.navy.mil

The oldest commissioned warship afloat, the U.S.S. *Constitution* saw action in the Mediterranean protecting American shipping from the Barbary pirates. In the War of 1812, she won fame and her nickname of "Old Ironsides" when cannonballs bounced off her in a battle with the British ship *Guerriere*. In the course of her active service, she won 42 battles, lost none, captured 20 vessels, and was never boarded by an enemy. She underwent a thorough overhaul in time for her 1997 bicentennial, enabling her to carry her own canvas into the wind for the first time in a century. On July 4 each year, she is taken out into the harbor for a turnaround that reverses her position at the pier to ensure equal weathering on both sides. A small museum documents her history.

U.S.S. *Constitution*, built in 1797, moored in Charlestown Navy Yard

Concord ⑨

First settled in 1635, Concord is linked with neighboring Lexington in the battles of April 19, 1775. Colonials favoring separation from Great Britain hid munitions here and British troops, seeking these supplies, marched on the town, passing first through Lexington *(see p119)*. The resulting battles in Concord, along with the Lexington skirmish, are considered the first of the American Revolution. Half a century later, with the gathering of American writers including essayist Ralph Waldo Emerson, Concord blossomed as the literary heart of the US. The homes of many writers of the era are now preserved as museums.

widely considered to have set off the war, as the Colonials drove three British companies from the bridge and chased them back to their occupation barracks in Boston.

Across the bridge is the famous **Minute Man** statue, crafted by Concord native Daniel Chester French (1850–1931). A short trail leads from the bridge to the North Bridge Visitor Center. A re-enactment of the battle takes place every year in April.

North Bridge in Minute Man National Historical Park

🏛 Monument Square
At Concord's center is Monument Square. The square was the focus of a battle between British troops and Colonists on what has become known as Patriots Day. Having seized the gun cache of rebel forces, British soldiers began burning them. Nearby Colonial forces saw the smoke and, believing the British were torching the town, rushed to Concord's defense.

🏛 Minute Man National Historical Park – North Bridge Visitor Center
174 Liberty St. *Tel (978) 318-7810.* ⬤ *Apr–Oct: 9am–5pm daily; Nov: 9am–4pm daily; Dec–Mar: 11am–3pm daily.* ⬤ *Jan 1, Thanksgiving, Dec 25.* ♿ www.nps.gov/mima

Although British troops met little resistance on Lexington Battle Green and managed to prevail in Concord center, they fared less well in the countryside. Colonial militia and citizen-soldiers (Minute Men) successfully hid their cannon and powder stashes from a contingent of British soldiers by burying the munitions in newly plowed fields. They then confronted British troops who were patrolling North Bridge. The so-called "shot heard round the world," memorialized in Emerson's "Concord Hymn" (1837), is

Minute Man statue in Concord

🏛 Emerson House
28 Cambridge Tpk. *Tel (978) 369-2236.* ⬤ *mid-Apr–late Oct: 10am–4:30pm Thu–Sat, noon–4:30pm Sun.* 🖼 www.emersonhouse.rwe.org
Following his graduation from Harvard, Ralph Waldo Emerson (1803–82) spent his early adulthood as a schoolteacher and then as a Unitarian minister. But as he grew away from religious orthodoxy and began to promulgate his Transcendental philosophy, Emerson withdrew from the ministry and moved to Concord, living first in The Old Manse where he wrote his manifesto *Nature*. On marrying Lydia Jackson in 1835, he settled into Emerson house, writing essays, organizing lecture tours, and entertaining friends and admirers as the honored "Sage of Concord". Emerson lived in this house until his death in 1882. Much of his furniture, writings, books, and family memorabilia are on display here.

Along the Battle Road, by John Rush, is located in the Minute Man Visitor Center

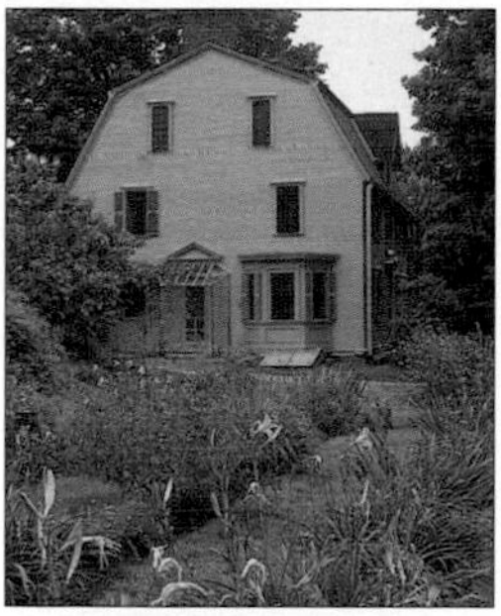

Concord's Old Manse: home to 19th-century literary giants

🏛 The Old Manse

269 Monument St.
Tel *(978) 369-3909.*
🕐 *mid-Apr–Oct: 10am–5pm Mon–Sat, noon–5pm Sun.* 📷 🛍

The parsonage by the North Bridge was built in 1770 by the grandfather of writer Ralph Waldo Emerson. Author Nathaniel Hawthorne (1804–64) lived here as a newlywed in 1842–45 and wrote *Mosses from an Old Manse* (1846), giving the house its name. On view are Emerson family possessions and period furniture. The garden was planted by essayist Henry David Thoreau (1817–62) as a wedding gift to Hawthorne.

🏛 Concord Museum

Jct of Lexington Rd and Cambridge Tpk. ***Tel*** *(978) 369-9609.* 🕐 *Jan–Mar: 11am–4pm Mon–Sat, 1–4pm Sun; Apr–Dec: 9am–5pm Mon–Sat, noon–5pm Sun (Jun–Aug: 9am–5pm Sun).* 📷 ♿ **www**.concordmuseum.org

Begun in 1850, the Concord museum contains one of the oldest and best-documented collections of Americana. Holdings include decorative arts from the 17th, 18th, and 19th centuries that can be traced to original Concord owners; the lantern that Paul Revere ordered hung to warn of the British advance; and American Revolution artifacts that include powder horns, muskets, cannonballs, and fifes. The museum is also the repository of the contents of Emerson's study, and the largest collection of personal items that belonged to essayist Henry David Thoreau. The "Why Concord?" exhibit traces the community from initial settlement some 10,000 years ago through the 20th century.

VISITORS' CHECKLIST

👥 *17,750.* ✈ *Boston.*
ℹ *58 Main St. (978) 369-3120.*
🎉 *Patriots Day (Apr).*
www.concordchamberofcommerce.org

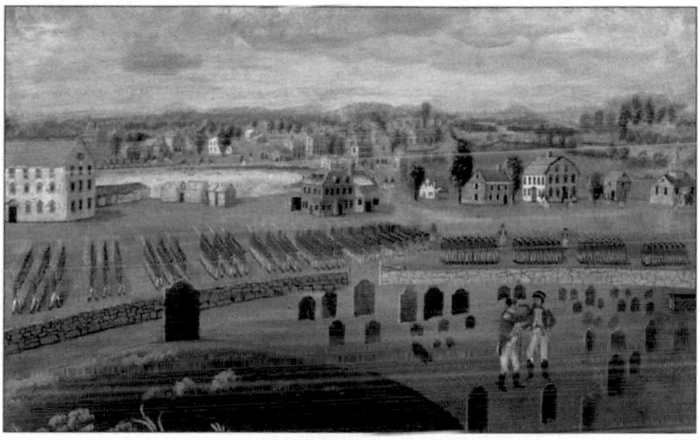

***A View of the Town of Concord April 19, 1775,* Concord Museum**

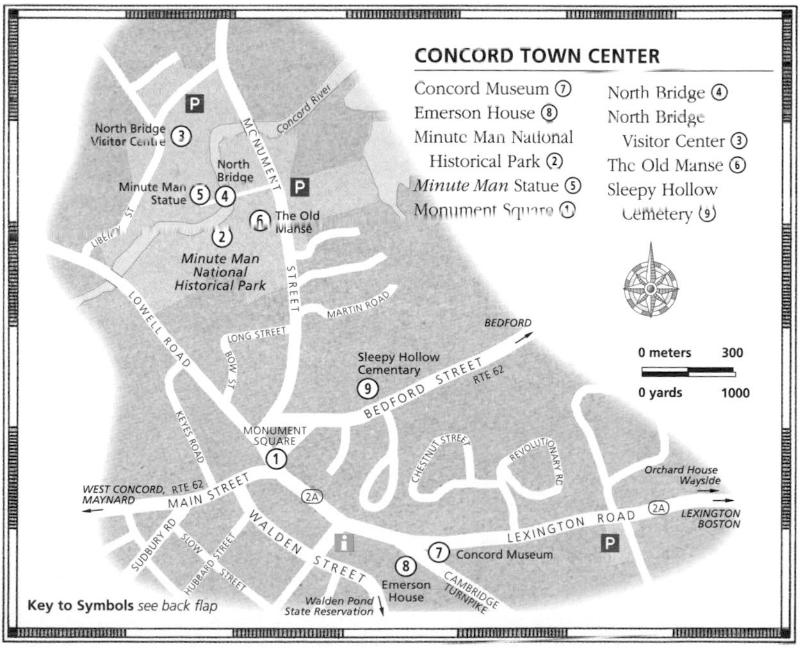
CONCORD TOWN CENTER
Concord Museum 7
Emerson House 8
Minute Man National Historical Park 2
Minute Man Statue 5
Monument Square 1
North Bridge 4
North Bridge Visitor Center 3
The Old Manse 6
Sleepy Hollow Cemetery 9
0 meters 300
0 yards 1000
North Bridge Visitor Centre
North Bridge
Minute Man Statue
The Old Manse
Minute Man National Historical Park
Concord River
MONUMENT STREET
LIBERTY ST
LOWELL ROAD
MARTIN ROAD
LONG STREET
BOW ST
BEDFORD
Sleepy Hollow Cementary
BEDFORD STREET
RTE 62
KEYES ROAD
MONUMENT SQUARE
CHESTNUT STREET
REVOLUTIONARY RD
Orchard House Wayside
WEST CONCORD, MAYNARD
RTE 62
MAIN STREET
2A
WALDEN STREET
LEXINGTON ROAD
LEXINGTON BOSTON
SUDBURY RD
SLOW STREET
HUBBARD STREET
Concord Museum
Emerson House
CAMBRIDGE TURNPIKE
Walden Pond State Reservation
Key to Symbols *see back flap*

Author's Ridge, Sleepy Hollow Cemetery

⚰ Sleepy Hollow Cemetery

Bedford St, east of Monument Sq.
○ *dawn–dusk daily.*

This rolling green cemetery
is the final resting place of
many Concord literary giants.
Pilgrims seek the graves of
Henry David Thoreau (1817–
62), Nathaniel Hawthorne
(1804–64), Louisa May Alcott
(1832–88), and Ralph Waldo
Emerson (1803–82), among
other notables, on "Author's
Ridge." They often leave
pebbles on Emerson's head-
stone, acorns on Thoreau's,
and pennies on the grave of
sculptor Daniel Chester French.
Although his most famous
work is the Lincoln Memorial
in Washington, DC, French
also sculpted the Civil War
Memorial in Sleepy Hollow.

⚏ Orchard House

399 Lexington Rd.
Tel (978) 369-4118. ○ *Apr–Oct:
10am–4:30pm Mon–Sat, 1–4:30pm
Sun; Nov–Mar: 11am–3pm Mon–Fri,
10am–4:30pm Sat, 1–4:30pm Sun.*
📷 📹 ○ *Jan 1–15, Easter,
Thanksgiving, Dec 25.*
www.louisamayalcott.org

Louisa May Alcott was the
most successful member of
the Alcott family, but in his
day, her father Bronson
was well-regarded as a
Transcendental philosopher
and founder of
the now-defunct
Concord School of
Philosophy. Orchard
House was the Alcott
family home from
1858–77, and Louisa
May set *Little Women*
(1868) here. Since
the house has been
little altered since
the Alcotts lived

in it, visitors often comment
that a tour is like walking
through the book.

**Room at Orchard House, the Alcott
family residence from 1858–77**

⚏ The Wayside

455 Lexington Rd.
Tel (978) 369-6993.
○ *May–Oct, call for hours.*

This National Historic Site
has a long literary history.
It was home to the Alcott
family while Louisa May was
growing up, and became the
only home ever owned by
author Nathaniel Hawthorne.
Children's author Margaret
Sidney (1844–1924) of *Five
Little Peppers* fame bought it
from Hawthorne's daughter.
Guided tours are offered at
limited hours by Minute Man
National Park rangers.

⚏ Walden Pond State Reservation

915 Walden St. *Tel (978) 369-3254.*
○ *Call for hours.* 📷 📹 ♿
www.mass.gov/dcr

Essayist Henry David Thoreau
(1817–62) lived at Walden Pond
from 1845 to 1847. It was here
that he compiled the material
for his seminal work *Walden;
or, Life in the Woods* (1854),
which called for a return to
simplicity and a respect for
nature, which he cast as the
source of all morality. Although
he depicted himself living in
isolation, Thoreau would visit
the Concord Center to have
Sunday dinners with the
Emerson family, and the pond
and its woodlands are no
more wilderness than they
were in Thoreau's day. His
significance in American
thought and letters, however,
led to the designation of the
pond as a National Historic
Landmark. The area is popular
for walking, fishing, and swimming, though the reservation
limits visitors to 1,000 people
at any one time. A bronze
statue of Thoreau stands outside a re-creation of his cabin.

Directly across busy Route
2 from Walden Pond is the
Walden Woods Project which
demonstrates the enduring
appeal of Thoreau's ideas. A
one-mile (1.6-km) walking
trail is punctuated by
aphoristic inscriptions in
granite from Thoreau's
writings, and bronze-tipped
columns devoted to such
issues as pacifism and
environmentalism. Within
Walden Woods is a "reflection
circle." The granite columns
surrounding it bear yet more
quotations from thinkers who
were influenced by Thoreau,
including civil rights leader
Martin Luther King, Jr. (1929–
68) and Sioux chief Luther
Standing Bear (1868–1939).

Fisherman on the tranquil waters of Walden Pond

Lexington ❿

The peaceful prosperity of the modern-day suburb of Lexington belies its role in the birth of American independence. On the village common at dawn on April 19, 1775, British regulars and Colonial militia exchanged shots. The skirmish proved to be the opening salvo of the American Revolution, and Lexington Battle Green has been hallowed ground for Americans ever since. Many visitors like to bicycle the 5.5 miles (9 km) from Alewife "T" station in Cambridge along the Minuteman Bikeway, which roughly parallels the British route on their march to Lexington.

VISITORS' CHECKLIST

🏠 31,550. 🚉 Boston. ℹ️ 1875 Massachusetts Ave. (781) 862-1450. 🎊 Patriots Day (Apr). www.lexingtonchamber.org

Minute Man Bikeway, part of the Minute Man National Historical Park

🏞 Minute Man National Historical Park – Minute Man Visitor Center

Rte 2A. **Tel** (781) 674-1920. ⏰ Apr–Oct: 9am–5pm daily, Nov: 9am–4pm daily. www.nps.gov/mima This 990-acre (400-ha) park, with access from both Concord (see pp116–18) and Lexington, preserves the site and interprets the story of the first battles of the American Revolution. It explains that British forces were seeking to uncover colonial munitions hidden in the countryside, and how both Massachusetts militia and citizen-soldiers, known as Minute Men, managed to rout the British regulars. The Visitor Center features a massive battle mural and a 22-minute multimedia show, Road to Revolution. A significant portion of the national park runs along the five-mile (8-km) Battle Road Trail. This is the path that was followed by British forces as they advanced from Lexington and marched on to Concord – the same route the forces took in retreat.

🏛 Lexington Battle Green

Tranquil churches surround the leafy green where, each year in April, historic re-enactors re-create the Battle of Lexington. The rest of the year, a statue of a Massachusetts militia man erected in 1900 recalls the event, as do the graves of seven of the eight colonial casualties.

Historic re-enactor

🏛 Historical Society Houses

Hancock-Clarke House 36 Hancock St; **Buckman Tavern** 1 Bedford St; **Munroe Tavern** 1332 Massachusetts Ave; **Tel** (781) 862-1703. ⏰ call for seasonal opening hours. 🖼 www.lexingtonhistory.org These three structures all played a role in the events of April 19, 1775 (now known as Patriots Day). **Buckman Tavern** served as the meeting place for the Massachusetts militia before the confrontation

and as a makeshift hospital for their wounded. Bostonian Paul Revere undertook his "midnight ride" to **Hancock-Clarke House** to warn patriots Samuel Adams and John Hancock, two of the signatories to the Declaration of Independence, of the approaching British (see p21). **Munroe Tavern** was a headquarters for British forces. All display artifacts from the Revolutionary era.

🏛 National Heritage Museum

33 Marrett Rd. (At intersection of Rte 2A and Massachusetts Ave.) **Tel** (781) 861-6559. ⏰ 10am–5pm Mon–Sat, noon–5pm Sun. 🔒 Jan 1, Thanksgiving, Dec 24–25. www.monh.org This museum, opened on the bicentennial of the Battle of Lexington, is devoted both to patriotic subjects and a celebration of American popular culture. Among its prized artifacts is a copy of the Lexington Alarm, a broadside detailing the events at Lexington and calling on American colonists to revolt against the British Crown.

Buckman Tavern, where militia met to plan their revolt against British forces

THREE GUIDED WALKS

Given the difficulties of driving in Boston, it is fortunate that its compact layout and ubiquitous sidewalks make it an ideal walking city. These three walks show the city's extremes – the dense riches of a university campus, the unexpected pleasures of an intensely residential neighborhood, and Boston's most famous walking tour along the historic Freedom Trail. While Harvard *(see pp112–7)* gets the lion's share of attention among the Boston-area universities, its younger neighbor in Cambridge, the Massachusetts Institute of Technology (MIT), is known for its modern art. South Boston is a secret often jealously guarded by its inhabitants. Although Dorchester Heights was a critical site in the American Revolution, few Freedom Trail walkers ever make the detour to appreciate the high vantage on Boston's outer harbor. In addition to these three walks, each of the five areas of Boston described in the *Area by Area* section of this book has a walk on its *Street-by-Street* map.

David Faragut statue

CHOOSING A WALK

The Three Walks
This map shows the location of the three guided walks in relation to the main sightseeing areas of Boston.

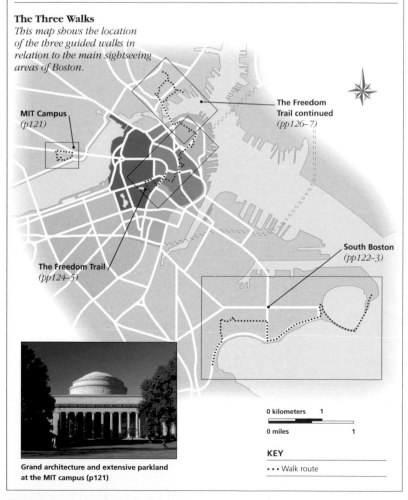

MIT Campus
(p121)

The Freedom Trail continued
(pp126–7)

The Freedom Trail
(pp124–5)

South Boston
(pp122–3)

0 kilometers 1

0 miles 1

KEY

••• Walk route

Grand architecture and extensive parkland at the MIT campus (p121)

A 45-Minute Walk on the MIT Campus

Perhaps best known for its advances in science and engineering, the Massachusetts Institute of Technology has embraced cutting-edge art and architecture as surely as it has pioneered artificial intelligence and robotics. This walking tour samples some of the best of modern and post-modern sculpture and buildings located around the campus. These highlights represent the institute's innovative use of unconventional materials and techniques.

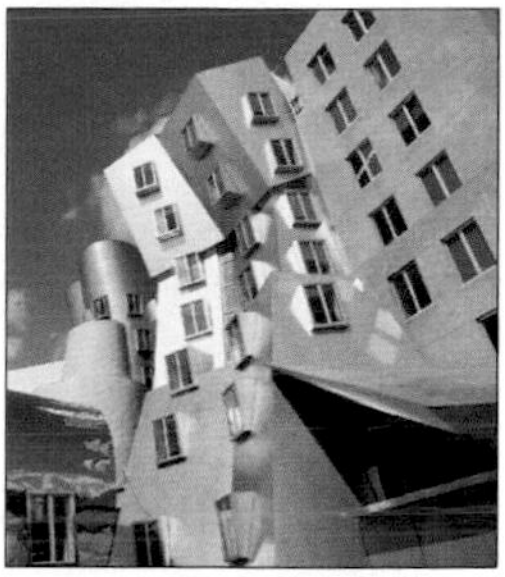

The Stata Center designed by Frank Gehry ⑨

From the Kendall/MIT "T" station, walk to Main Street and turn right. Take the second right down Wadsworth Street to the corner of Amherst Street where Pablo Picasso's *Figure Découpée* ① from 1963 stands in a small garden. Cross the intersection to the Tang Building, where Frank Stella's 1988 abstract wall relief of acrylic and enamel on aluminum, *Heads or Tails* ②, fills the wall at the base of the staircase atrium. Continue down Amherst Street and turn right onto Ames Street at the Media Lab Extension building. Next door, the sleekly banded white box with dark windows is the List Visual Arts Center ③, where galleries display changing exhibitions of innovative, contemporary art. Note Alexander Calder's intermediate model for his sculpture, *The Big Sail*, in the lobby ④. In the central atrium, Kenneth Noland's 1985 *Here-There* ⑤ carries the minimalist abstraction of the List building to its logical artistic extreme in a four-story interior wall mural.

Join the students rushing to classes as you cross Ames Street to the walkway that leads into the heart of the campus. Set at the edge of the sidewalk on the left is a complex sculpture of curves, angles, and twisted planes commissioned in 1975 from sculptor Louise Nevelson. Although painted, *Transparent Horizon* ⑥ was constructed of non-rusting corten steel. Continue past the Nevelson and look to the left for a view of Alexander Calder's fully realized, 40-ft- (12-m) high sculpture, *The Big Sail* ⑦.

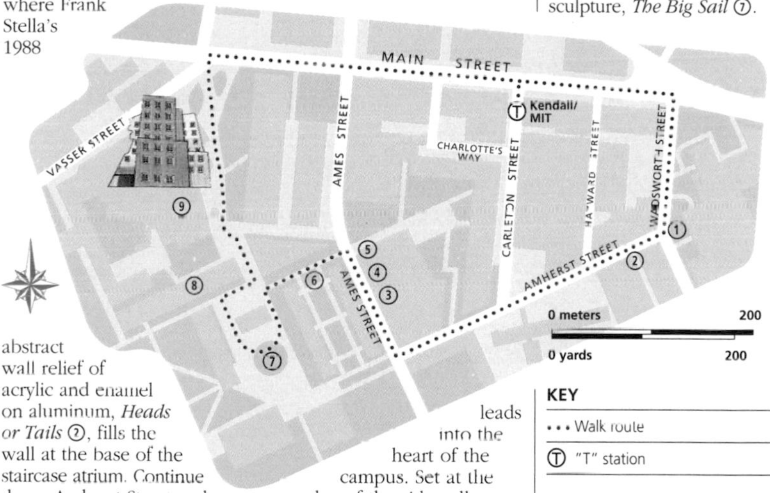

KEY

• • • Walk route

Ⓣ "T" station

Turn right to enter the Whitaker Building, where a projection screen in the ground-level corridor shows experimental film and video. The Media Test Wall ⑧, as the installation is called, is emblematic of the school's commitment to technology in the arts. Cross through the Whitaker building for a view of the south side of the Stata Center ⑨. Frank Gehry's metal-sheathed complex constitutes a research and teaching village devoted to computer, information, and intelligence sciences. Walk around the center to return to Main Street and the "T" station.

TIPS FOR WALKERS

Starting point: *Kendall/MIT "T"*
Length: *0.8 miles (1.3 km).*
Stopping-off points: *Amelia's Trattoria (111 Harvard St.) serves gourmet pizzas and pasta dishes.*
Visitor information: *See page 109 for museum opening hours.*

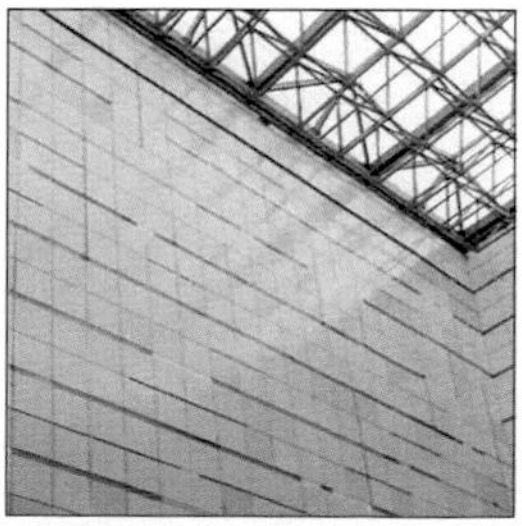

Here-There **mural (1985) by minimalist artist Kenneth Noland ⑤**

A Two-Hour Walk in South Boston

The harbor is the main attraction in quickly gentrifying South Boston. Initially populated by refugees from the mid-19th century Irish famine, the area evolved into the third-largest Irish-American community in the U.S. Recent gentrification has diversified the population and turned Victorian tenements into trendy condominiums. But the defining characteristic of South Boston has always been its relation to the harbor – a bevy of soft sand beaches and headlands that guard the entry to the Port of Boston. The steep hill to Dorchester Heights can be skipped in favor of a continued seaside promenade.

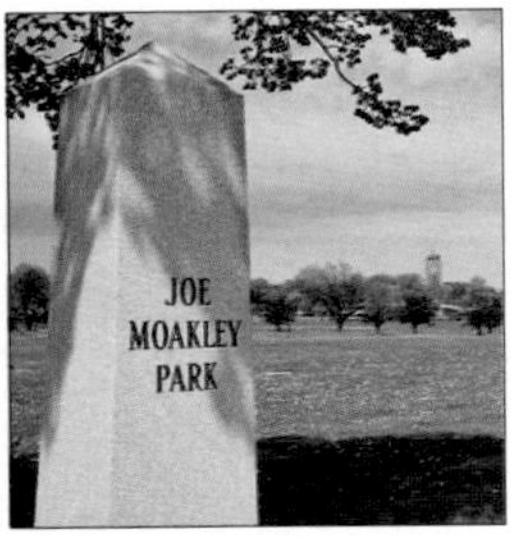

Stone column at the entrance to Joe Moakley Park ①

The last stop of the No. 5 bus is at the playing fields and green walkways of Joe Moakley Park ①, named after the late South Boston-born Congressman. Some of Moakley's sayings celebrate the neighborhood's identity and are etched on granite columns that can be found around the park. One such saying reads "Everyone I knew growing up in South Boston was baptized, issued a union card, and enrolled in the Democratic Party." Cross the park to the broad swath of fine brown sand known as Carson Beach ②, a public swimming beach with a bathhouse and bocce courts.

The steep walk up Old Harbor Street leads to the grand hilltop oval of Thomas Park, where the Dorchester Heights Monument ③ stands like a lighthouse to mark the spot where George Washington erected cannons in 1776 to force the British withdrawal from Boston. The massive building at one end of the park is South Boston High School ④. Walk along East 7th Avenue past newly renovated homes to L Street and turn right toward the harbor. Woody's L Street Tavern ⑤, Southie's most old-fashioned pub and the set for scenes in the film *Good Will Hunting*, is at the corner of East 8th Street.

At the foot of the street is the L Street Bath House ⑥, the toddler-friendly L Street Beach ⑦, and M Street Beach ⑧. The bath house, which actually stretches between K and M streets, was a municipal gift from notoriously corrupt mayor James Curley (last elected to office from jail) to his friends and cronies of South Boston. The bath house now serves a broad public. Walk east along William J. Day Boulevard as it winds past the yacht club and private moorings and concludes at Pleasure Bay. Standing sentinel over the harbor on the traffic circle connecting the boulevard to Farragut Road is a bronze of Admiral David Farragut ⑨, commander in chief of the US Navy during the Civil War.

Across the street is the section of South Boston beach known as the "Sugar Bowl" ⑩. This beach lines

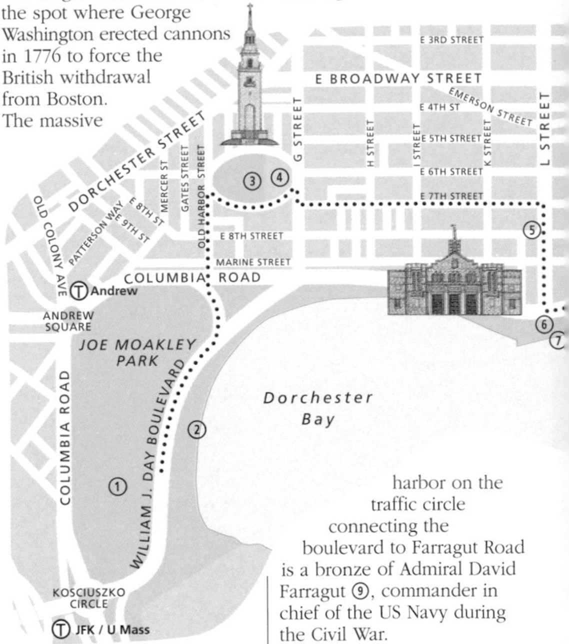

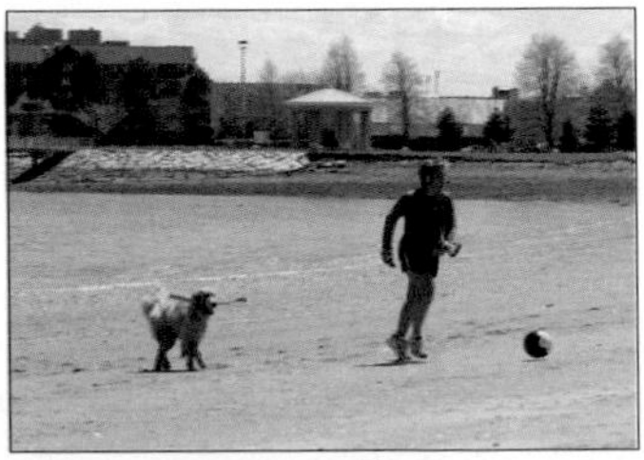

Time out on Carson Beach ②

TIPS FOR WALKERS

Starting point: *Joe Moakley Park*
Getting there: *No. 5 bus from Andrew Sq. to Moakley Park (McCormack Housing).*
Length: *3 miles (5km).*
Stops: *Sullivan's (next to Fort Independence) and* Nicole's Seaside Cafe *(at Carson Beach) serve fried clams.* Ruth & Leo's Deli & Seafood, *across from Moakley Park, offers more substantial fare.*

Canons at Fort Independence, Castle Island ⑭

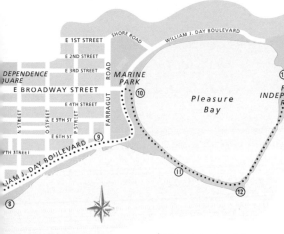

0 meters 500

0 yards 500

KEY

••• Walk route

Ⓣ "T" station

Pleasure Bay, a circular body of water protected from the harbor by an extensive breakwater, the Pleasure Bay Causeway ⑪. The causeway walk of nearly 1 mile (1.5 km) is a favorite spot for local mothers to show off their infants, as well as a good exercise route for joggers and speed walkers. Halfway along the causeway is the Head Island light pavilion ⑫, with picnic tables, benches, and sweeping views of the harbor, looking all the way down to the landmark gas storage tank in Dorchester. The tank was

first painted in rainbow colors by abstract artist Corita Kent in 1971.

The causeway concludes at Castle Island, which has not been a real island since the channel to the mainland was filled in 1891. Follow the seaside walkway which passes by a number of memorials to fallen South Boston firefighters, police officers, and soldiers. The

walkway brings you to a pointed obelisk monument ⑬. This granite-block shaft is a memorial to Donald McKay whose shipyard, directly across the channel, launched some of the fastest clipper ships of the mid-19th century and helped cement Boston as an international trading port. Bas-reliefs of some of McKay's most famous vessels are mounted near the base. The shipyard site is now Logan International Airport. Most planes coming to Boston make their final approach and touchdown on the runway directly opposite Castle Island.

Because Castle Island controls the throat of Boston harbor, it has been fortified since 1634. The current structure, Fort Independence ⑭, was erected in 1779 under George Washington's orders so that no enemy could ever again occupy Boston as the British had done. It never saw action, though it did serve as a prisoner of war camp during the Civil War. Author Edgar Allen Poe served here briefly in the 1820s and is said to have based one of his macabre tales, *A Cask of Amontillado*, on a fort legend of a man deliberately confined in a dungeon. (Just such a skeleton was uncovered during a renovation in 1905.) The No. 11 bus, which runs along Day Boulevard, will take you back to downtown Boston.

USS Constitution gliding past Fort Independence ⑭

A 90-Minute Walk along the Freedom Trail

Boston has more sites directly related to the American Revolution than any other city. The most important of these sites, as well as some relating to other freedoms gained by Bostonians, have been linked together as "The Freedom Trail." This 2.5-mile (4-km) walking route, marked in red on the sidewalks, goes from Boston Common to Bunker Hill in Charlestown *(see pp126–7)*. This first section weaves through the central city and Old Boston. See www.thefreedomtrail.org for more information.

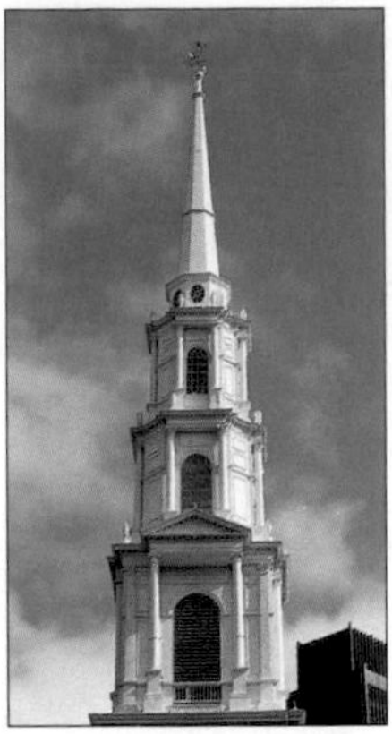

Elegant Georgian steeple of Park Street Church

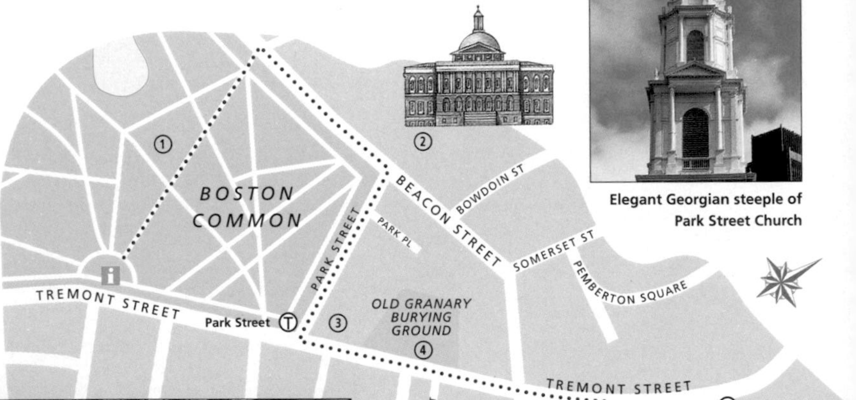
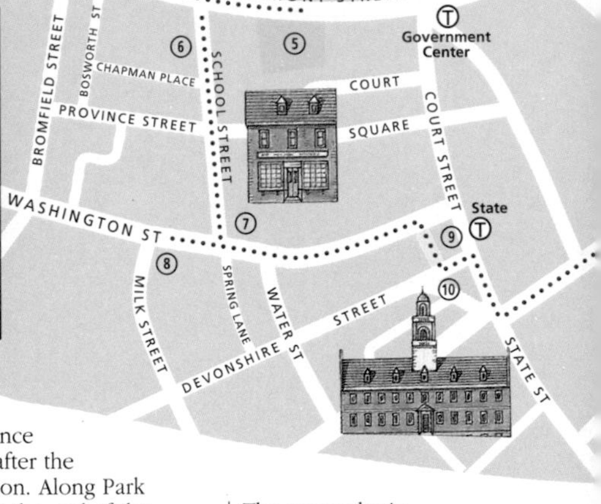

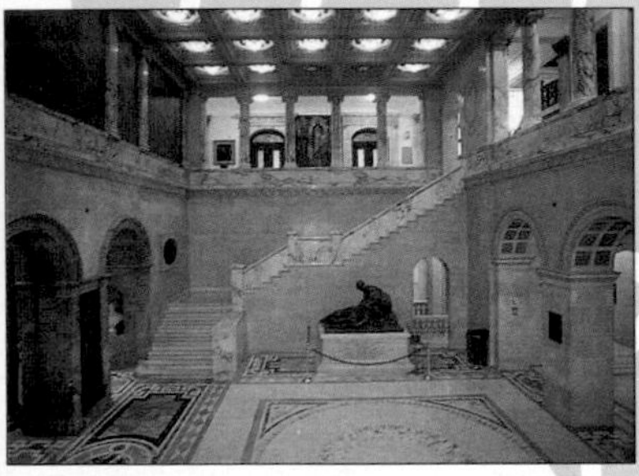

Nurses Hall in Massachusetts State House

Central City

The Freedom Trail starts at the Visitor Information Center on Boston Common [1] *(see pp46–7)*. This is where angry colonials rallied against their British masters and where the British forces were encamped during the 1775–76 military occupation. Political speakers still expound from their soap-boxes here, and Boston Common remains a center of much activity.

Walking toward the north-west corner of the Common gives a great view of the Massachusetts State House [2] *(see p50)* on Beacon Street, designed by Charles Bulfinch as the new center of state governance shortly after the Revolution. Along Park Street, at the end of the Common, you will come to Park Street Church [3] *(see p48)*, built in 1810 and a bulwark of the antislavery movement. The church took the place of an old grain storage facility, which in turn gave its name to the adjacent Granary Burying Ground [4], one of Boston's earliest cemeteries and the final resting place of patriots John Hancock and Paul Revere *(see p21)*. Continuing along Tremont Street you will come to King's Chapel and Burying Ground [5] *(see p58)*.

The atmospheric cemetery is Boston's oldest, containing, among others, the grave of colonial city founder John Winthrop. As the name suggests, King's Chapel was the principal Anglican church in Puritan Boston, and more than half of its congregation fled to Nova Scotia at the outbreak of the Revolution. The box pew on the right just inside the front entrance was reserved for condemned prisoners to hear their last sermons before going to the gallows on Boston Common.

Heart of Old Boston
Head back along Tremont Street and turn down School Street, where a hopscotch-like mosaic embedded in the sidewalk commemorates the site of the First Public School ⑥, established in 1635. At the end of the street is the Old Corner Bookstore ⑦ *(see p59)*, a landmark more associated with Boston's literary emergence of 1845– 65 than with the Revolution.

The Old South Meeting House ⑧, a short way to the south on Washington Street, is a graceful, white-spired brick church, modeled on Sir Christopher Wren's English country churches. As one of the largest meeting halls in Revolutionary Boston, "Old South's" rafters rang with many a fiery speech urging revolt against the British. It was a crucible

for free-speech debates and taxation protests. A few blocks along, the Old State House ⑨ presides over the head of State Street. The colonial government building, it also served as the first state legislature, and the merchants' exchange in the basement was where Boston's colonial shipping fortunes were made. The square in front of the Old State House is the Boston Massacre Site ⑩, where British soldiers opened fire on a taunting mob in 1770, killing five and providing propaganda for revolutionary agitators.

Follow State Street down to Congress Street and turn left to reach Faneuil Hall ⑪, known as the "Cradle of Liberty" for the history of patriotic speeches made in its public meeting hall. Donated to the city by Huguenot merchant Peter Faneuil, the building was built primarily as Boston's first central marketplace. Use the red stripe to negotiate your way down to North End and

the Paul Revere House ⑫ on North Square. Boston's oldest private residence, it was home to the man famously known for his "midnight ride" *(see p21)*. From here, walk to Hanover Street and turn right, following the red stripe towards the next point on the Freedom Trail, Old North Church *(see p126)*.

(see p59), (see p126), (see p21)

Faneuil Hall, popularly known as "the Cradle of Liberty"

Old State House, once the seat of colonial government

TIPS FOR WALKERS

Starting point: Boston Common. Maps available at Boston Common Visitors' Center.
Length: 2.5 miles (4 km).
Getting there: Exit at Park Street "T" station to start. Other "T" stations also located on route: State, Haymarket, and Government Center. Follow red stripe on sidewalk for the full route.

HAYMARKET
STREET
UNION STREET
BLACKSTONE STREET
SALEM STREET
HANOVER STREET
NORTH STREET
CLINTON STREET
RICHMOND STREET
NORTH STREET
GARDEN CT
HANOVER STREET
FLEET STREET
CLARK STREET
NORTH STREET
ATLANTIC AVENUE

0 meters ———— 200
0 yards ———— 200

KEY

••• Walk route

ⓣ "T" Station

🛈 Tourist information

The Freedom Trail continued

Distances begin to stretch out on the second half of the Freedom Trail as it meanders through the narrow streets of the North End, then continues over the Charles River to Charlestown, where Boston's settlers first landed. The key Revolutionary and colonial-era sites here embrace two wars – the War of Independence and the War of 1812.

View from Copp's Hill terrace, Copp's Hill Burying Ground ⑭

The North End

Following the Freedom Trail through the North End from Paul Revere House *(see p125)*, allow time to try some of the Italian cafés and bakeries along the neighborhood's main thoroughfare, Hanover Street. Cross through the Paul Revere Mall to reach Old North Church ⑬ *(see p71)*, whose spire is instantly visible over the shoulder of the statue of Paul Revere on horseback. Sexton Robert Newman famously hung two lanterns in the belfry here, signaling the advance of British troops on Lexington and Concord in 1775. The church retains its 18th-century interior, including the unusual box pews.

Gravestone at Copp's Hill Burying Ground

The crest of Copp's Hill lies close by on Hull Street. Some of Boston's earliest gallows stood here, and Bostonians would gather in boats below to watch the hangings of heretics and pirates. Much of the hilltop is covered by Copp's Hill Burying Ground ⑭. This was established in 1660, and the cemetery holds the remains of several generations of the Mather family – Boston's influential 17th- and 18th-century theocrats – as well as the tombstones of many soldiers of the Revolution slain in the fight for freedom.

Boston's first free African American community, "New Guinea," covered the west side of Copp's Hill. A broken column marks the grave of Prince Hall, head of the Black Masons, distinguished veteran of the Revolution, and prominent political leader in the early years of the Republic. The musketball-chipped tombstone of patriot Daniel Malcolm records that he asked to be buried "in a stone grave 10 feet deep" to rest beyond the reach of British gunfire.

Boston Inner Harbor

KEANY SQUARE

COMMERCIAL STREET

CHARLESTOWN BRIDGE

PRINCE STREET

HULL STREET

SNOWHILL STREET

SHEAFE STREET

PRINCE STREET

SALEM STREET

NORTH BENNETT STREET

TILESTON STREET

HULL STREET

COPP'S HILL BURYING GROUND ⑭

CHARTER STREET

FOSTER ST

ATLANTIC AVENUE

NORTH END PLAYGROUND

⑬

HANOVER STREET

KEY

••• Walk route

Ⓣ "T" station

Unusual box pews inside Old North Church ⑬

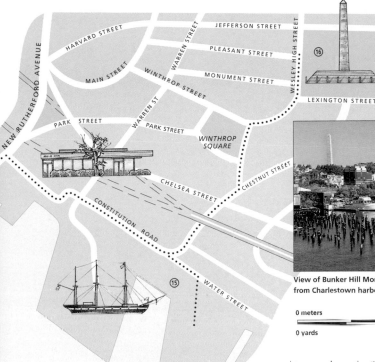

View of Bunker Hill Monument ⑯
from Charlestown harborfront

0 meters		200
0 yards		200

Charlestown

The iron bridge over the Charles River that links the North End in Boston with City Square in Charlestown dates from 1899. Across the bridge, turn right along Constitution Road, following the signs to Charlestown Navy Yard ⑮. The National Park Service operates the Visitor Center at Building 5, which has newly expanded exhibits explaining the historic role of the Navy Yard and the history of the warships – one from the late 18th century, another from the mid-20th century – that are berthed at its piers. The colonial navy had been no match for the might of Britain's naval forces during the Revolution, and building a more formidable naval force became a priority. This was one of several shipyards that were set up around 1800. Lying at her berth alongside Pier 1, the 200-year old wooden-hulled

Lion carving, U.S.S.
Constitution ⑮

U.S.S. Constitution is probably the most famous ship in U.S. history and still remains the flagship of the U.S. Navy. Built at Hartt's ship-yard in the North End, she was completed in 1797. In the War of 1812, she earned the nickname "Old Ironsides" for the resilience of her live oak hull against cannon fire. Fully restored for her bicentennial, the Constitution occasionally sails under her own power. The granite obelisk that

towers above the Charlestown waterfront is Bunker Hill Monument ⑯, commemorating the battle of June 17, 1775 that ended with a costly victory for British forces against an irregular colonial army that finally ran out of ammunition. British losses were so heavy, however, that the battle would presage future success for the colonial forces. As a monument to the first large-scale battle of the Revolution, the obelisk based on those of ancient Egypt, was a prototype for others across the U.S. Catch a bus from Chelsea Street back to the North End and city center.

Defensive guns at Charlestown Navy Yard ⑮ with view of the North End

TRAVELERS' NEEDS

WHERE TO STAY

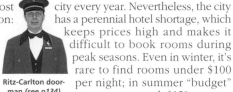

Ritz-Carlton doorman *(see p134)*

Boston offers the visitor almost every type of accommodation: modest guesthouses, luxury hotels, chain motels, Victorian brownstone bed and breakfasts, and elegant, designer "boutique" hotels. Many older hotels have been renovated to provide traditional charm with modern conveniences, while new hotels and B&Bs open in the city every year. Nevertheless, the city has a perennial hotel shortage, which keeps prices high and makes it difficult to book rooms during peak seasons. Even in winter, it's rare to find rooms under $100 per night; in summer "budget" rates can approach $150 or more. Information is available from Boston's tourist information offices *(see p175)*.

The elegant Omni Parker House *(see p133)*

WHERE TO STAY

The centrally located Back Bay has the greatest concentration of hotels and is convenient for tourists as well as business travelers. In the gentrified South End, nearby, an increasing number of restored Victorian brownstones have been converted to B&Bs. Accommodation in the Financial District, close to the waterfront, caters to business people during the week, but often offers good value to vacationers on the weekends. Across the Charles River, Cambridge has a large number of hotels, particularly around Harvard Square and Kendall Square. In more suburban Brookline, situated a little way west of Back Bay, there are several guesthouses, as well as a selection of more upscale B&Bs.

HOTEL GRADING AND FACILITIES

Boston does not have an official hotel grading system. While higher prices generally indicate more amenities, some lodgings in prime locations, or with unique historic features, may command prices that exceed what the facilities might otherwise warrant. B&Bs generally do not offer fitness facilities, business services, or restaurants, and may be somewhat less expensive, although some at the high end of the price scale now have amenities – and prices – that rival the best hotels. Most large hotels have at least a basic fitness room, while some have arrangements with nearby clubs for guest use. Swimming pools are less common, except at the big hotels, and outdoor pools generally open only between June and early September. One recent development that travelers may find beneficial is that Boston's hotels now house many of the city's top restaurants. High-speed internet access (wired and wireless) has also become increasingly common in hotels.

HOW TO BOOK

Most hotels have toll-free reservation numbers, and some offer discounts for internet booking. Room rates are often quoted for two people sharing a room, not including tax or breakfast, although some B&Bs provide a morning meal. Prepay only the first night in case the accommodation does not meet expectations. There are last-minute rooms during the winter months, but Boston hotels are busy in May and June for college graduations, July and August for summer vacations, and September and October for the fall season.

HIDDEN EXTRAS

If you have a car in Boston, you'll pay dearly for parking. Ask your hotel if parking is included; if not, budget at least $20-25 extra per day. Taxes in Boston will also add 12.45 percent to the hotel bill. If breakfast is not included, expect to spend at least $3 for coffee and a pastry in a nearby café or $15 and up for a full hotel breakfast.

Lobby of the Hyatt Regency Boston *(see p134)*

◁ City Palace Atrium in the Massachusetts State Transport Building

Glass Atrium of the Inn at Harvard
(see p131), Cambridge

DISCOUNTS

Hotel prices vary signifi-cantly with the seasons, with the lowest rates found in January and February. Through the year, many hotels catering to business travelers, such as in the Financial District, around Hynes Convention Center, and in Cambridge's Kendall Square, offer discount weekend rates. B&Bs may offer better prices mid week.

BED AND BREAKFAST

Boston has a good selection of small hotels and B&Bs, offering personal service and charm. If you are looking for a classic B&B – a room or two in the owner's home – contact one of Boston's B&B booking agencies. A recent trend is the "boutique" hotel, a small, elegantly appointed hotel, though prices at these reflect the level of service and luxury.

BUSINESS TRAVELERS

Business travelers will find that all major hotels provide fax and wireless internet access. Some new or newly refurbished hotels offer in-room fax machines, multiline phones, and private voice mail. It is wise to check that older hotels have the facilities you require.

DISABLED TRAVELERS

Disabled travelers may be most comfortable in the city's newer hotels that have been built to conform to access requirements. Some of the large older hotels have been refitted, but many small B&Bs have steps, narrow hall-ways, or other architectural

features that may make access difficult. For information about hotels, transportation, tour services, and other resources, contact the **Massachusetts Network of Information Providers for People with Disabilities**.

CHILDREN

Children are welcome in most of the larger hotels and often stay free in their parents' rooms. Some deluxe hotels provide child-friendly amenities, ranging from bed-time milk and cookies to the telephone "bedtime story line" at the Charles Hotel *(see p137)*. Suites are available in many big hotels giving families space to spread out. For families on more moderate budgets, some guesthouses, such as the Copley Inn *(see p134)*, offer apartment-style accommodations. Be aware that many B&Bs cannot accommodate young children.

Exterior of Irving House *(see p137)*, Cambridge

BUDGET OPTIONS

It can be hard finding budget accommodation in Boston. The **Boston Interna-tional Youth Hostel** has mostly six-bed dormitories, and there are some inexpen-sive chain hotels, such as **Days Inn**, in the suburbs, which offer functional lodging. The North Shore towns of Salem and Rockport, just north of Boston, have good selec-tions of mid-priced B&Bs and are accessible from the city by M.B.T.A. commuter rail – contact the **North of Boston Convention and Visitors' Bureau** for more details.

DIRECTORY

BED AND BREAKFAST AGENCIES

Bed and Breakfast Agency of Boston
Tel (617) 720-3540.
Tel (800) 248-9262.
www.boston-bnbagency.com

Bed and Breakfast Associates Bay Colony, Ltd.
P.O. Box 57166, Babson Park Branch, Boston, MA 02457.
Tel (781) 449-5302.
Tel (888) 486-6018.
Tel 08-234-7113 (toll-free from UK)
www.bnbboston.com

Host Homes of Boston
Box 117, Waban Branch, Boston, MA 02468.
Tel (617) 244-1308.
Tel (800) 600-1308.
www.hosthomesofboston.com

DISABLED TRAVELERS

Massachusetts Network of Information Providers for People with Disabilities
200 Trapelo Rd, Waltham, MA 02452. *Tel* (781) 642-0248.
Tel (800) 642-0249.
TTY (for people who cannot hear). *Tel* (800) 764-0200.
www.disabilityinfo.org

HOSTELS

Boston International Youth Hostel
12 Hemenway St **Map** 3 A3.
Tel (617) 536-9455.
www.bostonhostel.org

BUDGET AND CHAIN HOTELS

Days Inn
Several locations.
Tel (800) 329-7466.
www.daysinn.com

Best Western
Several locations.
Tel (800) 780-7234.
www.bestwestern.com

North of Boston Convention and Visitors' Bureau
17 Peabody Sq., Peabody, MA 01960.
Tel (978) 977-7760
www.northofboston.org

Choosing a Hotel

The hotels in this guide have been selected across a wide range for their good value, facilities, and location. These listings highlight some of the factors that may influence your choice. Hotels are listed by area, beginning with Beacon Hill and West End. All the entries are alphabetical within each price category.

PRICE CATEGORIES
For a standard double room per night, inclusive of breakfast, service charges, and any additional taxes.

$ Under $150
$$ $150–$200
$$$ $200–$250
$$$$ $250–$300
$$$$$ Over $300

BEACON HILL AND WEST END

John Jeffries House $
14 David G Mugar Way, 02114 **Tel** *(617) 367-1866* **Fax** *(617) 742-0313* **Rooms** *46*   **Map** 1 B3

This red brick building was opened in 1909 as housing for nurses at the Massachusetts Eye and Ear Infirmary. Hardwood floors, original moldings, and comfortable traditional furnishings give the feel of a well-lived-in townhouse. It is conveniently located at the foot of Beacon Hill. **www.johnjeffrieshouse.com**

Beacon Hill Hotel & Bistro $$$$
25 Charles St., 02114 **Tel** *(617) 723-7575* **Fax** *(617) 723-7525* **Rooms** *13*   **Map** 1 B4

Paris meets Beacon Hill in this smart townhouse renovation, steps from Boston Common and Public Garden. Rooms are fairly small but chic with soothing colors, plantation shutters, and flat panel televisions. There is a sitting room and a private roof deck. Rates include breakfast in the ground floor bistro. **www.beaconhillhotel.com**

Bulfinch Hotel $$$$$
107 Merrimac St., 02109 **Tel** *(617) 624-0202; (877) 267-1776* **Fax** *(617) 624-0211* **Rooms** *80*   **Map** 1 C2

This building near TD BankNorth Gardens boasts big Beaux-Arts windows that flood the sleek, contemporary rooms with light. The lobby is minimal, but the rooms and mini-suites have large beds and all the modern technology, including flat-screen televisions. **www.bulfinchhotel.com**

Charles Street Inn $$$$$
94 Charles St., 02114 **Tel** *(617) 314-8900; (877) 772-8900* **Fax** *(617) 371-0009* **Rooms** *9*   **Map** 1 B4

This Charles Street time capsule was built in 1860 as a demonstration showpiece for new homes under construction in the Back Bay. Victorian features such as carved marble fireplaces harmonize with European furnishings and modern whirlpool tubs. This is a good base for exploring the street's antiques shops. **www.charlesstreetinn.com**

Holiday Inn Select Government Center $$$$$
5 Blossom St., 02114 **Tel** *(617) 742-7630; (800) 465-4329* **Fax** *(617) 742-4192* **Rooms** *305*   **Map** 1 B3

The location is neither Beacon Hill nor Quincy Market, but a kind of no-man's land of government buildings. However, walking a few extra steps can yield significant savings. Functioning largely as a tour group and conference facility, this hotel has undergone a recent major renovation. **www.ichotelsgroup.com**

Onyx Hotel $$$$$
155 Portland St., 02114 **Tel** *(617) 557-9955; (866) 660-6699* **Fax** *(617) 557-0005* **Rooms** *112*   **Map** 1 C2

This sleekly contemporary boutique hotel features modest-sized rooms decorated in a warm palette of black, taupe, and Chinese-lacquer red. It has comfortable beds with feather and down pillows. There is a car service to the Financial District each morning. The hotel is pet-friendly. **www.onyxhotel.com**

OLD BOSTON AND THE FINANCIAL DISTRICT

Harborside Inn $$$$
185 State St., 02109 **Tel** *(617) 723-7500; (888) 723-7565* **Fax** *(617) 670-6015* **Rooms** *54*   **Map** 2 E3

This modest boutique hotel is housed in an 1858 granite spice warehouse building near Faneuil Hall Marketplace and the New England Aquarium. Rooms are small but stylish, with exposed brick walls, wooden floors, sleigh beds, and Oriental carpets. **www.harborsideinnboston.com**

Hilton Boston Financial District $$$$$
89 Broad St., 02110 **Tel** *(617) 556-0006; (800) 996-3426* **Fax** *(617) 556-0053* **Rooms** *362*   **Map** 2 E4

This 1928 Art Deco building was Boston's first skyscraper. A careful conversion in 1999 preserved such Art Deco features as marble floors in the lobby and bathrooms, and polished wood and brass details in the public areas. Rooms are traditionally furnished. It is situated on the edge of the Financial District. **www.hilton.com**

Key to Symbols *see back cover flap*

Langham Boston Hotel

⌨ P ⊞ ☰ 📺 $$$$$

*250 Franklin St., 02110 **Tel** (617) 451-1900 **Fax** (617) 423-2844 **Rooms** 325* **Map** 2 D4

The Langham occupies a Renaissance Revival palace which was constructed to house the Federal Reserve Bank. The painted dome and gilded vaults of the foyer hint at the 19th-century French decor in the rooms. The hotel's Julien restaurant (*see p143*) is housed in the former bank vault. **www.langhamboston.com**

Millennium Bostonian

⌨ P ⊞ 🏋 📺 $$$$$

*26 North St., 02109 **Tel** (617) 523-3600; (800) 343-0922 **Fax** (617) 523-2454 **Rooms** 201* **Map** 2 D3

This upscale hotel is housed in three former warehouse buildings. Rooms vary greatly in size, but all were updated in 2008 and now feature luxury linens and 42" LCD televisions. Some have balconies overlooking Faneuil Hall Marketplace. The lobby boasts a gas-burning fireplace for cool evenings. **www.millenniumhotels.com**

Nine Zero

⌨ P ⊞ 📺 $$$$$

*90 Tremont St., 02108 **Tel** (617) 772-5800; (866) 906-9090 **Fax** (617) 772-5810 **Rooms** 190* **Map** 4 F1

Poised between Beacon Hill and Downtown Crossing, the elegant Nine Zero prides itself on winning numerous design awards from the hotel and travel industries. Frette linens, Italian marble, and plenty of stainless steel and glass combine to create a comfortable atmosphere. **www.ninezero.com**

Omni Parker House

⌨ P ⊞ 🏋 📺 $$$$$

*60 School St., 02108 **Tel** (617) 227-8600; (888) 444-6664 **Fax** (617) 742-5729 **Rooms** 551* **Map** 2 D4

Memorabilia on display in the ornate lobby emphasizes Parker House's status as the oldest hotel in continuous operation in the US. Rooms were recently updated, though some remain compact. Boston cream pie was first served here and Parker's Restaurant and Parker's Bar are favorites with local politicians. **www.omniparkerhouse.com**

XV Beacon

⌨ P ⊞ 📺 $$$$$

*15 Beacon St., 02108 **Tel** (617) 670-1500; (877) 982-3226 **Fax** (617) 670-2525 **Rooms** 60* **Map** 1 C4

This chic hotel occupies a 1903 Beaux Arts office building. Furnishings mix traditional and contemporary styles. All rooms feature gas fireplaces, CD players, and 27" television sets, along with other luxury amenities. A complimentary chauffeured car service is available for trips within the city. **www.xvbeacon.com**

NORTH END AND THE WATERFRONT

Boston Harbor Hotel

⌨ P ⊞ ☰ 🏋 📺 $$$$$

*70 Rowes Wharf, 02110 **Tel** (617) 439-7000; (800) 752-7077 **Fax** (617) 330-9450 **Rooms** 230* **Map** 2 E4

Dramatic public spaces and large rooms are trademarks of this classically elegant hotel. Specify harbor or city view when booking. Located in the heart of the waterfront activity, this hotel is known for fine dining, a winter wine festival, and open air films and concerts on its outdoor decks in the summer. **www.bhh.com**

Intercontinental Hotel

⌨ $$$$$

*510 Atlantic Ave., 02210 **Tel** (866) 493-6495; (617) 747-1000 **Fax** (617) 217-5190 **Rooms** 424* **Map** 2 D5

A bold hotel clad in reflective blue glass and polished granite, the Intercontinental is located on the still-developing South Boston waterfront. Great harbor views and posh rooms are aimed squarely at executive travelers on expense accounts. High rack rates, however, are sometimes offset by excellent specials. **www.intercontinentalboston.com**

Marriott Long Wharf

⌨ P ⊞ ☰ 📺 $$$$$

*296 State St., 02109 **Tel** (617) 227-0800; (800) 228-9290 **Fax** (617) 227-2867 **Rooms** 412* **Map** 2 E3

This red-brick hotel stretches along Boston's original China Trade Wharf. Most rooms feature harbor or city skyline views. The seasonal outdoor terrace is a favorite with locals on weekend afternoons. This is a good base for exploring the waterfront or taking a ferry to the Harbor Islands. **www.marriottlongwharf.com**

Seaport Hotel

⌨ P ⊞ ☰ 🏋 📺 $$$$$

*1 Seaport Lane, 02210 **Tel** (617) 385-4000; (877) 732-7678 **Fax** (617) 385-4001 **Rooms** 426* **Map** 2 F5

This modern business hotel, connected by walkway to the World Trade Center, helped revitalize the waterfront district. Regular shuttles run to North Station and the Financial District. A water taxi to Long Wharf, the North End, and Charlestown is a fun way to tour the Freedom Trail (*see pp124–7*). **www.seaportboston.com**

CHINATOWN AND THE THEATER DISTRICT

Boston Park Plaza

⌨ P ⊞ 📺 $$$$

*64 Arlington St., 02116 **Tel** (617) 426-2000; (800) 225-2008 **Fax** (617) 426-5545 **Rooms** 941* **Map** 4 D2

Opened in 1927, and recently restored, this 15-floor hotel is the city's largest historic lodging. Two ballrooms and an elegant lobby make the Park Plaza the scene of many local celebrations, as well as business meetings and small conventions. Afternoon tea is served in Swan's Cafe. **www.bostonparkplaza.com**

Courtyard Boston Tremont Hotel ❄ [P] 🍴 $$$$$

275 Tremont St., 02116 ***Tel*** *(617) 426-1400; (800) 321-2211* ***Fax*** *(617) 482-6730* ***Rooms*** *315* ***Map*** *4 E2*

Renovation of this 1920s tower hotel in the Theater District was completed in early 2006. The dramatic lobby features marble columns, carved granite details, and glittering crystal chandeliers. Guest rooms are more simply furnished but updated with modern amenities including walk-in showers. **www.marriott.com/city/boston-hotels**

Four Seasons ❄ [P] 🍴 ≋ 🏋 $$$$$

200 Boylston St., 02116 ***Tel*** *(617) 338-4400; (800) 819-5053* ***Fax*** *(617) 423-0154* ***Rooms*** *274* ***Map*** *4 D2*

Low-key contemporary luxury draws rock stars, authors, corporate businesspeople, and visiting dignitaries. The lobby-level Bristol Lounge offers afternoon tea and a full dining menu for children. The Four Seasons is conveniently situated on a corner of the Public Garden at the edge of the Theater District. **www.fourseasons.com**

Hyatt Regency Boston Financial District ❄ [P] 🍴 ≋ 🏋 $$$$$

1 Avenue de Lafayette, 02116 ***Tel*** *(617) 912-1234* ***Fax*** *(617) 451-2198* ***Rooms*** *471* ***Map*** *4 D2*

The Hyatt offers spacious rooms with modern decor and is located close to the up-and-coming Ladder District, with several fine restaurants and night-time entertainment venues nearby. It is also one block from the Downtown Crossing shops. It caters to business travelers but also has good-value weekend specials. **regencyboston.hyatt.com**

Radisson Boston ❄ [P] 🍴 ≋ 🏋 $$$$$

200 Stuart St., 02116 ***Tel*** *(617) 482-1800; (888) 201-1718* ***Fax*** *(617) 451-2750* ***Rooms*** *356* ***Map*** *4 D2*

A Theater District location makes this Radisson a popular choice for bus tour groups, while proximity to Chinatown makes it convenient for inexpensive and late-night dining. The hotel hosts many small conferences for nearby medical and dental schools, and rooms are fitted with oversized work desks. **www.radisson.com/bostonma**

Ritz-Carlton Boston Common ❄ [P] 🍴 ≋ 🏋 $$$$$

10 Avery St., 02111 ***Tel*** *(617) 574-7100; (800) 241-3333* ***Fax*** *(617) 574-7200* ***Rooms*** *193* ***Map*** *4 E2*

Boston's new Ritz-Carlton, opened in 2001, occupies a prime corner of Boston Common. This is a good alternative for those seeking the trademark pampering of Ritz hotels, but who prefer a more modern decor and sensibility. There is a multi-screen cinema and fine dining on offer. **www.ritzcarlton.com**

BACK BAY AND SOUTH END

Commonwealth Court Guest-House $

284 Commonwealth Ave., 02116 ***Tel*** *(617) 424-1230; (888) 424-1230* ***Fax*** *(617) 424-1510* ***Rooms*** *17* ***Map*** *3 A2*

On the corner of Gloucester Street, the Commonwealth is convenient to upper Back Bay, especially the Hynes Convention Center and Berklee College of Music. The former private brownstone residence oozes historic architectural detail. Rooms are often rented by the week or month and include kitchenettes. **www.commonwealthcourt.com**

463 Beacon Street Guest House [P] $$

463 Beacon St., 02116 ***Tel*** *(617) 536-1302* ***Fax*** *(617) 247-8876* ***Rooms*** *20* ***Map*** *3 A2*

This Back Bay brownstone is a handsome building closer to the Charles River Esplanade than Back Bay attractions. It offers budget lodging in the form of studio rooms and small furnished apartments by day, week, or month. All rooms have at least limited cooking facilities. It is popular with young European travelers. **www.463beacon.com**

Chandler Inn ❄ $$

26 Chandler St., 02116 ***Tel*** *(617) 482-3450; (800) 842-3450* ***Fax*** *(617) 542-3428* ***Rooms*** *55* ***Map*** *4 D3*

Located in the South End just two blocks from Tremont Street's restaurant row, this newly renovated and tastefully decorated budget inn is well-situated for walking around Back Bay. The immediate neighborhood is primarily a low-rise residential area, giving the Chandler a homely feel in the heart of the city. **www.chandlerinn.com**

Copley Inn $$

19 Garrison St., 02116 ***Tel*** *(617) 236-0300; (800) 232-0306* ***Fax*** *(617) 536-0816* ***Rooms*** *20* ***Map*** *3 B3*

A former rooming house literally in the shadow of Copley Place, this renovated budget lodging features studio rooms, each with a queen bed, fully equipped kitchenette, and private bath. Clean and bright, the decor is utilitarian but some rooms retain charming old-fashioned touches, such as decorative fireplaces. **www.copleyinn.com**

Charlesmark Hotel ❄ 🍸 [P] $$$

655 Boylston St., 02116 ***Tel*** *(617) 247-1212* ***Fax*** *(617) 247-1224* ***Rooms*** *33* ***Map*** *3 C2*

Very much in the mode of a contemporary European boutique hotel, the Charlesmark occupies an 1892 Back Bay townhouse on Copley Square. Custom-made designer furniture, light-toned woodwork, imported Italian tile, and European lighting fixtures decorate the 33 rooms. The Charlesmark offers good value. **www.thecharlesmark.com**

Hotel 140 ❄ [P] 🍴 🏋 $$$

140 Clarendon St., 02116 ***Tel*** *(617) 585-5600; (800) 714-0140* ***Fax*** *(617) 585-5699* ***Rooms*** *54* ***Map*** *3 C3*

Literally around the corner from the Back Bay Amtrak rail station, Hotel 140 is a stylish budget-priced renovation of America's first YWCA building. Rooms are small but the trendy minimalist design makes efficient use of space. There is a secure key card access system for both rooms and elevator. **www.hotel140.com**

Key to Price Guide *see p132* **Key to Symbols** *see back cover flap*

Midtown Hotel ⇅ [P] 🍴 🏊 $$$

220 Huntington Ave., 02115 ***Tel*** *(617) 262-1000; (800) 343-1177* ***Fax*** *(617) 262-8739* ***Rooms*** *159* ***Map*** *3 B4*

A rarity in Back Bay, this is a classic 1960s-era motor inn. Renovated rooms offer simple style and good value in an otherwise expensive area. The outdoor swimming pool and low-cost parking are significant bonuses. The on-site Italian café has a child-friendly menu. **www.midtownhotel.com**

Newbury Guest-House ⇅ [P] $$$

261 Newbury St., 02116 ***Tel*** *(617) 437-7666; (800) 437-7668* ***Fax*** *(617) 670-6100* ***Rooms*** *32* ***Map*** *3 B2*

When three Victorian homes were linked to form this cozy inn, owners were careful to preserve such period details as ceiling medallions, parquet floors, and decorative fireplaces. The rooms feature a comfortable mix of older furniture. Newbury Street can be noisy so ask for a room at the back. **www.newburyguesthouse.com**

Clarendon Square Inn [P] $$$$$

198 West Brookline St., 02118 ***Tel*** *(617) 536-2229* ***Rooms*** *3* ***Map*** *3 C4*

Located in the heart of the South End in a 19th-century townhouse, Clarendon Square Inn offers exquisite interior decor and a relaxed atmosphere. Just one queen bed per room makes it best for couples. The rooftop hot tub is a relaxing summer amenity. **www.clarendonsquare.com**

The Colonnade Hotel ⇅ [P] 🍴 🏊 👪 🏋 $$$$$

120 Huntington Ave., 02116 ***Tel*** *(617) 424-7000; (800) 962-3030* ***Fax*** *(617) 425-3222* ***Rooms*** *285* ***Map*** *3 B3*

The spacious and comfortable rooms at the Colonnade have been updated in modern style with rich, soothing colors. This family-friendly hotel is also favored by upscale bus groups. Amenities include a rooftop pool and a ground-level bistro. **www.colonnadehotel.com**

Copley Square Hotel ⇅ [P] 🍴 $$$$$

47 Huntington Ave., 02116 ***Tel*** *(617) 536-9000; (800) 225-7062* ***Fax*** *(617) 421-1402* ***Rooms*** *143* ***Map*** *3 C3*

Opened in 1891 as the first hotel in Back Bay, this establishment underwent a $14-million renovation in 2008. All rooms are smoke-free and feature efficient workspaces as well as fine linens and big TVs. Ask for an interior room for the utmost tranquility. Basement-level Saint is one of the city's trendiest nightspots. **www.copleysquarehotel.com**

Eliot Suites Hotel ⇅ [P] 🍴 🏋 $$$$$

370 Commonwealth Ave., 02215 ***Tel*** *(617) 267-1607; (800) 443-5468* ***Fax*** *(617) 536-9114* ***Rooms*** *95* ***Map*** *3 A2*

The suites with separate sleeping and sitting rooms here are equally convenient for guest musicians playing at nearby Symphony Hall, business people, and families (children under 18 stay free). Guests enjoy complimentary access to Boston Sports Club at Fenway Park. Restaurant Clio *(see p148)* is one of the city's best. **www.eliothotel.com**

Fairmont Copley Plaza Hotel ⇅ [P] 🍴 $$$$$

138 St. James Ave., 02116 ***Tel*** *(617) 267-5300; (800) 257 7544* ***Fax*** *(617) 267-7668* ***Rooms*** *383* ***Map*** *3 C2*

A red carpet leads guests into the opulent lobby of this 1912 Boston landmark, the sister hotel to New York's Plaza. Interior rooms can be small, but a recent $34 million restoration updated the traditional style of dark woods and rich fabrics. Extravagant furnishings help make the Oak Room the city's favorite steak house. **www.fairmont.com**

Jurys Boston Hotel ⇅ [P] 🍴 🍸 🏋 $$$$$

350 Stuart St., 02116 ***Tel*** *(617) 266-7200* ***Fax*** *(617) 266-7203* ***Rooms*** *225* ***Map*** *3 D2*

This Irish boutique hotel occupies a limestone-faced former Boston Police headquarters building. Feather pillows and duvets, heated towel racks, and 24-hour room service make this modest-priced hotel feel like a luxury stay. It is convenient to both Back Bay and South End. **www.jurys-boston-hotels.com**

Lenox Hotel ⇅ [P] 🍴 🏋 $$$$$

61 Exeter St., 02116 ***Tel*** *(617) 536-5300; (800) 225-7676* ***Fax*** *(617) 236-0351* ***Rooms*** *214* ***Map*** *3 D2*

This landmark hotel, just off Copley Square behind the Boston Public Library, features sumptuous Edwardian detail in its public areas. Several deluxe corner suites with wood-burning fireplaces rival any upscale room in town. Mahogany furniture, marble baths, and muted tones create a soothing, elegant atmosphere. **www.lenoxhotel.com**

Taj Boston Hotel ⇅ [P] 🍴 👪 🏋 $$$$$

15 Arlington St., 02116 ***Tel*** *(617) 536-5700; (877) 482-5267* ***Fax*** *(617) 536-1335* ***Rooms*** *273* ***Map*** *4 D2*

Opened in 1927, this was the first hotel of the Ritz-Carlton chain, and the progenitor of Ritz style. The property became part of the Taj Hotel Group in 2007, but continues to emphasize elegance and excellent service. **www.tajhotels.com**

FARTHER AFIELD

Beechtree Inn $

83 Longwood Ave., Brookline, 02446 ***Tel*** *(617) 277-1620; (800) 544-9660* ***Rooms*** *10*

This rambling Victorian home is located in a leafy neighborhood near Longwood Medical Center and the Green Line's "E" branch. The rooms have an old-fashioned decor with solid furnishings and a television set, but some rooms share bathrooms. Read a book and sip tea under the backyard apple tree. **www.thebeechtreeinn.com**

Ramada Inn Boston   🖥 P 🍴 ≈ 🏃   Ⓢ

800 Morrissey Blvd., Dorchester, 02122 **Tel** *(617) 287-9100* **Fax** *(617) 265-9287* **Rooms** *177*

The Ramada Inn is well located for making daytrips into the city. The hotel offers a free shuttle to Logan Airport, JFK/UMass stop on the T's Red Line, and to the World Trade Center. It is a convenient spot for travelers also planning to go to Cape Cod. **www.ramada.com**

Constitution Inn   🖥 P ≈ 🍽   ⓈⓈ

150 Third Ave., Charlestown, 02129 **Tel** *(617) 241-8400; (800) 495-9622* **Fax** *(617) 241-2856* **Rooms** *147* **Map** *2 D1*

Convenient to the Freedom Trail *(see pp124–7)*, this unique property offers the lowest rates to Armed Services personnel. However, it also welcomes casual visitors and its well-maintained rooms, fitness center, pool, and sauna are a good deal for all. The staff are especially welcoming. **www.constitutioninn.org**

Days Hotel Boston   🖥 P 🍴 ≈ 🏃 🍽   ⓈⓈ

1234 Soldiers Field Rd., 02135 **Tel** *(617) 254-1234; (800) 329-7466* **Fax** *(617) 254-4300* **Rooms** *117*

This hotel along the Charles River provides easy access to the popular river banks and their jogging paths. The newly renovated rooms are cheerful and spacious. Fitness buffs may want to undertake the one-mile walk to Harvard Square. **www.dayshotelboston.com**

A Friendly Inn   P   ⓈⓈ

1673 Cambridge St., Cambridge, 02138 **Tel** *(617) 547-7851* **Fax** *(617) 547-0202* **Rooms** *17*

Visiting scholars, prospective students, and parents visiting their Ivy League offspring tend to frequent this aptly named bed and breakfast. It is located in a quiet residential neighborhood just north of Harvard Yard and east of Harvard Divinity School. **www.afinow.com**

Isaac Harding House   P   ⓈⓈ

288 Harvard St., Cambridge, 02138 **Tel** *(617) 876-2888; (877) 489-2888* **Fax** *(617) 497-0953* **Rooms** *14*

This bed and breakfast occupies an 1860s Victorian house in a quiet Cambridge residential neighborhood halfway between Central and Harvard squares. Public areas combine comfort with elegance. Guest rooms are spacious and bright, and some share baths. Free parking is available. **www.harding-house.com**

Bertram Inn   P   ⓈⓈⓈ

92 Sewall Ave., Brookline, 02446 **Tel** *(617) 566-2234; (800) 295-3822* **Fax** *(617) 277-1887* **Rooms** *5*

This large Craftsman-style home, built in 1907, has an elegant parlour and antiques-filled rooms. Some of the bedrooms feature working wood-burning fireplaces. Located two miles from the center of Boston, Bertram Inn is a perfect retreat from the hubbub of the city. **www.bertraminn.com**

Best Western Roundhouse Suites   🖥 P 🏃 🍽   ⓈⓈⓈ

891 Massachusetts Ave., 02118 **Tel** *(617) 989-1000; (888) 468-3562* **Rooms** *92*

This unique 1900s round building was transformed into an all-suites hotel in 2001. Sofa beds, microwaves, and refrigerators make Roundhouse Suites an appealing option for families. A shuttle service is available and parking is free for those who arrive by car. **www.bestwesternboston.com**

Gryphon House   P   ⓈⓈⓈ

9 Bay State Rd., 02215 **Tel** *(617) 375-9003; (877) 375-9003* **Fax** *(617) 425-0716* **Rooms** *8*

Built in the Richardsonian Romanesque style, this 1895 townhouse in a quiet neighborhood features unusually large guest rooms. All have fireplaces and wet bars, and some have river views. Guests can walk two blocks to Kenmore "T" station or continue on foot to sites in Back Bay or Fenway. **www.gryphonhouseboston.com**

Hampton Inn   🖥 P 🍽   ⓈⓈⓈ

191 Monsignor O'Brien Highway, Cambridge, 02141 **Tel** *(617) 494-5300* **Fax** *(617) 494-6569* **Rooms** *114*

This new budget hotel is a five-minute walk from the Lechmere terminus of the T's Green Line, which makes it reasonably convenient for the Museum of Science and TD BankNorth Gardens. Bonuses include free breakfast and parking, and loaner bicycles. **www.hamptoninn.com**

Holiday Inn Express   🖥 P 🍽   ⓈⓈⓈ

250 Monsignor O'Brien Hwy., Cambridge, 02141 **Tel** *(617) 577-7600; (800) 972-3381* **Fax** *(617) 354-1313* **Rooms** *112*

Close to the Lechmere "T" stop, this hotel is also designed for business travelers who arrive by car. It is one of the rare newer hotels to offer rooms for smokers and a choice of room sizes. On-site parking is limited, however free parking is offered across the street. **www.ichotelsgroup.com**

Hotel Tria   🖥 P 🍴 ≈ 🍽   ⓈⓈⓈ

220 Alewife Brook Pkwy., Cambridge, 02138 **Tel** *(617) 491-8000; (866) 333-8742* **Fax** *(617) 491-4932* **Rooms** *69*

Though outside the usual tourist districts, this small hotel is big on contemporary style and comfort. Guest-pleasing perks include fresh cookies in the afternoon and hand-cut scented soaps. Children under 18 stay free. There is a complimentary shuttle service to Alewife on the T's Red Line and to Harvard Square. **www.hoteltria.com**

Hyatt Harborside   🖥 P ≈ 🍽   ⓈⓈⓈ

101 Harborside Dr., East Boston, 02128 **Tel** *(617) 568-1234* **Fax** *(617) 567-8856* **Rooms** *270*

Located on the East Boston waterfront near Logan Airport, this modern hotel was designed to maximize harbor views from the lobby, restaurant, and indoor pool. Half of the spacious rooms also have harbor views. The water taxi to downtown docks nearby. **www.harborside.hyatt.com**

Key to Price Guide *see p132* **Key to Symbols** *see back cover flap*

Irving House [P] $$$

24 Irving St., Cambridge, 02138 ***Tel*** *(617) 547-4600; (877) 547-4600* ***Fax*** *(617) 576-2814* ***Rooms*** *44*

This bed and breakfast is housed in a large, wood-framed Victorian building with a welcoming front porch. Rooms vary greatly in size and some share baths. Its friendly service, quiet location, and proximity to Harvard Yard and Harvard Square make it a favorite with visiting scholars on a budget. **www.irvinghouse.com**

Kendall Hotel ⇅ [P] 🍴 🧒 $$$

350 Main St., Cambridge, 02142 ***Tel*** *(617) 577-1300; (866) 566-1300* ***Fax*** *(617) 577-1377* ***Rooms*** *77*

The memorabilia here celebrates this boutique hotel's former life as a century-old Queen Anne-style firehouse. Eleven of the guest rooms were once the firemen's dormitory. The rest of the spacious rooms occupy newer extensions. It is convenient to Massachusetts Institute of Technology and the T's Red Line. **www.kendallhotel.com**

Mary Prentiss Inn [P] $$$

6 Prentiss St., Cambridge, 02140 ***Tel*** *(617) 661-2929* ***Fax*** *(617) 661-5989* ***Rooms*** *20*

The strong architectural features of this 1843 Greek Revival mansion are accentuated by the bold wallpapers, period furniture, antiques, and rich fabrics. Some rooms have wood-burning fireplaces and whirlpool tubs. Breakfast is served in the parlor or on the outdoor terrace in summer. **www.maryprentissinn.com**

Harvard Square Hotel ⇅ [P] 🍴 $$$$

110 Mt. Auburn St., Cambridge, 02138 ***Tel*** *(617) 864-5200; (800) 458-5886* ***Fax*** *(617) 864-2409* ***Rooms*** *73*

This four-story motor-inn boasts an excellent location in the midst of Harvard Square. There is a small lobby and basic but comfortable guest rooms featuring light wood furnishings and warm colors. Register for special deals offered only by e-mail. **www.harvardsquarehotel.com**

Charles Hotel ⇅ [P] 🍴 🏊 🧒 🏋 $$$$$

1 Bennett St., 02138 ***Tel*** *(617) 864-1200; (800) 882-1818* ***Fax*** *(617) 864-5715* ***Rooms*** *294*

Handmade quilts on the beds add a cozy touch to the restrained modern decor. The hotel's location on the edge of Harvard Square is a plus. A top-notch jazz club, restaurant, and hip bar serve visitors and locals alike. The weekly farmers market and outdoor dining enliven the hotel's plaza in warm weather. **www.charleshotel.com**

Hotel Commonwealth ⇅ [P] 🍴 🏋 $$$$$

500 Commonwealth Ave., 02215 ***Tel*** *(617) 933-5000; (866) 784-4000* ***Fax*** *(617) 266-6888* ***Rooms*** *150*

The opening of this ultra-modern hotel in 2002 signaled the gentrification of student-oriented Kenmore Square. French Second Empire decor is combined with hi-tech amenities. The Foundation Lounge is a popular drinking spot. Lunch and dinner are served outdoors in good weather. **www.hotelcommonwealth.com**

Hotel Marlowe ⇅ [P] 🍴 🏋 $$$$$

25 Edwin H. Land Blvd., Cambridge, 02141 ***Tel*** *(617) 868-8000; (800) 825-7140* ***Fax*** *(617) 868-8001* ***Rooms*** *236*

Next to the Cambridgeside Galleria, this sleek hotel has something for everyone: fitness center, a complimentary wine reception each evening by the fireplace in the lobby, and special packages for pets. A short walk to the Charles River, Museum of Science, and the T's Green Line. **www.hotelmarlowe.com**

Hyatt Regency Cambridge ⇅ [P] 🍴 🏊 🏋 $$$$$

575 Memorial Dr., Cambridge, 02138 ***Tel*** *(617) 492-1234; (800) 233-1234* ***Fax*** *(617) 491-6906* ***Rooms*** *415*

This pyramid-shaped hotel cuts a dramatic profile along the Charles River and is perfectly situated for sunset views from a number of the guest rooms. Take advantage of the Charles River pathways by renting a mountain bike from the hotel. A regular shuttle service is available. **cambridge.hyatt.com**

Inn at Harvard ⇅ [P] 🍴 $$$$$

1201 Massachusetts Ave., Cambridge, 02138 ***Tel*** *(617) 491-2222; (800) 458-5886* ***Fax*** *(617) 520-3711* ***Rooms*** *113*

The four-story atrium of this modern hotel was modeled on Isabella Stewart Gardner's Italian-style palazzo turned museum. Rooms are comfortably appointed and filled with period furniture. Access to the nearby Harvard Faculty Club and its dining room is extended to all guests. **www.theinnatharvard.com**

Le Méridien Cambridge ⇅ [P] 🍴 🏋 $$$$$

20 Sidney St., Cambridge, 02139 ***Tel*** *(617) 577-0200; (800) 543-4300* ***Fax*** *(617) 494-8366* ***Rooms*** *210*

Built as the Hotel @ MIT, the high-tech Méridien is an interface between investors and the professors, biotech engineers, and electronics visionaries at the adjacent Massachusetts Institute of Technology. Sleekly contemporary, it is also handy to the music bars and ethnic restaurants of Cambridge's Central Square. **www.starwoodhotels.com**

Royal Sonesta Hotel ⇅ [P] 🍴 🏊 🧒 🏋 $$$$$

5 Cambridge Hwy., Cambridge, 02142 ***Tel*** *(617) 806-4200; (800) 766-3782* ***Fax*** *(617) 806-4232* ***Rooms*** *400*

The Royal Sonesta boasts a prime location on the pathway along the Charles River. Many of the comfortable rooms have river views and public areas are noted for outstanding art works. It is within easy walking distance to the T's Green Line. Family packages often include bicycles. **www.sonesta.com/boston**

Sheraton Commander ⇅ [P] 🍴 🏋 $$$$$

16 Garden St., Cambridge, 02138 ***Tel*** *(617) 547-4800; (800) 325-3535* ***Fax*** *(617) 234-1396* ***Rooms*** *175*

Harvard Square's original hotel, built in 1927, sits across from Cambridge Common and a short walk from Harvard Yard. Though the hallways are narrow and some rooms are small, consistent refurbishment maintains the hotel's comfortable style. The restaurant specializes in traditional New England fare. **www.sheraton.com/commander**

RESTAURANTS, CAFÉS, AND BARS

For a number of years Boston had a reputation of serving stodgy, old New England fare. Today, however, this is no longer the case, as the city now has a wide variety of exciting places to eat. Along with more traditional cuisine, Boston restaurants show many diverse influences, with immigrant restaurateurs and innovative chefs transforming local restaurant culture. Celebrated chefs also bring traditional

Sign for a downtown seafood restaurant

Boston cuisine to life for modern palates, and restaurants all delight in fresh New England produce. The top restaurants serve a medley of styles, such as French and Italian, often using other Mediterranean and Asian accents. For other flavors of the world, Boston has many Indian, Southeast Asian, Latin American, Caribbean, and Japanese restaurants, which are located in small neighborhoods and fashionable streets alike.

Murals at the Casablanca restaurant, a Cambridge institution *(see p149)*

EATING THE BOSTONIAN WAY

If your lodgings don't include breakfast, join locals on their way to work and have a bagel and a cup of steaming coffee in one of the city's many delis and coffee bars. Most places also offer pastries, muffins, coffee cake, tea, and fruit juices. Diners offer richer, more substantial breakfasts of bacon, eggs, potatoes, and toast, with a "bottomless" cup of coffee – one with free refills.

Lunches in Boston may also be a simple sandwich or a larger meal in a restaurant, depending on how much time you have, and how hungry you are. Business districts abound with lunch options – join office workers Downtown at a lunch counter for a grinder (long filled roll).

Dinner is the biggest meal of the day for Bostonians. The most exclusive and elegant

restaurants are in the Financial District and Downtown. Those in the Back Bay, North End and South End tend to be trendy and youthful, while in Cambridge they are more relaxed, reflecting the area's laid-back atmosphere. The website www.bostonchefs.com is useful for menus and prices.

OPENING HOURS

The types of meals served at many restaurants vary according to the type of establishment and its location. Many downtown lunch counters are open only for breakfast and lunch, while some finer restaurants are open only for dinner. Some restaurants close for a few hours between lunch and dinner, while smaller family-run places may stay open throughout the afternoon, making them a good bet for eating at more unusual times. Generally, lunch is served from 11:30am to 2:30pm, and dinner from 5:30 to 10:30pm. Massachusetts state law prohibits the sale of alcohol, including beer and wine, after 2am, so bars and most restaurants will close by then. There

are some very late night restaurants in Chinatown and Kenmore Square, supported mostly by the ravenous crowds leaving dance clubs and bars. On Sundays, restaurants begin serving alcohol at noon. Cocktails at brunch are very popular, especially in the South End.

Attractive exterior of the Terramia restaurant *(see p144)*

PAYING AND TIPPING

Most restaurants with table service will bring you your bill at the end of the meal. The bill will have a 5 percent state meals tax added to the total. All restaurants with table service expect you to leave a tip for your waiter, who is paid a very low rate

The fashionable Sonsie restaurant in Boston's Back Bay *(see p146)*

A typically Italian atmosphere is created at Caffé Vittoria *(see p150)*

with the expectation that tips will fill out their salary. The standard tip is 20 percent of the pre-tax bill. If service is especially good or bad, adjust the tip accordingly. If paying by credit card, you may include the tip in the charged amount. Fast food restaurants may have optional tip jars next to the cashier.

BOOKING

Finer restaurants often require a reservation, though in most cases (especially on weeknights) reservations can be made at short notice. There are a few very popular places that do not accept reservations, and customers must put their names on the waiting list. The host will tell you how long you can expect to wait.

ALCOHOL AND SMOKING

The tide has turned in favor of non-smokers throughout Greater Boston, with complete bans on indoor smoking in public places including restaurants and bars. Outdoor smoking is also prohibited at playgrounds and other posted areas.
    Twenty-one is the legal drinking age, so under-age travelers should be aware that they will be denied access to most bars. They will not be able to order wine with dinner in restaurants, either. If there is any doubt that a person is old enough, proof will be required, so use your I.D. or passport if asked.

ETIQUETTE

Bostonians tend to dress casually when dining out. Restaurants that enforce dress codes usually require a reservation, so ask when booking. For the top dining rooms, a jacket and tie for men is expected. Ladies may wear slacks, though skirts or dresses are more traditional. Formal evening wear is uncommon but not out of place in the finer restaurants. Cell phone use is strongly discouraged.

CHILDREN

Children are welcome in most mid-range restaurants, although in the business areas restaurants are often less

accustomed to them. Avoid restaurants that feature a large bar and young crowds, as they are less likely to permit under 21's on the premises.

DISABILITIES

A number of restaurants in Boston and Cambridge are accessible by wheelchair *(see pp142–9)*, and many more are accessible to people with other disabilities. Doors may be fitted with an automatic opener, and rest rooms usually include the appropriate stalls and sinks.

FAST FOOD

Being a college city, Boston is teeming with fast food options. Sandwiches come in infinite varieties, the classic sandwich being found along with "wraps" (fillings wrapped up in a flatbread), "grinders" (long rolls stuffed with meats), and gourmet sandwiches on baguette or *focaccia*. Pizza is another ubiquitous meal, and bagels, spread with cream cheese, are a popular snack eaten on the go. Burritos are hearty portable meals of meat, beans, and cheese rolled into a flour tortilla. Downtown and Harvard Square are good places for fast food, with their many lunch counters catering to business people. These are reliable and easy on the wallet.

Enjoying a beer outside at one of Quincy Market's bars *(see p64)*

The Flavors of Boston

Geography and history have given New England some fine and highly distinctive culinary traditions. Its long coastline accounts for the region's abundance of superb seafood. Early settlers brought dishes from England, such as boiled dinners and puddings, that remain popular to this day, as do a range of staples introduced to them by Native Americans, such as corn, maple syrup, and cranberries. The ethnic make-up of Boston has also led to some surprising culinary highlights. Thanks to a large Italian community, Boston boasts some of the best and most authentic pizza in America, and the large Irish population ensures there are plenty of hearty Irish dishes to enjoy.

New England apples

Lobster meal at one of Boston's seafood restaurants

GIFTS FROM THE SEA

Seafood is king in New England. The cold waters along the coast yield a bounty of delicious fish such as scrod (young cod), haddock, and swordfish. Lobster is a particularly coveted delicacy. Tanks of live lobsters are shipped to restaurants all around America, but nowhere are

they as succulent and sweet as they are in their home region. Several of Boston's best restaurants serve mouth-watering lobster dishes, where diners can pick their own freshly-caught lobster from a tank, then sit back and relax while it is steamed or boiled, according to their wishes. Lobster dishes are usually served up with an accompaniment of melted butter for dipping the meat into and cups of clear, steaming seafood broth.

THE MIGHTY CLAM

No food is more ubiquitous in New England than clams. They are served in so many different ways: steamed, stuffed, baked, minced in fish cakes or in the famous New England clam chowder. The large hard-shelled quahog clam – a delicacy from nearby Rhode Island – is used to make stuffed clams known as "stuffies". Many regional states have their own

Corn on the cob   Baked potato   Steamed clams   Melted butter   Boiled lobster

A typical New England clambake dinner

LOCAL DISHES AND SPECIALITIES

Like most Americans, New Englanders tend to have a light lunch and their main meal in the evening. Perhaps because of the cold winters, breakfasts are hearty. Some New England dining experiences are too good to miss. At least one breakfast should include wild blueberry pancakes or muffins, and another an omelette made with tangy Vermont cheddar. Other musts are a lunch of lobster roll (chunks of sweet lobster meat in a mayonnaise-based dressing, stuffed into a toasted bun), New England clam chowder,

Maple Syrup and one of the region's famous clambake dinners. A visit to Boston is hardly complete without sampling the superb local scrod and its rich, classic Boston cream pie, both found on menus all over the city, along with Vermont's favorite ice cream, Ben and Jerry's.

Blueberry pancakes *Small wild blueberries are stirred into batter to make a stack of these thick pancakes.*

Colorful display of pumpkins at a local farmers' market

NEW AMERICAN CUISINE

Boston's best chefs are masters of "New American" cuisine, emphasizing the use of the freshest ingredients, in-season fruits and vegetables, and light, healthy sauces. Often dishes have touches of Mediterranean and Asian spices. Seasonal menus include game in winter and fall, and fresh seafood year round. In the growing season, many dishes also feature fresh fruit and berries. To ensure freshness, produce comes from nearby growers. Presentation is important, with dishes planned to please the eye as well as the palate.

version of clam chowder. Boston has a distinctive interpretation of this broth, made with a cream sauce, potatoes, and onions, which makes it much richer than the clear tomato based version served in Manhattan.

19th century, molasses from the Caribbean was used as a sweetener, and it is still added to many traditional sweet treats, such as Indian pudding, a delicious slow-baked confection of spiced cornmeal, molasses, and milk.

SWEET OFFERINGS

Sugar maples, which bring a dazzling display of color to the hillsides in autumn, yield yet another bonus in late winter. They can then be tapped and their sap boiled down to produce maple syrup. This is served on pancakes and made into candy (sweets) and sauces. New England's vast acres of wild blueberries, along with its many apple orchards and pumpkin fields, also lend themselves to a variety of delectable desserts. In the

Freshly picked wild blueberries, from the bumper summer harvest

WHAT TO DRINK

Poland Spring water This bottled water from Maine is popular with Bostonians.

Frappé A New England-style milk shake made with ice cream and chocolate syrup.

Westport Rivers wines These are always a favorite at the annual Boston wine festivals.

Samuel Adams and Harpoon beers New England's best known brands are brewed in Boston.

Micro-brewery beers Sample Boston Beer Works' "Boston Red," named after the city's Red Sox baseball team, or any one of the English-style pale ales made by Tremont Brewery.

Baked scrod *Fillets of young cod (scrod) are rolled in breadcrumbs, baked, and then served with tartare sauce.*

New England clam chowder *Fresh clams, either left whole or chopped, and chunks of potato fill this creamy soup.*

Boston cream pie *Layers of sponge cake, sandwiched with egg custard, are topped with chocolate icing.*

Choosing a Restaurant

The restaurants in this guide have been selected for their good value, exceptional food, or interesting location. These listings highlight some of the factors that may influence your choice, such as whether you can opt to eat outdoors or if the venue offers live music. Entries are alphabetical within each price category.

PRICE CATEGORIES
Include a three-course meal for one, half a bottle of house wine, and all unavoidable extra charges such as sales tax and service.
$ Under $20
$$ $20–$30
$$$ $30–$45
$$$$ $45–$60
$$$$$ Over $60

BEACON HILL AND WEST END

Panificio
144 Charles St., 02114 **Tel** (617) 227-4340
Map 1 B3
$$

A popular bakery that specializes in rustic Italian breads and also structures light meals, served all day, from their baked goods. Piles of meat and heaps of vegetables fill the sandwiches, but the soups are less hearty. Look out for fancy egg dishes such as frittatas, French toast, and different versions of eggs Benedict at the weekend brunches.

Artú
89 Charles St., 02114 **Tel** (617) 227-9023
Map 1 B3
$$$

The secret weapon of this casual eatery is the ferociously hot oven, which produces sumptuous roast pork and lamb that go perfectly with such grilled Italian vegetables as marinated eggplant. Prepare for a long wait at lunch: savvy office workers come here for sandwiches. Dinner is quieter, and more romantic. Closed lunch Mon, Sun.

Figs
42 Charles St., 02114 **Tel** (617) 742-3447
Map 1 B4
$$$

This small, casual eatery (a side operation of a local superchef) launched Boston's love for grilled pizzas. The signature pizza is topped with caramelized figs, prosciutto, and gorgonzola cheese, and the rich baked pastas are extremely popular too. The portions are so generous that virtually every entrée provides enough food to feed two people.

Lala Rokh
97 Mt. Vernon St., 02114 **Tel** (617) 720-5511
Map 1 B4
$$$

North Africa's fine cuisine was born in Persia, and dining at Lala Rokh is like taking a gastronomic tour through the greatest hits of Persian cuisine. Dishes are redolent of herbs, citrus, and exotic spices, often featuring lamb and game birds. Most of the desserts are built around dates and nuts.

Ma Soba
156 Cambridge St., 02114 **Tel** (617) 973-6680
Map 1 C3
$$$

As the name suggests, Ma Soba focuses on noodle dishes, often blending notes from different Asian cuisines to create a pan-Asian fusion. Korean dishes, such as the marinated *beef bolgogi* (grilled beef), tend to be the best executed, though Ma Soba also prepares some of the best and most reasonably-priced sushi in Boston.

Paramount Deli-Restaurant
44 Charles St., 02114 **Tel** (617) 720-1152
Map 1 B4
$$$

This hangout has been a comfort-food destination since 1937. The busiest times are at breakfast and during the day when there is a cafeteria-style service. The evening table service emphasizes stir-fries and unfussy American bistro dishes, usually a grilled piece of meat atop a starch and graced with a light sauce. All the meals provide good value.

Beacon Hill Bistro
25 Charles St., 02114 **Tel** (617) 723-1133
Map 1 B4
$$$$

Located in the Beacon Hill Hotel *(see p132)*, this Irish-run restaurant features American staples for breakfast and lunch but offers an American interpretation of French bistro cuisine at night. Steak-frites, for example, is made with New York strip steak, while local codfish gets a Mediterranean treatment with roasted tomatoes and Greek olives.

Bin 26 Enoteca
26 Charles St., 02114 **Tel** (617) 723-5939
Map 1 B4
$$$$

True to its name, this stylishly contemporary restaurant puts a strong emphasis on its extensive wine list, with delicious *stuzzichini* ("small bites") to munch while enjoying a glass of wine. The cuisine is predominantly Italian and definitely more adventurous than traditional. Try the cocoa pasta with wild mushrooms.

Grotto
37 Bowdoin St., 02114 **Tel** (617) 227-3434
Map 4 E1
$$$$

Visitors to Boston rarely find Grotto because it is tucked into a brownstone north of the State House. It is worth seeking out this fine northern Italian restaurant with spot-on service and a chef who emphasizes simple combinations of intensely flavored ingredients. The fixed-price menu is good value.

Key to Symbols *see back cover flap*

No. 9 Park
P & $$$$$
9 Park St., 02108 **Tel** *(617) 742-9991*
Map *1 C4*

Sports stars, state politicians, and hard-charging business people frequent this upscale room near the State House for bold American bistro food accompanied by an imaginative list of unusual wines. The chef-owner has a magical touch with duck, so the duck special of the night is often worth trying.

OLD BOSTON AND THE FINANCIAL DISTRICT

Durgin Park
🏃 & 🎵 $$$
340 Faneuil Hall Marketplace, 02109 **Tel** *(617) 227-2038*
Map *2 D3*

Legendary for its generous portions, Durgin Park began in 1826 as a lunch hall for produce and meat market workers. Family-style seating at long tables in the dining room makes for lively conversation. Traditional favorites include baked beans, Indian pudding, and grilled prime rib of beef big enough to hang over the edge of the plate.

The Times Irish Pub and Restaurant
& 🎵 $$$
112 Broad St, 02110 **Tel** *(617) 357-8463*
Map *2 E4*

While the taps mainly run Irish brews, the kitchen is far more eclectic. Office types throng the bar for sandwiches and burgers at lunch, but come evening, the menu shifts toward carefully prepared diner fare such as dense meatloaf, fried chicken, garlic mashed potatoes, and old-fashioned stews. Of course, they all go well with a pint of stout.

Union Oyster House
🏃 & $$$
41 Union St., 02110 **Tel** *(617) 227-2750*
Map *2 D3*

Some dishes have probably not changed much since Daniel Webster was a regular in the 1830s, and people still point to the booth where John F. Kennedy used to have Sunday brunch and read the paper. Apart from Boston scrod, the best bet by far is the raw bar. Savor the differences in oysters from various waters of the world.

Café Fleuri
P & 🍴 $$$$
250 Franklin St., 02110 **Tel** *(617) 451-1900*
Map *2 D4*

This restaurant is situated in the Langham Boston Hotel *(see p133)*. When the Langham group took over this grand hotel from its French predecessors, it shifted the main dining to the bright and airy Café Fleuri in the upstairs atrium and expanded the menu to include more casual food such as panini and pizzas.

Vinalia
& 🎵 $$$$
101 Arch St., 02110 **Tel** *(617) 737-1777*
Map *4 F1*

Wines by the glass from all over the world are the big draw here, with most diners picking a wine first and some accompanying food second. Downtown workers often stop early for a glass of red and a small pizza or a dinner salad. Regular diners arrive mid-evening for the wood-grilled meats and fish and the hefty bistro desserts.

Oceanaire
$$$$$
40 Court St., 02108 **Tel** *(617) 742-2277*
Map *2 D5*

Part of a small national chain of upmarket fish restaurants, Oceanaire retains the marble glamor of the bank that once occupied this space, while offering up a constantly changing menu of outstanding seafood. Unlike most Boston seafood restaurants, Oceanaire makes no bones about flying in fish not available from local waters. Closed at lunch.

Radius
P & $$$$$
8 High St., 02110 **Tel** *(617) 426-1234*
Map *2 D5*

This restaurant is often ranked as one of America's temples of trendy cuisine. The kitchen imbues dishes with explosive sensuality for those who can afford both the prices and the calories. Solo diners can join the convivial crowd at an elevated bar in one corner of the room. Closed lunch Sat; Sun.

Umbria
P & 🎵 $$$$$
295 Franklin St., 02110 **Tel** *(617) 338-1000*
Map *2 E4*

Umbria is known as "the green heart of Italy," and this fine-dining venue with attached nightclub remains strikingly true to the regional cuisine with such dishes as duck and chestnut filled pasta, wild game in a red wine sauce, and mixed seafood in savory broth. Many ingredients are imported directly from Italy. For a quiet meal, dine early.

NORTH END AND THE WATERFRONT

Ernesto's Pizzeria
🏃 $
69 Salem St., 02113 **Tel** *(617) 523-1373*
Map *2 D4*

This simple pizza shop with plastic seating offers 24 different combinations of toppings and delivers to most Boston hotel rooms, beating the pizza chains at their own game. The signature *mala femina* pie is topped with artichoke hearts, fresh tomatoes, and blue cheese.

Antico Forno

93 Salem St., 02113 **Tel** *(617) 723-6733*

$$$

Map 2 D2

With its statue of San Rocco, its mural of Tuscany, and its beehive wood-fired brick oven, Antico is popular with North End residents who frequent this underground room for the Neopolitan pizzas. The oven also works wonders with roasted meats and baked pasta dishes. A wood grill supplies smoke and flavor to many fish dishes as well.

Barking Crab

88 Sleeper St., 02110 **Tel** *(617) 426-CRAB*

$$$

Map 2 E5

Although it is open all year, this Fort Point Channel restaurant is best in summer, when diners can sit outdoors at picnic tables and wield heavy stones to crush lobster and crab shells. Local cod, haddock, flounder, tuna, halibut, clams, and crab are available fried, steamed, or broiled. The Boston skyline views are an added bonus.

La Famiglia Giorgio's

112 Salem St., 02113 **Tel** *(617) 367-6711*

$$$

Map 2 D2

Upbeat Italian meals with generous portions at a price that will not break the bank. Great for couples and families on a casual night out. The menu is simple: pizzas, pastas with a choice of sauces, and filling chicken or veal dishes. Unlike many North End restaurants, they do serve dessert and coffee.

Maurizio's Ristorante Italiano

364 Hanover St., 02113 **Tel** *(617) 367-1123*

$$$

Map 2 E2

The Sardinian chef-owner has an affinity for fish dishes, and the menu features Sardinian and Ligurian white wines that complement the bold flavors. The handmade filled pastas (like lobster ravioli) are tender and luscious. There is an open kitchen and close quarters on the main floor, as well as a basement room below. Closed lunch Mon–Fri.

Pomodoro

319 Hanover St., 02113 **Tel** *(617) 367-4348*

$$$

Map 2 E2

The tiny Pomodoro often has long lines of diners waiting for tables. The eponymous tomato sauce is one of the North End's best, and the kitchen shines with its vegetable dishes. Even dedicated meat-eaters will find pleasure in a meal of cold grilled vegetable antipasti, great bread, and a warming bowl of soup.

Bricco

241 Hanover St., 02113 **Tel** *(617) 248-6800*

$$$$

Map 2 E2

Bricco's kitchen keeps finding new twists on traditional Italian cooking, like spicing up steamed mussels with smoked red pepper and braised broccoli rabe. The windows swing wide open onto busy Hanover Street to make Bricco a popular spot for socializing over Venetian-style sardines or saddle of rabbit. Closed lunch.

Carmen

33 North Sq., 02113 **Tel** *(617) 742-6421*

$$$$

Map 2 E2

This cozy little trattoria specializes in small dishes for those who just want a bite while sipping wine – maybe a bowl of mussels or some oil-drizzled cheese. Fine pasta dishes with classic sauces are also available. Close quarters and below-street seating combine to give Carmen a romantic atmosphere. Closed lunch (except Fri and Sat).

Sel de la Terre

255 State St., 02109 **Tel** *(617) 720-1300*

$$$$

Map 2 E3

A study in contrasts, this casually elegant dining room near the Aquarium specializes in the rustic dishes of Provence. The fish dishes make good use of produce sold at the morning fish auction a few piers down the harbor. There are also great breads and charcuterie, and the boulangerie by the door sells breakfast breads and lunchtime sandwiches.

Terramia

98 Salem St., 02113 **Tel** *(617) 523-3112*

$$$$

Map 2 D2

This snug trattoria (the sister restaurant to Antico across the street) eschews the red-sauce neighborhood heritage in favor of Piemontese roasted meats (including game), deeply savory dishes with dark mushrooms and caramelized onions, and bright Ligurian-style seafood lightly dressed with capers and lemon. There is sadly no coffee or dessert.

Mare Organic

135 Richmond St., 02113 **Tel** *(617) 723-4273*

$$$$$

Map 2 F3

Acclaimed as one of the top 10 new restaurants in the US when it opened, Mare features classic Italian coastal cuisine, including rarities such as barbecued octopus. The chef uses deep-water fish, locally farmed shellfish, and organic meats and vegetables. The chic contemporary design helps to create a gallery-like setting. Closed lunch.

Meritage

70 Rowes Wharf, 02110 **Tel** *(617) 439-3995*

$$$$$

Map 2 E4

Exquisite regional and seasonal contemporary American dishes are laid out on the menu to match choices from the extensive wine list. Thus, the list leads with dishes for sparkling wines and light whites, proceeds through robust reds and ends with rich desserts or a platter of fine cheeses matched to ports and Sauternes.

Prezza

24 Fleet St., 02113 **Tel** *(617) 227-1577*

$$$$$

Map 2 E1

Prezza bases its menus on the mountain and shore cuisine of Abruzzi, with delicate handmade pastas and chunky meat and fish dishes cooked on a wood-burning grill. Roughly four dozen Italian and New World wines by the glass complement the food. Unlike many neighboring restaurants, Prezza makes its own desserts. Closed lunch.

Key to Price Guide *see p142* **Key to Symbols** *see back cover flap*

CHINATOWN AND THE THEATER DISTRICT

Xinh Xinh⠀⠀⠀⠀⠀⠀⠀⠀⠀⠀⠀⠀⠀⠀⠀⠀⠀⠀⠀⠀⠀⠀⠀⠀⠀⠀⠀⠀Ⓢ
7 Beach St., 02111 **Tel** *(617) 422-0501*⠀⠀⠀⠀⠀⠀⠀⠀⠀**Map** *1 C5*

Popular with many of Boston's Vietnamese residents, Xinh Xinh (pronounced "sin-sin") is a Saigon-style bistro offering the soothing noodle soups that many Western diners associate with Vietnamese cuisine and also classic dishes such as lemongrass chicken with rice-paper wrappers and smoky, tangy roasted whole quail.

Chau Chow City⠀⠀⠀⠀⠀⠀⠀⠀⠀⠀⠀⠀⠀⠀⠀⠀🚻🚹⠀⠀ⓈⓈ
83 Essex St., 02111 **Tel** *(617) 338-8158*⠀⠀⠀⠀⠀⠀⠀**Map** *1 C5*

Modern Hong Kong seafood dishes, such as scallops with green beans and macadamia nuts, top the menu on the lower two floors, while the third level is the reigning king of Boston's dim sum palaces. Shrimp dumpling is the benchmark of good dim sum, and this one is a perfect tender wrapper around sweet and crunchy shrimp.

Peach Farm⠀⠀⠀⠀⠀⠀⠀⠀⠀⠀⠀⠀⠀⠀⠀⠀⠀⠀⠀⠀⠀⠀ⓈⓈ
4 Tyler St., 02111 **Tel** *(617) 482-1116*⠀⠀⠀⠀⠀⠀⠀⠀**Map** *4 F2*

In the heart of Chinatown and popular with the locals. The sound of Hong Kong pop music fills the series of interconnected rooms and you should step inside the door to peruse the live tanks. Chinese seafood is its specialty, such as sesame jellyfish and salt and pepper eel, or just ask for what is fresh. Open late.

Shabu-Zen⠀⠀⠀⠀⠀⠀⠀⠀⠀⠀⠀⠀⠀⠀⠀⠀⠀⠀⠀⠀⠀⠀ⓈⓈ
16 Tyler St., 02111 **Tel** *(617) 292-8828*⠀⠀⠀⠀⠀⠀⠀**Map** *2 D5*

"Shabu-shabu" means "swish-swish" – the sound chopsticks make as they swirl raw vegetables and slivers of meat and fish in hot broth. Season your chicken broth with scallions, soy sauce, and hot pepper, settle on a meat or fish and a type of noodles, and assemble your own dinner. Perfect for diners who always wanted their sushi cooked.

Taiwan Cafe⠀⠀⠀⠀⠀⠀⠀⠀⠀⠀⠀⠀⠀⠀⠀⠀⠀⠀📄⠀⠀ⓈⓈ
34 Oxford St., 02111 **Tel** *(617) 426-8181*⠀⠀⠀⠀⠀⠀**Map** *4 F2*

Locals flock here for Taiwanese comfort food that makes few concessions to western tastes. If you are hunting for homestyle delicacies such as duck tongue, steamed taro, or meatballs in clay hot pots, this small second-story restaurant is the place. Luncheon specials (fish ball soup, for example) are a rare steal. Cash only.

Jacob Wirth Company Restaurant⠀⠀⠀⠀⠀🚻🚹🎹⠀⠀ⓈⓈⓈ
31 Stuart St., 02116 **Tel** *(617) 338-8586*⠀⠀⠀⠀⠀⠀**Map** *1 B5*

This Boston landmark *(see p85)* has been around since 1868, and is an old-fashioned restaurant best known for its bratwurst with sauerkraut and homemade potato salad. The sauerbraten may not be up to Munich standards, but the price is right and the evening piano bar can be a lot of fun.

Legal Seafoods⠀⠀⠀⠀⠀⠀⠀⠀⠀⠀⠀⠀⠀🚻🚹⠀⠀ⓈⓈⓈⓈ
26 Park Plaza, 02116 **Tel** *(617) 426-4444*⠀⠀⠀⠀⠀⠀**Map** *4 E2*

Now that Legal has gone national with airport restaurants, this flagship of the local chain is less of a novelty, but it is still a national leader in setting quality standards for fresh fish. This location features an extensive wine cellar and a lounge popular for Back Bay business lunches and after-dinner drinks. It also offers a gluten-free menu for celiacs.

Teatro⠀⠀⠀⠀⠀⠀⠀⠀⠀⠀⠀⠀⠀⠀⠀⠀⠀⠀🅿🚹⠀⠀ⓈⓈⓈⓈ
177 Tremont St., 02111 **Tel** *(617) 778-6841*⠀⠀⠀⠀⠀**Map** *4 E2*

The high arched mosaic ceiling and open kitchen of this erstwhile synagogue-turned-restaurant creates a theatrical atmosphere worthy of the name. Reservations aren't required, but make one if you need to eat in time for a curtain opening. Teatro offers a light grill menu and broad selection of northern Italian seafood and veal dishes.

blu⠀⠀⠀⠀⠀⠀⠀⠀⠀⠀⠀⠀⠀⠀⠀⠀🅿🚹🏧⠀⠀ⓈⓈⓈⓈⓈ
4 Avery St., 02111 **Tel** *(617) 375-8550*⠀⠀⠀⠀⠀⠀⠀**Map** *4 E2*

Fitting in very nicely with the chic sports club on the same level of the Ritz-Carlton Boston Common Hotel *(see p134)*, this Ladder District pioneer features light, fresh, delicately nuanced New American cuisine. The exuberantly post-modern architecture and artistic presentation create a dramatic sense of occasion for a big night out.

Locke-Ober⠀⠀⠀⠀⠀⠀⠀⠀⠀⠀⠀⠀⠀⠀⠀🅿🍸⠀⠀ⓈⓈⓈⓈⓈ
3 Winter Place, 02108 **Tel** *(617) 542-1340*⠀⠀⠀⠀⠀**Map** *1 C4*

The original 1890s décor has been lusciously restored in this bastion of fine dining in Old Boston. Locke-Ober did not permit women until the 1970s, but now its kitchen is run by a female chef-owner who fills the giant footsteps of Escoffier with modern interpretations of culinary classics. Closed Sat lunch; Sun.

Pigalle⠀⠀⠀⠀⠀⠀⠀⠀⠀⠀⠀⠀⠀⠀⠀⠀🅿🚹🏧⠀⠀ⓈⓈⓈⓈⓈ
75 Charles St. South., 02116 **Tel** *(617) 423-4944*⠀⠀⠀**Map** *4 E2*

This intimate room with rich, deep colors and antique chandelier exudes the Parisian bistro look. It also has the food to match the décor. The Theater District location makes Pigalle bustle with a pre-show crowd, so reserve for 8pm or later to have the time to savor the crackling roast duck or the chunky *cassoulet* (stew). Closed lunch; Mon.

BACK BAY AND SOUTH END

Mike's City Diner　　　　　　　　　🍽🚶　　　　　　Ⓢ
1714 Washington St., 02118 **Tel** *(617) 267-9393*　　**Map** *3 C5*

Show up early – very early. Mike's is open 6am–3pm every day, and there is usually a line of customers outside the door waiting for the breakfast specials, rendered with a little more care and finesse than you would normally expect. Political candidates always come by for a photo op during the quadrennial presidential nominating race.

Parish Cafe　　　　　　　　　　🚶♿🚻　　　　ⓈⓈ
361 Boylston St., 02116 **Tel** *(617) 247-4777*　　**Map** *3 B2*

Think of this casual bar-restaurant as a sampler of Boston's most famous chefs. The owners convinced each to dream up a signature sandwich, and the results are unusual, lobster salad on pepper brioche, for one. Landing one of the few outdoor tables can be hard so come early or sit at the bar inside.

Steve's　　　　　　　　　　　　　🚶　　　　　ⓈⓈ
316 Newbury St., 02116 **Tel** *(617) 267-1817*　　**Map** *3 A3*

Maybe the cheapest place to eat well in Back Bay, Steve's is an old-fashioned Greek restaurant where spinach-feta pastries, eggplant dishes, and salads studded with dark olives are the standard fare. Steve's gets a deal on locally-caught octopus, since few other restaurants serve it, but aficionados rave loudest about the lamb dishes.

B&G Oysters　　　　　　　　　　　　　　　ⓈⓈⓈ
550 Tremont St., 02116 **Tel** *(617) 423-0550*　　**Map** *4 D4*

A side venture of the famed chef of No. 9 Park, this subterranean spot for mollusk lovers consists of a marble bar surrounded by stools and an open stainless steel kitchen that preps the raw bar offerings. At least a dozen varieties of oysters are available at any given time. There is also a broad selection of sparkling and mineral-rich white wines.

Brasserie Jo　　　　　　　　　🅿🚶♿🚻　　ⓈⓈⓈ
120 Huntington Ave., 02116 **Tel** *(617) 425-3240*　　**Map** *3 B3*

One advantage of this Alsatian restaurant in the Colonnade Hotel *(see p135)* is that you can get a meal from dawn until after midnight. French beers are on tap, and the menu is replete with all the brasserie classics from steak-frites to *tarte tatin* (form of apple pie). This place is popular after-work for sharing glasses of kir and a plate of pâté.

Ciao Bella　　　　　　　　　　　🚶♿🚻　　ⓈⓈⓈ
240 Newbury St. #A, 02116 **Tel** *(617) 536-2626*　　**Map** *3 A3*

The outdoor tables on Newbury Street at Fairfield are as big a draw as the reasonably priced retro Italian-American menu that runs from minestrone to chicken parmesan. Local sports figures and visiting minor celebrities often seem to end up eating here, so the paparazzi provide some good additional street entertainment.

Firefly American Bistro　　　　　　🚶🚻　　ⓈⓈⓈ
130 Dartmouth St., 02116 **Tel** *(617) 262-4393*　　**Map** *3 C3*

Burgers, sandwiches, salads, and soups highlight the lunch menu at this fun spot across from Back Bay train station. Come night-fall, the menu switches to bistro meals like steamed mussels, signature "pot pie" crepes filled with peas, carrots, and chicken breast chunks in creamy bechamel. Sunday brunch is very popular. Closed Sun dinner.

Jasper White's Summer Shack　　　　🚶♿　　ⓈⓈⓈ
50 Dalton St., 02116 **Tel** *(617) 867-9955*　　**Map** *3 A3*

The Back Bay venue of this chain of casual seafood restaurants, started by one of New England's best chefs, sits right above a bowling alley and within easy walking distance of Symphony Hall and Fenway Park. Look out for the daily fish specials and weekend brunches featuring White's signature lobster hash.

Masa　　　　　　　　　　　　🅿🚶♿　　ⓈⓈⓈ
439 Tremont St., 02116 **Tel** *(617) 338-8884*　　**Map** *4 D3*

A rarity in Boston, Masa draws inspiration from the new gourmet cuisine pioneered in the American Southwest. The chef is apt to serve mushrooms in a pumpkin seed mole sauce or grilled trout with a chile-pepper rub. This is not a salsa-and-chips tequila bar, but Masa does pour tasting flights of different styles of tequila. Closed lunch Mon–Fri.

Orinoco　　　　　　　　　　　　　　　　ⓈⓈⓈ
477 Shawmut Avenue, 02118 **Tel** *(617) 369-7075*　　**Map** *3 C5*

This dining room with a tin ceiling in an 1890s building is the hot spot for listening to the new wave in Latin music while enjoying *arepas* (meat-filled grilled corn muffins) and plantain-stuffed *empanadas*. There is limited seating and no reservations.

Sonsie　　　　　　　　　　　🅿🚶♿🚻　　ⓈⓈⓈ
327 Newbury St., 02116 **Tel** *(617) 351-2500*　　**Map** *3 A3*

Everybody loves the look of this upper-Newbury Street stalwart, especially when they swing open the glass doors in the summer and the outdoor tables fill up with patrons more interested in being seen than in eating the truly delicious food. Most dishes hail from the French and Italian rivieras, with the occasional Indochinese delight.

Key to Price Guide *see p142* **Key to Symbols** *see back cover flap*

Tapeo

    🏵🏵🏵

266 Newbury St., 02116 **Tel** *(617) 267-4799*

Map *3 B2*

Authentically Spanish, this restaurant and tapas bar specializes in small plates that would be served with a glass of sherry in Spain. One of the few restaurants in Boston to serve true *jamón serrano* (the Spanish answer to Italian prosciutto), Tapeo also prepares exquisite bites like boneless pheasant breast and garlicky squid. Closed lunch Mon–Fri.

Bouchée

    🏵🏵🏵

159 Newbury St., 02116 **Tel** *(617) 450-4343*

Map *3 B2*

Boston's love affair with French food goes back at least to the American Revolution, and Bouchée delivers all the classics you'd look for in a Parisian brasserie, from steak *frites* and *coq au vin* to *bouillabaisse* and *cassoulet*. The excellent French wine list gets past the obvious names to include many lesser-known appellations. Open daily.

Rocca

    🏵🏵🏵🏵

50 Harrison Ave., 02118 **Tel** *(617) 451-5151*

Map *1 C5*

Boston's only restaurant focusing on Ligurian cuisine (the herb-infused dishes and ocean-oriented food of Genoa and the Italian Riviera), Rocca stands out by serving intensely flavored but light Italian food. The lively scene is fueled in part by an excellent cocktail bar and on-site parking, which is almost unheard of in the South End. Closed lunch.

Sibling Rivalry

    🏵🏵🏵🏵

525 Tremont St., 02116 **Tel** *(617) 338-5338*

Map *4 D4*

The name refers to the two vastly different menus by brothers who have achieved chef stardom elsewhere in the country. Located on the ground level of a fashionably designed luxury condo complex, Sibling Rivalry offers a choice of French food as favored by one brother, and American cuisine as favored by the other.

Stephanie's on Newbury

    🏵🏵🏵🏵

190 Newbury St., 02116 **Tel** *(617) 236-0990*

Map *3 B2*

Stephanie's has become an institution with its dinner salads and pasta dishes that are so big that diners routinely leave with "doggie bags" for the next meal. Signature plates include smoked salmon potato pancakes and meatloaf layered with cheese and caramelized onions. The restaurant offers some of Back Bay's best outdoor tables.

Toro

    🏵🏵🏵🏵

1704 Washington St., 02118 **Tel** *(617) 536-4300*

Map *3 C5*

The name is a bilingual pun of the Spanish for "bull" and the Japanese for bluefin tuna belly sashimi – no surprise, given the chef-owner's love of Spanish tapas and Japanese sushi and sashimi bars. The food is a hybrid of the two. Sushi is much less expensive here than at the chef's upscale restaurant Clio. Closed lunch

Tremont 647

    🏵🏵🏵🏵

647 Tremont St., 02118 **Tel** *(617) 266-4600*

Map *3 C4*

The extensively tattooed chef-owner is no shrinking violet, and his style of cooking favors big portions, bold flavors, and lots of smoke with the meat. South End trend followers are always stopping in to determine what's *au courant*, whether it is high-alcohol caipirinhas or the weekend pajama brunches when diners show up in sleepwear.

Union Bar & Grille

    🏵🏵🏵🏵

1357 Washington St., 02118 **Tel** *(617) 423-0555*

Map *4 D4*

An anchor for the rapidly gentrifying SoWa (south of Washington) neighborhood, this restaurant is popular with owners of the stylish new loft conversions. A sleek restaurant serving unpretentious American food, its attentive service, sharp design, and deft bar make it a hit with those who love to dine out. Closed lunch.

Via Matta

    🏵🏵🏵🏵

79 Park Plaza, 02116 **Tel** *(617) 422-0008*

Map *4 D2*

"Crazy Street" is as good a name as any for this hip bar-restaurant scene on the back side of Park Square. The food is solidly northern Italian – risottos and game from the Piedmont, tender veggie plates from Liguria, roasted meats of Tuscany, and heavenly sauces and cheeses from Emilia Romagna. The menu changes daily.

Aujourd'hui

    🏵🏵🏵🏵🏵

200 Boylston St., 02116 **Tel** *(617) 351-2037*

Map *4 D2*

A strong contender for the city's best restaurant, Aujourd'hui overlooks the Public Garden from broad windows in the Four Seasons hotel *(see p134)*. The menu features contemporary interpretations of French *haute cuisine* and an extensive wine list. Book well ahead, especially for Sunday brunch, and dress up to enjoy the sense of occasion.

Azure

    🏵🏵🏵🏵🏵

61 Exeter St., 02118 **Tel** *(617) 933-4800*

Map *3 B2*

While the chef is known for his bold treatments of grilled meats like lamb steak marinated in pomegranate juice, North Atlantic and Alaskan seafood dishes are the real stars. They are usually set off by an unusual fruit or vegetable, such as a mound of sweet and sour eggplant. The portions are large and Azure also serves a hearty breakfast.

Clio

    🏵🏵🏵🏵🏵

370-A Commonwealth Ave., 02215 **Tel** *(617) 536-7200*

Map *3 A2*

Clio's chef-owner is widely celebrated as one of country's most inventive chefs. Small plates and appetizers often feature arcane Asian spices, dabs of various caviars, and decorative techniques worthy of an origami master. Entrées are simpler, with the emphasis on exquisite cuts of meat and fish. Closed lunch; Mon.

Grill 23
P & T $$$$
161 Berkeley St., 02116 **Tel** *(617) 542-2255*   **Map** *4 D2*

Although a horde of chain steakhouses has descended on Boston in recent years, Grill 23 has been the genuine article since 1983. Beef is certified hormone- and antibiotic-free, and the bar serves exquisite martinis. The constantly evolving menu is based on seasonal availability. The 900-plus label wine list is among the city's best. Closed lunch.

Hamersley's Bistro
P & ☴ $$$
553 Tremont St., 02116 **Tel** *(617) 423-2700*   **Map** *4 D4*

A French country restaurant translated into an urban setting adjacent to the Boston Center for the Arts. Chicken roasted with garlic, lemon, and parsley under the skin has been a signature dish for decades. The summertime tables on the plaza are some of the most sought-after in the city.

Icarus
P ☆ & ♬ T $$$$
3 Appleton St., 02116 **Tel** *(617) 426-1790*   **Map** *4 D4*

New American cuisine is the forte of this classy room, often cited as the South End's most romantic restaurant. The chef-owner is very active in the Slow Food movement and its efforts to build sustainable local farming and fishing. The menu descriptions, therefore, include information on who grew or caught the ingredients. Closed lunch.

Oak Room
P & T $$$
138 St. James Avenue, 02116 **Tel** *(617) 267-5300*   **Map** *1 A5*

The aromas that strike you as you enter are seared beef and old money. The oak paneling helps preserve the Edwardian men's club atmosphere in this venerable steak house where even the small portions could feed two. The anteroom bar is one of the most elegant in the city.

Sorellina
P & T $$$$
1 Huntington Avenue, 02116 **Tel** *(617) 412-4600*   **Map** *3 A4*

Contemporary northern Italian cuisine is on offer in this impressive restaurant with its highly designed decor. Dishes range from the traditional, such as herb-roasted chicken and plain, grilled steaks, to the more adventurous, such as venison carpaccio with cherries. Closed lunch.

FARTHER AFIELD

Mr. Bartley's Burger and Salad Cottage
☰ ☆ & ☴ $
1246 Massachusetts Ave., Cambridge, 02138 **Tel** *(617) 354-6559*

Harvard Square's quintessential burger shop specializes in whopping pieces of meat. Some sandwiches have humorous names linked to a celebrity or politician, but most importantly, the prices are right, the food is fresh, and it fills you up. On weekends, it can take up to an hour to get in the door to order.

El Pelon Taqueria
☆ & ☴ $$
92 Peterborough St., 02111 **Tel** *(617) 262-9090*

In a world of fake Mexican restaurants, an authentic taqueria tends to stand out. There's nothing fancy about the tacos, tortas, and quesadillas except the freshness of the vegetables, but the level (and type) of chile seasoning is exactly right, as are the prices. Located in the Fenway near Boston University's large student population.

Forest Cafe
& $$
1682 Massachusetts Ave., Cambridge, 02138 **Tel** *(617) 661-7810*

The mother cuisine of Mexico comes from Oaxaca, and so do the dishes at Forest Cafe. Do not let the bikers and beery regulars at the bar dissuade you from sitting down in the cheerful Mexican cantina, on the left as you enter. Several classic mole sauces are usually on the menu, and the grilled fish and pork dishes are worth special attention.

Le's
☆ & $$
36 Dunster St., Cambridge, 02138 **Tel** *(617) 864-4100*

Asian students at Harvard head to this congenial restaurant for bowls of Vietnamese soup known as *pho*. A big bowl of noodles and broth with beef, chicken, or seafood is perhaps the ultimate comfort food, but Le's also offers a range of other noodle dishes, as well as healthy and inexpensive entrées and rice plates.

Tanjore
☆ & $$
18 Eliot St., Cambridge, 02138 **Tel** *(617) 868-1900*

Located on the river side of Harvard Square, Tanjore, owned by a local family, is the most eclectic of Indian restaurants. The menu carefully identifies the regions from which all the dishes come, from the mild dosas of the south to the coastal vindaloos to the tandoori dry roasts of the north. Authentic Indian desserts are available.

Betty's Wok & Noodle
☆ & $$$
250 Huntington Ave., 02116 **Tel** *(617) 424-1950*   **Map** *3 A4*

Offering tongue-in-cheek dining close to the Huntington Theatre and Symphony Hall, Betty's is decorated in 1950s retro chic. The menu, though, is all about modern choice. Pick a rice or noodle base, then a protein (fish, chicken, tofu), then a sauce to create your own combo dish. Traditional American desserts include chocolate layer cake.

Key to Price Guide *see p142* **Key to Symbols** *see back cover flap*

Paolo's Trattoria

251 Main St., Charlestown, 02129 **Tel** *(617) 242-7229*

The heart and soul of Paolo's is somewhere in the Adriatic, halfway between Greece and Italy. Ostensibly Italian, the menu makes extensive use of kalamata olives, feta and local goat cheese, and both dried and fresh figs. Wood oven pizzas include chef's signature *Amore*, topped with scallops, spinach, and two kinds of cheese.

Petit Robert Bistro

468 Commonwealth Ave., 02215 **Tel** *(617) 375-0699*

Once you have eaten here, you will wonder how any other restaurant in the neighborhood can stay in business. French bistro fare in French bistro portions (smaller than American) by a French Master Chef at these prices is a steal. Simple, clean executions of the classics from *coquilles St-Jacques*, to steak-frites, to profiteroles.

Casablanca

40 Brattle St., Cambridge, 02138 **Tel** *(617) 876-0999*

Few Harvard alumni can return without a nostalgic meal at this Bogart-themed boîte. Casablanca approaches Mediterranean cuisine from North Africa, so cumin and coriander figure prominently in the lamb and bulgar meatballs, and spicy hummus is often a side dish. The bar in the rear is a watering hole for local literati. Closed Sun lunch.

East Coast Grill

1271 Cambridge St., Cambridge, 02139 **Tel** *(617) 491-6568*

The chef that runs this colorful, casual restaurant is one of the country's acknowledged masters of open-fire grilling, having written seven books and counting. Grilled fish with tropical salsas, pulled barbecued pork, and icy oysters are among the greatest hits. The Bloody Mary bar inevitably draws an overflow crowd during Sunday brunch. Closed lunch.

Great Bay

500 Commonwealth Ave., 02215 **Tel** *(617) 532-5300*

This seafood restaurant in the Hotel Commonwealth (see p137) treats regional and local catch with elegance and restraint, matching tarragon to lobster, for example, or chorizo sausage to dayboat codfish. Diners interested in less formal plates can enjoy fish tacos, lobster and crab rolls, or plates of ceviche at the bar. Closed lunch.

Les Zygomates

129 South St., 02111 **Tel** *(617) 542-5108*

Map *4 F2*

The name refers to the facial muscles involved in smiling, which is what most diners will be doing when they discover the relaxed French bistro fare, the live jazz, and the extensive selection of wines by the glass. The wine bar is located in the old Leather District close to South Station. The menu always includes a few vegetarian entrées.

Oleana

134 Hampshire St., Cambridge, 02139 **Tel** *(617) 497-1239*

Oleana's chef-owner is the winner of many culinary accolades. Her dishes are inspired by the cuisines of all sides of the Mediterranean Sea, so she is likely to wax Lebanese in one dish, Moroccan in the next, and Catalan in another. Aromatic spices and intense sauces characterize most dishes. There is a nightly vegetarian tasting menu. Closed lunch.

Temple Bar

1688 Massachusetts Ave., Cambridge, 02138 **Tel** *(617) 547-5055*

This local hangout between Harvard and Porter Squares takes the kitchen as seriously as it does the busy bar. Burgers, sandwiches, and gourmet pizzas (lamb and roasted tomatoes, for example) are always available, but evening entrées are more ambitious New American bistro fare presented with considerable panache. Closed lunch.

Craigie Street Bistrot

5 Craigie Circle, Cambridge, 02138 **Tel** *(617) 497-5511*

The Burgundy-trained chef-owner creates new dishes each day based on the fish, meat, and dairy produce deliveries. House terrines, pâtés, and preserved vegetables provide some constancy, but each night's featured dishes tend to be surprises. Bargain fixed-price meals are available most nights, either very early or very late. Closed lunch.

Olives

10 City Square, Charlestown, 02129 **Tel** *(617) 242-1999*

Map *1 C1*

Home base for superchef Todd English, Olives pioneered a style of rustic Italian/Mediterranean cooking in Boston. Bold baked pastas and giant roasts of meat and fish pour out of the kitchen with admirable consistency. Its Charlestown location is near USS Constitution at the end of the Freedom Trail and there is a vigorous bar scene. Closed lunch.

Rialto

1 Bennett St., Cambridge, 02138 **Tel** *(617) 661-5050*

High-end, sophisticated décor makes this the special event restaurant of choice around Harvard Square. But Rialto is friendly and more relaxed than most *haute cuisine* temples. The chef takes a luscious approach to the classic Mediterranean cuisines, where rosemary is magic and basil an herb to conjure with. Closed lunch.

Sandrine's Bistro

8 Holyoke St., Cambridge, 02138 **Tel** *(617) 497-5300*

It is hard to resist the Alsatian flatbread topped with farmer's cheese blended with spices, and bacon, mushrooms, or asparagus – and those are just starters on this classical Alsatian menu. Here charcuterie is king and cabbage isn't eaten until it is sauerkraut. Modestly priced daily menu, as well as pull-out-the-stops tasting menu. Closed Sun lunch.

Cafés and Bars

The social fabric of Boston is held together through its abundance of places to meet with friends and while away the hours. A city with a rich mix of students, working folk, and executives provides a selection of cafés and bars that cater to all tastes, and to people who keep all hours. There are places where you can find a pick-me-up, rest your feet, and meet local people. A further selection of bars is listed on pp162–3.

CAFÉS

Cafés tend to cluster in a few areas of the city, most notably Harvard Square and its environs, the South End, the North End, and Beacon Hill. **Crema Café**, one of the newest in Harvard Square's long line of cafés, serves both hot and iced tea, along with delicious pastries and sandwiches. The Italian-style **Café Paradiso** features light food and Italian sodas in a trendier, more hurried atmosphere. For an especially genteel treat, make your way to **L.A. Burdick's Handmade Chocolates** and order a sampler plate of their innovative chocolates or one of their superb buttery fruit tarts. They also have some fine teas, including herbals. There are two branches of the **1369 Coffeehouse**, which are spacious, upbeat and frequented by a clientele of all ages, who come mainly for the excellent cookie bars.

The South End's secluded cafés are home to a thriving café society. Many are popular with the vibrant gay community *(see p163)* that has made its home in this neighborhood, but also happily welcome all visitors, regardless of sexual preference. **The Garden of Eden**, with its cozy, provincial decor, is a perfect place to start the day, reading the newspapers and enjoying the croissants they bake for breakfast daily, or one of their many original sandwiches. **Flour Bakery & Café** makes artisanal breads, generous sandwiches and warming soups, as well as fine pastries. **Berkeley Perk** is colorful and spacious, with a wide selection of juices, quality sodas, and sweet treats.

Cafés cluster around the main thoroughfares of the North End, where many local restaurants do not even bother to serve coffee or dessert because the cafés in this lively Italian neighborhood do it so much better – espresso or cappuccino with *tiramisu* or *cannoli* are a must. **Caffè Vittoria**, decorated in marble and chrome, has a wide array of pastries and liqueurs, and its own cigar parlor. **Caffè Pompei** is a more chaotic place, which features murals of its doomed namesake crowding the walls. While many like **Mike's Pastry** for their *cannoli*, it is said that the best are found alongside the nougat at **Maria's Pastry Shop**, which sadly does not have seating. **Lulu's Bake Shop** is known for its tempting variety of cupcakes. On Beacon Hill, **Café Vanille** has a range of exquisite Parisian pastries.

TEA ROOMS

A couple of grand hotels have preserved a genteel tradition of offering afternoon tea: **The Bristol Lounge** at the Four Seasons Hotel serves a lovely tea (especially enjoyable if you are seated by the fireplace), while on weekends the **Taj Boston** continues the formal afternoon tea tradition established by its predecessor the Ritz-Carlton, complete with a full Old World service. More recently, tea has found aficionados among the college-aged crowd, and a number of tea houses designed for the younger and more budget-conscious flourish in Harvard Square and on Newbury Street. **Tea-luxe**, which has a branch on Newbury Street

and in Harvard Square, lets customers peruse an impressive catalog of hundreds of teas from around the world. Fine Asian teas, with a touch of tranquillity and a hint of enlightenment, are the specialty at **Dado Tea**, which is situated both in and east of Harvard Square in Cambridge. Near the theater district and in Harvard Square is **Finale**, famous for specializing in producing the most delicious desserts.

ICE CREAM PARLORS

Bostonians eat more ice cream, per person, year round, than anyone else in America. They are highly discerning customers, and fiercely loyal to their favorite parlor. Many restaurants make a point of serving one of the locally made ice creams with their dessert menus. When ordering ice cream, you can get it served in a dish with a spoon, or in a cone to lick. You get a choice of wafer cone (light, crispy, slightly bland) or a sugar cone (thin, crisp, sweet cookie wafer). Some may decide to order one of the enormous waffle cones, which is really just an overgrown sugar cone custom-made for the truly indulgent. Parlors are open most of the day and late into the evening. In central Boston the best ice creams are hard to find, but Newbury Street *(see p93)* has some of the best options. **J.P. Licks** is an old favorite, its bizarre tiled decor a landmark. The New England ice cream giant **Ben and Jerry's** has several parlors featuring all their flavors.

Farther out of town, Harvard Square has some great ice-cream parlors. Old college friends often reunite over a heaped cone at **Herrell's**, trying the latest flavors while chatting in what was once a bank vault. Steve Herrell is credited with starting Greater Boston's craze for premium ice cream, which is also satisfied by newcomer **Lizzy's Ice Cream**. Try the Charles River Crunch (dark chocolate ice cream with almond toffee nuggets).

Competition for most inventive flavors is stiff. For example, **Christina's** in Inman Square makes the best green tea ice cream in the city, as well as a wide range of other flavors, ranging from the sublime to the simply gooey.

A little farther afield, **Ron's Gourmet Homemade Ice Cream & Bowling** features specialty flavors such as peanut sunrise, as well as a chance to work off some calories on their candlepin bowling lanes.

BARS

The legal drinking age in Boston is 21, and you may be asked to show proof of identification *(see p174)*.

Boston has scores of bars which offer live music and other types of entertainment *(see also pp162–3)*. Those listed here are a good place to relax and simply have a drink, though some of them can still be quite lively.

For good, down-to-earth bars, you cannot go wrong with the youthful **Shay's Pub**

and Wine Bar, The Sevens, the slightly tacky **Purple Shamrock,** the well-heeled **21st Amendment,** or the kitschy lounge paradise of **The Good Life. Parker's Bar** at the Omni Parker House Hotel has the atmosphere of a gentleman's club, while around the city are dotted a number of good wine bars, notably **Les Zygomates** and **Troquet. Jacob Wirth** *(see p85),* which is also a restaurant, is situated in the Theater District and has good beer and a lively ambience.

DIRECTORY

CAFÉS

Berkeley Perk
69 Berkeley St. **Map** 4 D3.
Tel (617) 426-7375.

Café Paradiso
1 Elliot Square, Cambridge.
Tel (617) 742-1768.

Café Vanille
119 Mt Vernon St. **Map** 1 B4. *Tel (617) 523-9200.*

Caffè Pompei
280 Hanover St. **Map** 2 E2. *Tel (617) 227 1562.*

Caffè Vittoria
290–296 Hanover St. **Map** 2 E2.
Tel (617) 227-7606.

Crema Café
27 Brattle St., Cambridge.

Flour Bakery & Café
1595 Washington St. **Map** 3 C5. *Tel (617) 267-4300.*

The Garden of Eden
571 Tremont St. **Map** 4 D4.
Tel (617) 247-8377.

L.A. Burdick's Handmade Chocolates
52 Brattle St.,Cambridge.
Tel (617) 491-4340.

Lulu's Bake Shop
227 Hanover St.
Map 2 E2.
Tel (617) 720-2200.

Maria's Pastry Shop
46 Cross St. **Map** 2 D3.
Tel (617) 523-1196.

Mike's Pastry
300 Hanover St. **Map** 2 E2.
Tel (617) 742-3050.

1369 Coffeehouse
1369 Cambridge St., Cambridge.
Tel (617) 576-1369.
757 Massachusetts Ave.
Tel (617) 576-4600.

TEA ROOMS

The Bristol Lounge
200 Boylston St.
Map 4 D2.
Tel (617) 338-4400.

Dado Tea
955 Massachusetts Ave., Cambridge.
Tel (617) 497-9061.
50 Church St., Cambridge.
Tel (617) 547-0950.

Finale
1 Columbus Ave.
Map 1 B5.
Tel (617) 423-3184.
30 Dunster St., Cambridge.
Tel (617) 441-9797.

Taj Boston
15 Arlington St.
Map 4 D2.
Tel (617) 536-5700.

Tea-Luxe
Brattle St., Cambridge.
Tel (617) 441-0077
108 Newbury St.
Map 3 C2.
Tel (617) 927-0400.

ICE CREAM PARLORS

Ben and Jerry's
174 Newbury St.
Map 3 B2
Tel (617) 536-5456.
20 Park Plaza.
Map 4 D2.
Tel (617) 426-0890.
36 John F. Kennedy St., Cambridge.
Tel (617) 864-2828.

Christina's
1255 Cambridge St.
Tel (617) 492-7021.

Herrell's
15 Dunster St., Cambridge.
Tel (617) 497-2179.

J.P. Licks
352 Newbury St.
Map 3 A3.
Tel (617) 236-1666.

Lizzy's Ice Cream
29 Church St., Cambridge.
Tel (617) 354-2911.

Ron's Gourmet Homemade Ice Cream & Bowling
1231 Hyde Park Ave., Hyde Park, MA 02136.
Tel (617) 364-5274.

BARS

The Good Life
28 Kingston St.
Map 2 D5.
Tel (617) 451-2622.

Jacob Wirth
31–37 Stuart St.
Map 4 E2.
Tel (617) 338-8586.

Les Zygomates
129 South St.
Map 4 F2.
Tel (617) 542-5108.

Parker's Bar
60 School St.
Map 2 D4.
Tel (617) 227-8600.

Purple Shamrock
1 Union St.
Map 2 D3.
Tel (617) 227-2060.

The Sevens
77 Charles St.
Map 1 B3.
Tel (617) 523-9074.

Shay's Pub and Wine Bar
58 John F. Kennedy St., Cambridge.
Tel (617) 864-9161.

Troquet
140 Boylston St.
Map 4 E2.
Tel (617) 695-9463.

21st Amendment
150 Bowdoin St.
Map 1 C3.
Tel (617) 227-7100.

SHOPPING IN BOSTON

Shopping in Boston has evolved dramatically in recent years. Long known as an excellent center for antiques, books, and quality clothing, the city's shopping options now cover a much broader spectrum, influenced both by its booming economy and its large, international student population. From the fashionable boutiques of Newbury Street, to the many stores selling cosmopolitan home furnishings

Red Sox baseball cap

or ethnic treasures, to the varied art and crafts galleries, Boston caters to every shopping need. Whether you are looking for the latest fashion accessory, an unusual antique, or a special souvenir, choices abound to accommodate every sense of style and budget. Boston is no longer simply traditional, and now holds its own in providing a vibrant, eclectic and world-class shopping experience.

Large glass atrium of the busy Prudential shopping mall

SALES

There are two major sale seasons in Boston: July, when summer clothes go on sale to make room for fall fashions, and January, when any winter clothing and merchandise is cleared after the holidays. Most stores also have a sale section or clearance rack throughout the year.

PAYMENT AND TAXES

Major credit cards and traveler's checks with identification are accepted at most stores. There is a tax of 5 percent on all purchases except groceries and clothing, although any item of clothing over $175 will be taxed.

OPENING HOURS

Most stores open at 10am and close at 6pm from Monday to Saturday, and from noon to 5 or 6pm on Sunday. Many stores stay open later on Thursday nights,

and most department stores stay open until 7:30 or 8pm throughout the week. Weekday mornings are the best times to shop. Saturdays, lunch hours, and evenings can be very busy.

SHOPPING MALLS

Shopping malls – clusters of shops, restaurants, and food courts all within one large and open complex – have become top destinations for shopping, offering variety, dining, and entertainment. With long winters and a fair share of bad weather, New Englanders flock to malls to

Farm produce on display on Charles Street

shop, eat, and, in the case of teenagers, simply hang out.

Copley Place, with its elegant restaurants, and more than 75 shops over two levels, is based around a dazzling 60-ft (18-m) atrium and waterfall. Across a pedestrian overpass, **Shops at Prudential Center** encompasses **Saks Fifth Avenue** department store, a food court, and many smaller specialty shops. The most upscale mall in town, **Heritage on the Garden** looks out over Boston's Public Garden, and features the boutiques of top European designers, fine jewelers, and stores selling other luxury goods. Outside the center of town, across the Charles River, **Cambridgeside Galleria** has over 100 shops and a pond-side food court. For last-minute purchases, **Boston Landing**, at Logan Airport (Terminal C), has shops, restaurants, banking, and internet access.

DEPARTMENT STORES

There are four major department stores in Boston offering a large and varied selection of clothing, accessories, cosmetics, housewares, and gifts. Some also have restaurants and beauty salons, and provide a variety of personal shopping services. For those wanting to shop at several stores, **Concierge of Boston** provides a shopping service in metropolitan Boston. At

Downtown Crossing *(see p82)*, a bustling shopping district between Boston Common and the Financial District, generations of Bostonians once shopped at Filene's, now closed. The department store's underground cut-price offspring, **Filene's Basement**, pioneered the "automatic markdown," in which goods are discounted more heavily the longer they remain unsold. This branch of Filene's Basement is closed through 2009 for renovations.

Directly across the street, **Macy's**, the legendary New York emporium, offers an equally impressive array of fashions, cosmetics, housewares, and furnishings.

Heading uptown, through Boston Common and Public Garden to Boylston Street, you can spot the Prudential Tower, centerpiece of a once nondescript but recently revitalized complex of shops, offices, and restaurants. This includes the venerable and elegant **Saks Fifth Avenue**, which caters to its upscale clientele with renowned service, a luxurious ambiance, and strikingly stylish displays. For the ultimate high fashion, high profile shopping experience, stop by **Neiman Marcus**,

which specializes in haute couture, precious jewelry, furs, and gifts. The store is well known for its Christmas catalog, with presents that have included authentic Egyptian mummies, vintage airplanes, a pair of two-million-dollar diamonds, and robots to help out around the house – or mansion. Other Copley Place merchants include Ralph Lauren, Christian Dior, Louis Vuitton, Gucci, and Emporio Armani, as well as Boston's first outlet of popular Manhattan trendsetter, Barney's.

DISCOUNT AND OUTLET STORES

Dedicated bargain hunters may want to consider making a day trip to one of New England's famed outlet centers, where many top designers and major brand manufacturers offer last-season and overstocked clothing and goods at big discounts. Generally sold at 20 to 30 percent less than their regular retail prices, some items can be found reduced by as much as 75 percent. **Wrentham Village**

Boutiques of genteel Newbury Street

Brattle Bookshop's sign

Premium Outlets are about 40 miles (65 km) south of Boston. The stores here sell designer clothing, housewares, and accessories from many of the leading manufacturers.

Kittery, 50 miles (80 km) north of Boston, is an even larger outlet destination, with more than 125 shops selling everything from footwear and designer clothes, to sports equipment, perfume, books, china, glass, and gifts. There are also numerous restaurants.

Freeport, Maine, is one of the largest and most famous outlet centers, being home to the renowned outdoor equipment specialist **L.L. Bean**. Over two hours' drive from Boston, it is only worth the journey for the dedicated shopper, or for those already visiting Maine.

DIRECTORY

SHOPPING MALLS

Boston Landing
Terminal C,
Logan International
Airport, East Boston.
www.massport.com

Cambridgeside Galleria
100 Cambridgeside Pl.,
Cambridge.
Tel (617) 621-8666.

Copley Place
100 Huntington Ave.
Map 3 C3.
Tel (617) 369-5000.
www.simon.com

Heritage on the Garden
300 Boylston St. **Map** 4 D2.
Tel (617) 426-9500.

Shops at Prudential Center
800 Boylston St. **Map** 3 B3.
Tel (800) 746-7778.
www.prudential center.com

DEPARTMENT STORES

Concierge of Boston
165 Newbury Street.
Map 3 C2.
Tel (617) 266-6611.
www.concierge.org

Filene's Basement
426 Washington St. **Map** 4 F1. *Tel (617) 542-2011.*

Macy's
450 Washington St. **Map** 4 F1. *Tel (617) 357-3000.*

Neiman Marcus
5 Copley Place, 100 Huntington Ave. **Map** 3 C3. *Tel (617) 536-3660.*

Saks Fifth Avenue
Prudential Center. **Map** 3 B3. *Tel (617) 262-8500.*

DISCOUNT AND OUTLET STORES

Freeport Merchants Association
Freeport, Maine.

Tel (207) 865-1212.
Tel (800) 865-1994.
www.freeportusa.com

Kittery Outlets
Route 1, Kittery, Maine.
Tel (888) 548-8379.
www.thekitteryoutlets. com

L.L. Bean
Route 1, Freeport, Maine.
Tel (877) 552-3268.

Wrentham Village Premium Outlets
1 Premium Outlets Blvd,
Wrentham.
Tel (508) 384-0600.

Fashion

From chain stores stocked with popular brand labels to specialists selling vintage clothing, Boston offers choices in every area of fashion. Well-heeled shoppers frequent high-fashion boutiques, students flock to vintage emporiums, bargain hunters converge at Filene's Basement, and businessmen visit both traditional outlets and the many fashionable men's outfitters. In this stylish, international city, many stores feature fine clothes from Italy, France, England, and Japan, along with the more prevalent fashions from top American designers.

MIXED FASHION

Many stores in Boston offer quality clothing for both men and women. **Louis Boston**, housed in an elegant building on Berkeley Street that once contained Boston's Museum of Natural History, has long been known as the city's most exclusive men's outfitters. It now also features similarly beautiful clothing for women. **Barney's New York**, a branch of the world famous Manhattan fashion icon, offers an extensive range of cutting edge designer labels.

Nearby on Newbury Street, **Giorgio Armani**, **Riccardi**, and **Burberry** all cater to the well-heeled, who love to browse through their extravagantly stylish and outrageously expensive clothing and accessories. **Alan Bilzerian** attracts celebrities in search of both his own label and the latest avant-garde looks from Europe and Japan. Donna Karan's **DKNY** features a wider range of fashion, from casual sportswear to glamorous evening attire, as well as housewares and baby clothes. In Cambridge, **American Apparel** features casual sportswear for men and women. **Urban Outfitters** offers an eclectic collection of clothing and accoutrements for the young and trendy, and stocks Kikit, Girbaud, and Esprit. America's favorite chain, **Gap**, has simple styles which remain stylish enough for movie stars, yet affordable for the masses. **Banana Republic** is ideal for those after a sleeker more modern look.

The Swedish retailer **H&M**, which stocks trend-setting fashion for adults and children at affordable prices, has shops both downtown and in Back Bay. The Back Bay store is particularly known for its large selection of accessories. For clothing more suited to the great outdoors, visit **Eddie Bauer**, which sells a range of no-nonsense sporting gear, or **Patagonia**, a mecca for serious climbers, skiers, and sailors, which also carries sophisticated, high-tech sporting equipment.

Visitors don't mind going a little out of the way for huge discounts (up to 70 percent) on athletic and street shoes and apparel at the **New Balance Factory Outlet** store. The locally based athletic-shoe company stocks virtually every size – short and narrow to long and wide.

WOMEN'S FASHION

No woman need leave Boston empty-handed, whether her taste is for the *haute couture* of **Chanel** in Boston's Taj Hotel or the earthy ethnic clothing at **Nomad**. Newbury Street is filled with sumptuous, high-fashion boutiques, including **Kate Spade**, **Betsy Jenney**, and **Max Mara**, Italy's largest and most luxurious ready-to-wear manufacturer for women. Casual clothes with optimistic mottoes are the specialty of **Life is Good**, while **Oilily**, the Dutch boutique, blazes with colorful prints and youthful designs. On Boylston Street, **Ann Taylor** is undoubtedly the first choice for refined, modern career clothes, while **Talbots**, a Boston institution, features enduring classics. **Anthropologie** stocks an eclectic mix of exotic and whimsical clothing and accessories from around the world.

In Harvard Square, **Oona's** has been selling vintage clothing for 35 years, while **A Taste of Culture** offers beautiful knit and woollen garments from Peru. **Clothware** features natural-fiber clothes from local designers, and **Settebello** carries elegant European apparel and accessories.

MEN'S FASHION

Gentlemen seeking a quintessential New England look need go no farther than **Brooks Brothers** on Newbury Street, longtime purveyors of traditional, high-quality men's and boys' wear.

America's foremost fashion house, **Polo/Ralph Lauren** offers top-quality and highly priced sporting and formal attire, while **Jos. A. Bank Clothiers** sells private label merchandise as well as most major brands at discounted prices.

Academics and college students alike head to Cambridge, where the venerable **Andover Shop** and **J. Press** provide a selection of Ivy-League essentials of impeccable quality.

DISCOUNT AND VINTAGE CLOTHES

The legendary Boston bargain emporium **Filene's Basement** has been selling a broad selection of discounted clothing for over 90 years. It is still unique among other discount stores for its frenzied atmosphere and its discount system, which reduces prices by 25% after 14 days, 50% after 21 days, and 75% after 28 days. After 35 days the clothes go off to charity. Bargain hunters are eagerly waiting for the store to reopen in 2010 after restoration of the 1912 building. First among the other discount chains is **Marshall's**, promising "brand names for less" and offering bargains on clothing, shoes, housewares, and accessories.

Vintage aficionados will love the vast collections at **Bobby from Boston**, a longtime costume source for Hollywood and top fashion designers. In Cambridge, **Keezer's** has provided generations of Harvard students with everything from used tuxedos to sports jackets and loafers. **Second Time Around**, with consignment shops in both Cambridge and Boston, offers a select array of top-quality, gently worn contemporary clothing for women.

SHOES AND ACCESSORIES

Many stores in Boston specialize in accessories and footware. **Helen's Leather** on Charles Street is well known for leather jackets, briefcases, purses, shoes, and Birkenstock sandals, as well as its huge selection of Western boots. At Downtown Crossing, **Foot Paths** carries a range of shoes from Timberland, Kenneth Cole, Rockport, and others.

Stylish Spanish shoes and bags are the specialty at **Stuart Weitzman** at Copley Place, while the adventurous will find more fashionable and unusual shoes at **Berk's** and **The Tannery** in Cambridge. For sports gear, the large and opulent **Niketown** on Newbury Street shows video re-runs of sports events while shoppers peruse the latest designs in athletic clothing and footwear.

DIRECTORY

MIXED FASHION

Alan Bilzerian
34 Newbury St.
Map 4 D2.
Tel *(617) 536-1001.*

American Apparel
47 Brattle St., Cambridge.
Tel *(617) 661-2770.*

Banana Republic
28 Newbury St. **Map** 4 D2.
Tel *(617) 267-3933.*

Barney's New York
Copley Place. **Map** 3 C3.
Tel *(617) 385-3300.*

Burberry
2 Newbury St. **Map** 3 C2.
Tel *(617) 236-1000.*

DKNY
37 Newbury St. **Map** 3 C2.
Tel *(617) 236-0476.*

Eddie Bauer
500 Washington St. **Map** 2 D4. **Tel** *(617) 423-4722.*

Gap
201 Newbury St. **Map** 3 C2. **Tel** *(617) 267-4055.*

Giorgio Armani
22 Newbury St. **Map** 3 C2.
Tel *(617) 267-3200.*

H&M
350 Washington St.
Map 4 F1.
Tel *(617) 482-7081.*
100 Newbury St. **Map** 3 C2. **Tel** *(617) 859-3192.*

Louis Boston
234 Berkeley St.
Map 3 C2.
Tel *(617) 262-6100.*

New Balance Factory Outlet
40 Life St., Brighton.
Tel *(877) 623-7867.*

Patagonia
346 Newbury St. **Map** 3 A3. **Tel** *(617) 424-1776.*

Riccardi
116 Newbury St. **Map** 3 C2. **Tel** *(617) 266-3158.*

Urban Outfitters
361 Newbury St. **Map** 3 A3. **Tel** *(617) 236-0088.*

WOMEN'S FASHION

Ann Taylor
800 Boylston St. **Map** 3 B3.
Tel *(617) 421-9097.*

Anthropologie
799 Boylston St. **Map** 3 B3.
Tel *(617) 262-0545.*

A Taste of Culture
1160 Massachusetts Ave., Cambridge.
Tel *(617) 868-0389.*

Betsy Jenney
114 Newbury St. **Map** 3 C3. **Tel** *(617) 536-2610.*

Chanel
5 Newbury St. **Map** 4 D2.
Tel *(617) 859-0055.*

Clothware
52 Brattle St., Cambridge
Tel *(617) 661-6441.*

Kate Spade
117 Newbury St. **Map** 3 C2. **Tel** *(617) 262-2632.*

Life is Good
285 Newbury St. **Map** 3 B2. **Tel** *(617) 262-5068.*

Max Mara
69 Newbury St. **Map** 3 C2.
Tel *(617) 267-9775.*

Nomad
1741 Massachusetts Ave., Cambridge.
Tel *(617) 497-6677.*

Oilily
32 Newbury St.
Map 4 D2.
Tel *(617) 247-9299.*

Oona's
1210 Massachusetts Ave., Cambridge.
Tel *(617) 491-2654.*

Settebello
52 Brattle St., Cambridge.
Tel *(617) 864-2440.*

Talbots
500 Boylston St.
Map 3 C2.
Tel *(617) 262-2981.*

MEN'S FASHION

Andover Shop
22 Holyoke St.,
Cambridge.
Tel *(617) 876-4900.*

Brooks Brothers
46 Newbury St.
Map 4 D2.
Tel *(617) 267-2600.*

Jos. A. Bank Clothiers
399 Boylston St.
Map 4 D2.
Tel *(617) 536-5050.*

J. Press
82 Mount Auburn St., Cambridge.
Tel *(617) 547-9886.*

Polo/Ralph Lauren
93/95 Newbury St.
Map 3 C2.
Tel *(617) 424-1124.*

DISCOUNT AND VINTAGE CLOTHES

Bobby from Boston
19 Thayer St. **Map** 4 E4.
Tel *(617) 423-9299.*

Filene's Basement
426 Washington St.
Map 4 F1.
Tel *(617) 542-2011.*

Keezer's
140 River St., Cambridge.
Tel *(617) 547-2455.*

Marshall's
500 Boylston St. **Map** 3 C2.
Tel *(617) 262-6066.*

Second Time Around
176 Newbury St. **Map** 3 B2. **Tel** *(617) 247-3504.*

SHOES AND ACCESSORIES

Berk's
50 John F. Kennedy St., Cambridge.
Tel *(617) 492-9511.*

Foot Paths
489 Washington St.
Map 4 F1.
Tel *(617) 338-6008.*

Helen's Leather
110 Charles St. **Map** 1 B3.
Tel *(617) 742-2077.*

Niketown
200 Newbury St. **Map** 3 B2. **Tel** *(617) 267-3400.*

Stuart Weitzman
Copley Place. **Map** 3 C3.
Tel *(617) 266-8699.*

The Tannery
39 Brattle St., Cambridge.
Tel *(617) 491-1811.*

Antiques, Fine Crafts, and Gifts

Visitors hoping to take home a special memento will find an enormous number of antique, craft, and gift stores in Boston. From the huge antique markets and cooperatives, to specialty shops selling everything from rugs to rare books, there are abundant opportunities to indulge a passion for the past. Those favoring more contemporary *objets d'art* will find crafts guilds, galleries, and gift shops selling unique glassware, ceramics, textiles, jewelry, and much more produced by New England artisans, as well as items from every corner of the world.

ANTIQUES

Charles Street is Boston's antiques Mecca, with more antique stores than any other part of town. The neighborhood is extremely affluent with many exclusive and expensive stores, though the occasional bargain may be found in some of the larger stores. One of the larger places is **Antiques at 80 Charles**, which has three floors of merchandise ranging from silver tea sets to jewelry, paintings, clocks, and collectables. **Upstairs Downstairs** also sells "affordable antiques," and has four rooms full of furniture, lamps, prints, and a large selection of smaller items.

Collectors of fine Asian antiques should not miss **Alberts-Langdon, Inc.** and **Judith Dowling Asian Art**, for everything from screens and scrolls to lacquer-ware, ceramics, paintings, and furniture from all over Japan. A prime source for antique pine and painted furniture, **Danish Country** carries antique *armoires* and other furniture from Scandinavia, as well as Royal Copenhagen china and tall case clocks. The shop also carries Chinese lacquered antique furniture that blends well with the Scandinavian pieces.

Antique jewelry from around the world is a specialty at **Marika's Antiques Shop**, along with paintings, glass, porcelain, and silver. Collectors of Art Deco furniture and decorative pieces inevitably gravitate to **A Room with a Vieux Antiques**, where the owners do most of their buying in France. **Twentieth Century Ltd.** excels particularly in glittery costume jewelry from top designers. They also offer pieces in sterling silver.

In Cambridge, **Reside** specializes in mid-20th century modern furniture and accessories, with ethnic pillows and weavings. For an eclectic mix of antiques both fine and funky from the 19th century to the 1950s, head to **Easy Chairs**.

ANTIQUE MARKETS AND COOPERATIVES

If browsing through mountainous inventories with the broadest range of quality, price, and stock is your idea of heaven, then there are several multi-dealer antiques emporiums worth exploring. On Charles Street, **Boston Antiques Cooperative I and II** has everything from quilts, candlesticks, and wicker furniture to chandeliers and furniture. In the Leather District, situated near South Station, is **JMW Gallery**, which specializes in fine 19th- and early 20th-century American furniture, ceramics, and printed materials associated with the Arts and Crafts Movement. In Cambridge, **Cambridge Antique Market** encompasses more than 100 dealers, offering estate antiques, collectibles, furniture, jewelry, and a vast selection of many other items.

If you have scoured Charles Street, scrutinized the cooperatives and still not found what you are looking for, try **Skinner Inc.** in Boston or **F.B. Hubley Company** in Cambridge, both of which hold auctions throughout the year featuring furniture and fine arts.

SPECIALTY DEALERS

Collectors in pursuit of more specific pieces will find shops in Boston that specialize in everything from nautical antiques to rare books, maps, jewelry, and rugs. Fine antiques and jewelry featuring Victorian and Art Nouveau designs are beautifully displayed and described by the knowledgeable staff at **Small Pleasures**. Vintage watches from Rolex, Cartier, Vacheron, Constantia, and others are a specialty at **Time and Time Again** watch emporium; while **The Bromfield Pen Shop** has been purveyor of thousands of new, antique, and limited edition pens for over 50 years. For nautical antiques, including model ships and marine paintings, **Lannan Ship Model Gallery** boasts an extensive and high quality inventory. Antique rugs, carpets, and tapestries from around the world are the mainstay at **Decor International**, and at **Mario Ratzki Oriental Rugs**, which has a discriminating selection of antique Persian carpets and tribal rugs from the 1860s to the 1930s. Bibliophiles will also find an extraordinary range of stores in Boston. In business since 1825, **Brattle Book Shop** (*see p83*) is the oldest and best known, with a huge selection of used, out-of-print and rare books, magazines, and vintage photographs. Rare books in the fine arts are the focus of **Ars Libri Ltd.**, while **Eugene Galleries** features antiquarian maps, prints, and etchings, in addition to its comprehensive selection of books. Mystery and thriller fans have been said to get a murderous glint in their eyes when looking through the new and used volumes at **Kate's Mystery Books**, where Boston-area writers hang out when avoiding the word processor. Also in Cambridge, **Schoenhof's Foreign Books** and **Grolier Poetry Book Shop** cater to those seeking specialty volumes. The **Bryn Mawr Bookstore** stocks used books and some rare volumes covering every conceivable subject.

FINE CRAFTS

Collectors with a more contemporary bent will find several distinguished galleries and shops featuring a wide variety of American crafts by both local and nationally recognized artists. **Mobilia** in Cambridge has a national reputation for its jewelry, ceramics, and other objects. The **Society of Arts and Crafts**, established in 1897, has a shop and gallery, with exhibits from the 350 artists it represents. Works are largely in wood, fiber, metal, glass, and mixed media. The **Cambridge Artists' Co-operative**, owned and run by over 250 artists, offers an eclectic collection of items, ranging from hand-painted silk jackets to ornaments and other larger items. **The Artful Hand Gallery** also has a range of fine items, again crafted primarily by American artists.

GIFTS

In addition to the plethora of souvenir shops that threaten to drown tourists in tasteless, predictable merchandise, Boston has numerous shops specializing in original and distinctive gifts that you will not find anywhere else. On Newbury Street browse the **International Poster Gallery**, for original, vintage posters from the 19th and 20th centuries. In Cambridge, **Joie de Vivre** has a fantastic collection of toys, clocks, jewelry, jack-in-the-boxes, and much more beside. Next door, **Paper Source** carries a selection of fine handmade papers, gift wrap, rubber stamps, and other materials for creative indulgence.

DIRECTORY

ANTIQUES

Alberts-Langdon, Inc.
126 Charles St. **Map** 1 B3.
Tel (617) 523-5954.

Antiques at 80 Charles
80 Charles St. **Map** 1 B4.
Tel (617) 742-8006.

Danish Country
138 Charles St. **Map** 1 B3.
Tel (617) 227-1804.

Easy Chairs
375 Huron Ave.,
Cambridge.
Tel (617) 491-2131.

Judith Dowling Asian Art
133 Charles St. **Map** 1 B3
Tel (617) 523-5211.

Marika's Antiques Shop
130 Charles St. **Map** 1 B3.
Tel (617) 523-4520.

Reside
266 Concord Ave.,
Cambridge.
Tel (617) 547-2929.

A Room with a Vieux Antiques
20 Charles St. **Map** 1 B4.
Tel (617) 973-6600.

Twentieth Century Ltd.
73 Charles St. **Map** 1 B4.
Tel (617) 742-1031.

Upstairs Downstairs
93 Charles St. **Map** 1 B4.
Tel (617) 367-1950.

ANTIQUES MARKETS AND COOPERATIVES

Boston Antiques Cooperative I and II
119 Charles St. **Map** 1 B3.
Tel (617) 227-9810.

Cambridge Antique Market
201 Msgr. O'Brien Hwy,
Cambridge.
Tel (617) 868-9655.

F.B. Hubley Company
364 Broadway,
Cambridge.
Tel (617) 876-2030.

JMW Gallery
144 Lincoln St.
Map 4 F2.
Tel (617) 338-9097.

Skinner Inc.
63 Park Plaza. **Map** 1 C4.
Tel (617) 350-5400.

SPECIALTY DEALERS

Ars Libri Ltd.
500 Harrison Ave.
Map 4 E4.
Tel (617) 357-5212.

Brattle Book Shop
9 West St. **Map** 1 C4.
Tel (617) 542-0210.

The Bromfield Pen Shop
5 Bromfield St. **Map** 1 C4.
Tel (617) 482-9053.

Bryn Mawr Bookstore
373 Huron Ave.,
Cambridge.
Tel (617) 661-1770.

Decor International
61 North Beacon St.,
Allston.
Tel (617) 262-1529.

Eugene Galleries
76 Charles St. **Map** 1 B4.
Tel (617) 227-3062.

Grolier Poetry Book Shop
6 Plympton St.,
Cambridge.
Tel (617) 547-4648.

Kate's Mystery Books
2211 Massachusetts Ave.,
Cambridge.
Tel (617) 491-2660.

Lannan Ship Model Gallery
99 High St. **Map** 2 E5.
Tel (617) 451-2650.

Mario Ratzki Oriental Rugs
40 Charles St. **Map** 1 B4.
Tel (617) 227-3592.

Schoenhof's Foreign Books
76A Mt. Auburn St.,
Cambridge.
Tel (617) 547-8855.

Small Pleasures
142 Newbury St. **Map** 3 C2. **Tel** (617) 267-7371.

Time and Time Again
73 Newbury St.,
2nd Floor. **Map** 3 B2.
Tel (617) 266-6869.

FINE CRAFTS

The Artful Hand Gallery
Copley Place. **Map** 3 C3.
Tel (617) 262-9601.

Cambridge Artists' Cooperative
59a Church St.,
Cambridge.
Tel (617) 868-4434.

Mobilia
358 Huron Ave.,
Cambridge.
Tel (617) 876-2109.

Society of Arts and Crafts
175 Newbury St. **Map** 3 B2. **Tel** (617) 266-1810.

GIFTS

International Poster Gallery
205 Newbury St. **Map** 3 B2. **Tel** (617) 375-0076.

Joie de Vivre
1792 Massachusetts Ave.,
Cambridge.
Tel (617) 864-8188.

Paper Source
1810 Massachusetts Ave.,
Cambridge.
Tel (617) 497-1077.

ENTERTAINMENT IN BOSTON

From avant-garde performance art to serious drama, and from popular dance music to live classical performances, Boston offers an outstanding array of entertainment options, with something to appeal to every taste: the Theater District offers many excellent plays and musicals, the Wang Theater hosts many touring productions, and Symphony Hall

Quincy Market entertainer

is home of the renowned Boston Symphony Orchestra. Boston is also well acquainted with jazz, folk music, and blues as well as being a center for more contemporary music, played in big city nightclubs. In summer, entertainment often heads outdoors, with many open-air plays and concerts, such as the famous Boston Pops at the Hatch Shell.

PRACTICAL INFORMATION

The best sources for information on current films, concerts, theater, dance, and exhibitions include the Thursday *Calendar* section of the *Boston Globe* and the Friday entertainment weekly, the *Boston Phoenix*. Even more up-to-date listings can be found on the World Wide Web at the following sites: www.boston.city search.com; the *Boston Globe* (www. boston.com); *Boston Phoenix* (www.bostonphoenix.com).

Boston entertainment listings magazines

BOOKING TICKETS

Tickets to popular musicals, theatrical productions, and touring shows often sell out far in advance, although theaters sometimes have a few returns

or restricted-view tickets available. You can either get tickets in person at theater box offices, or use one of the ticket agencies in Boston. For advance tickets these are **Ticketmaster** and **Live Nation Tickets**. Tickets can be purchased from both of these agencies over the telephone, in person, or online. Half-price tickets to most noncommercial arts events as well as to some commercial productions are available from 11am on the day of the performance at **BosTix** booths. Purchases must be made in person and only cash is accepted. BosTix also sells advance full-price tickets. Special Boston entertainment discount vouchers, available from hotel lobbies and tourist offices, may also give a saving on some shows.

Tchaikovsky's *Nutcracker*, danced by the Boston Ballet *(see p160)*

DISTRICTS AND VENUES

Musicals, plays, comedies, and dance are generally performed at venues in the Theater District, although larger noncommercial theater companies are distributed throughout the region, many being associated with colleges and universities.

The area around the intersection of Massachusetts and Huntington Avenues hosts a concentration of outstanding concert venues, including Symphony Hall, Berklee Performance Center at Berklee College of Music, and Jordan Hall at the New England Conservatory of Music.

Many nightclub and dance venues are on Lansdowne and other streets by Fenway Park and around Boylston Place in the Theater District. The busiest areas for bars and small clubs offering live jazz and rock music are Central and Harvard Squares in Cambridge, Davis Square in Somerville, and Allston. The principal gay scene in Boston is found in the South End, with many of the older bars and clubs in neighboring Bay Village.

Boston's Symphony Orchestra performing at Symphony Hall *(see p160)*

OPEN-AIR AND FREE ENTERTAINMENT

The best free outdoor summer entertainment in Boston is found at the Hatch Shell *(see p92)* on the Charles River Esplanade. The Boston Pops *(see p160)* performs here frequently during the week around July 4, and all through July and August jazz, pop, rock, and classical music is played. On Friday evenings from late June to the week before Labor Day, the Hatch Shell also shows free big-screen family films.

Music is also performed during the summer months at the **Bank of America Pavilion** on the waterfront, which holds live jazz, pop, and country music concerts. City Hall Plaza and Copley Plaza have free concerts at lunchtimes and in the evenings, and the **Museum of Fine Arts** *(see pp104–107)*

Free open-air music concert outside New City Hall

operates a summer musical concert series in its courtyard. Most of the annual concerts and recitals of the **New England Conservatory of Music** are free, although some require advance reservations.

Other open-air entertainment includes a series of free plays staged on Boston Common by the **Commonwealth Shakespeare Company** in July and August, and ticketed performances of various plays by the **Publick Theater** at Christian Herter Park on the Charles River.

An area that has more unusual open-air entertainment is Harvard Square, famous for its nightly and weekend scene of street performers.

Many recording artists paid their dues here, and other hopefuls still flock to the square in the vain hope of being discovered – or at least of earning the cost of dinner.

Details of all free entertainment happening in the city are listed in the *Calendar* section of Thursday's *Boston Globe*.

DISABLED ACCESS

Many entertainment venues in Boston are wheelchair accessible. **Very Special Arts Massachusetts** offers a full Boston arts access guide. Some places, such as **Jordan Hall**, the **Cutler Majestic Theater**, and the **Wheelock Family Theater**, have listening aids for the hearing impaired, while the latter also has signed and described performances.

Entrance to the Shubert Theatre *(see p160)*

DIRECTORY

BOOKING TICKETS

BosTix
Faneuil Hall Marketplace.
Map 2 D3.
Copley Square.
Map 3 C2.
Tel (617) 482-2849.
www.bostix.com

Live Nation Tickets
Downtown Crossing.
Map 1 C4.
Various outlets.
Tel (800) 431-3462.
www.livenation.com

Ticketmaster
Various outlets.
Tel (617) 931-2000.
www.ticketmaster.com

OPEN-AIR/FREE ENTERTAINMENT

Bank of America Pavilion
290 Northern Ave.,
South Boston. **Map** 2 F5.
Tel (617) 728-1600.
www.bankofamerica
pavilion.com

Commonwealth Shakespeare Company
Parkman Bandstand,
Boston Common. **Map** 1
C4. *Tel* (617) 482-9393.
www.freeshakespeare.org

Museum of Fine Arts
465 Huntington Ave.
Tel (617) 369-3306.
www.mfa.org

New England Conservatory of Music
290 Huntington Ave.
Tel (617) 585-1260.
www.newengland
conservatory.edu

Publick Theater
Christian A. Herter Park,
1175 Soldiers Field Rd.,
Brighton. *Tel* (617)
933-8600. **www**.publick
theater.com

DISABLED ACCESS

Cutler Majestic Theater
219 Tremont St. **Map**
4 E2. *Tel* (617) 824-8000.
www.maj.org

Jordan Hall
30 Gainsborough St.
Tel (617) 585-1260.

Very Special Arts Massachusetts
China Trade Center,
2 Boylston St.
Map 4 E2.
Tel (617) 350-7713.
TTY (617) 350-6836.
www.vsamass.org

Wheelock Family Theater
200 Riverway,
Brookline.
Tel (617) 879-2300.
TTY (617) 879-2150.
www.wheelock.edu

The Arts in Boston

Performing arts are vital to Boston's cultural life. Since the 1880s, the social season has revolved around openings of the Boston Symphony Orchestra and many Brahmins *(see p45)* occupy their grandparents' seats at performances. In the past, theaters in Boston were heavily censored *(see p87)*, but today's Bostonians are avid theatergoers, patronizing commercial venues for plays bound to, or coming from, Broadway and attending ambitious contemporary drama at repertory theaters. Many noncommercial theater and dance companies perform in smaller venues in local neighborhoods and at the colleges. Although some theaters are closed on Mondays, there is rarely a night in Boston without performing arts.

CLASSICAL MUSIC AND OPERA

Two cherished Boston institutions, the **Boston Symphony Orchestra** and its popular-music equivalent, the Boston Pops, have a long history of being led by some of America's finest conductors. The BSO performs a full schedule of concerts at Symphony Hall from October through April. The Boston Pops takes over for May and June, performing at the Charles River Esplanade *(see p92)* for Fourth of July festivities that are the highlight of the summer season.

The students and faculty of the **New England Conservatory of Music** present more than 450 free classical and jazz performances each year, many in Jordan Hall *(see p159)*. **Boston Lyric Opera** has assumed the task of reestablishing opera in Boston, through small-cast and light opera at venues around the city.

Boston's oldest musical organization is the **Handel & Haydn Society**, founded in 1815. As the first American producer of such landmark works as Handel's *Messiah* (performed annually since 1818), Bach's *B-Minor Mass* and *St. Matthew Passion*, and Verdi's *Requiem*, H & H is one of the country's musical treasures. Since 1986, the society has focused on performing and recording Baroque and Classical works using the period instruments for which the composers

wrote. H & H gives regular performances in Boston at Symphony Hall, Jordan Hall, and Cutler Majestic Theatre.

Classical music is ubiquitous in Boston. **Emmanuel Music**, for example, performs the entire Bach cantata cycle at regular services at Emmanuel Church on Newbury Street. The Isabella Stewart Gardner Museum *(see p103)* hosts a series of chamber music concerts, continuing a 19th-century tradition of professional "music room" chamber concerts in the homes of the social elite.

The **Celebrity Series** brings world-famous orchestras, soloists, and dance companies to Boston, often to perform at Jordan Hall, as well as several other venues. Some 40 to 50 events are organized.

THEATER

Though much diminished from its heyday in the 1920s, when more than 40 theaters were in operation throughout Boston, the city's Theater District *(see pp80–89)* today still contains a collection of some of the most architecturally eminent, and still commercially productive, early theaters in the United States. Furthermore, during the 1990s, many of the theaters that are currently in use underwent programs of restoration to their original grandeur, and visitors today are bound to be impressed as they catch a glimpse of these theaters' past glory.

The main, commercially run theaters of Boston – the **Colonial**, **Wilbur**, and **Shubert** theaters, the **Opera House** and the **Wang Theatre** *(see pp84–7)* – often program Broadway productions that have aleady premiered in New York and are touring the United States. They also present Broadway "try outs" and local productions.

In stark contrast to some of the mainstream shows on offer in Boston, the most avant-garde contemporary theater in the city is performed at the **American Repertory Theater (ART)**, an independent, non-commercial company associated with Harvard University *(see pp112–3)*. ART often premieres new plays, particularly on its second stage, but is best known for its often radical interpretations of traditional and modern classics. By further contrast, the **Huntington Theatre**, allied with Boston University, is widely praised for its traditional direction and interpretation. For example, the Huntington was the co-developer of Pulitzer-Prize winning plays detailing 20th-century African American life, by the late August Wilson, an important chronicler of American race relations.

Several of the smaller companies, including **Lyric Stage**, devote their energies to showcasing local actors and directors and often premiere the work of Boston-area playwrights. Many of the most adventurous companies perform on one of the four stages at the **Boston Center for the Arts**.

DANCE

The city's largest and most popular resident dance company, the **Boston Ballet** performs an ambitious season of classics and new choreography between October and May at the Opera House *(see p83)* and other venues. The annual performances of the *Nutcracker* during the Christmas season are a Boston tradition. The somewhat more modest

José Mateo's Ballet Theater has earned a reputation for developing a strong and impressive program of repertory choreography. The company performs in the attractive neo-Gothic Old Cambridge Baptist Church, which is situated near Harvard Square. Modern dance in Boston is represented by many small companies, collectives, and independent choreographers, who often perform in the **Dance Complex** and **Green Street Studios** in Cambridge. Boston also hosts many other visiting dance companies, who often put on performances at the **Cutler Majestic Theater**.

CINEMA

Situated in Harvard Square, close to Harvard Yard (*see pp110–111*), the **Brattle Theater**, one of the very last repertory movie houses in the Greater Boston area, primarily shows classic films on a big screen. For example, the Brattle was instrumental in reviving moviegoers' interest in the Humphrey Bogart, black-and-white classic *Casablanca*. Something of a Harvard institution, the Brattle has long served as a popular "first date" destination for couples with a shared passion for the movies.

Serious students of classic and international cinema patronize the screening programs of the **Harvard Film Archive**. The **Kendall Square Cinema** multiplex is the city's chief venue for non-English language films, art films and documentaries. Multiplex theaters showing mainstream, first-run Hollywood movies are found throughout the Boston area. Some of the most popular are **Loews Theaters**, located at Boston Common, and the **Regal Fenway 13** in the suburb of Brookline. Tickets for every kind of movie in Boston are often discounted for first shows of the day on weekends and all weekday shows before 5pm.

DIRECTORY

CLASSICAL MUSIC AND OPERA

Boston Lyric Opera
various venues.
Tel (617) 542-6772.
www.blo.org

Boston Symphony Orchestra
Symphony Hall,
301 Massachusetts Ave.
Map 3 A4.
Tel (617) 266-1200, (617) 266-1492. www.bso.org

Celebrity Series
various venues.
Tel (617) 482-6661.
www.celebrityseries.org

Emmanuel Music
Emmanuel Church,
15 Newbury St.
Map 4 D2.
Tel (617) 536-3356.
www.emmanuelmusic.org

Handel & Haydn Society
various venues.
Tel (617) 266-3605.
www.handelandhaydn.org

New England Conservatory of Music
Jordan Hall,
30 Gainsborough St.

Map 3 A4.
Tel (617) 585-1260.
www.newenglandconservatory.edu

THEATER

American Repertory Theater
Loeb Drama Center,
64 Brattle St.,
Cambridge.
Tel (617) 547-8300.
www.amrep.org

Boston Center for the Arts
539 Tremont St. **Map** 4 D3.
Tel (617) 933-8600.
www.bostontheaterscene.com

Colonial Theatre
106 Boylston St. **Map** 4 E2.
Tel (617) 426-9366.
www.broadwayacrossamerica.com

Huntington Theatre
264 Huntington Ave.
Map 3 B4. *Tel (617) 266-0800.* www.huntingtontheatre.org

Lyric Stage
140 Clarendon St.
Map 3 C3.
Tel (617) 585-5678.
www.lyricstage.com

Opera House
539 Washington St.
Map 4 E1.
Tel (617) 931-2787.
www.broadwayacrossamerica.com

Shubert Theatre
265 Tremont St.
Map 4 E2.
Tel (617) 482-9393.
www.citicenter.org

Wang Theatre
270 Tremont St. **Map** 4 E2. *Tel (617) 482-9393.* www.citicenter.org

Wilbur Theater
246 Tremont St. **Map** 4 E2. *Tel (617) 426-1083.* www.broadwayacrossamerica.com

DANCE

Boston Ballet
various venues.
Tel (617) 695-6950.
www.bostonballet.org

Cutler Majestic Theater
219 Tremont St.
Map 4 E2. *Tel (617) 824-8000.* www.maj.org

Dance Complex
536 Massachusetts Ave.,
Cambridge.
Tel (617) 547-9363.
www.dancecomplex.org

Green Street Studios
185 Green St, Cambridge.
Tel (617) 864-3191.
www.greenstreetstudios.org

Jose Mateo's Ballet Theater
400 Harvard St,
Cambridge.
Tel (617) 354-7467.
www.ballettheatre.org

CINEMA

Brattle Theater
40 Brattle St., Cambridge.
Tel (617) 876-6837.

Harvard Film Archive
24 Quincy St.,
Cambridge. *Tel (617) 495-4700.*
hcl.harvard.edu/hfa/

Kendall Square Cinema
1 Kendall Square,
Cambridge.
Tel (617) 499-1996.

Loews Theaters
Boston Common.
Map 4 E2.
Tel (617) 423-3499.

Regal Fenway 13
201 Brookline Ave.
Tel (617) 424-6266.

Music and Nightlife

Boston's mix of young professionals and tens of thousands of college students produces a lively nightlife scene, focused on live music, clubs, and bars. Ever since the 1920s, Boston has been especially hospitable to jazz, and it still has an interesting jazz scene, with Berklee College of Music playing an important part. Cambridge is an epicenter of folk and acoustic music revivals and alt-rock, while Lansdowne Street near Fenway Park *(see p166)* is the main district for nightclubs. Virtually every neighborhood has a selection of friendly bars, often with live music.

ROCK MUSIC

With the Lansdowne Street nightlife scene in the midst of a complete renovation, **Church** is helping to fill the gap in the Fenway neighborhood with live local bands from Wednesday through to Saturday and DJs on Sunday. With four performance spaces, the **Middle East** in Cambridge's Central Square leads the alternative rock scene, featuring both local bands and touring newcomers. Larger rock concert venues are the **Orpheum Theater** and the arena seating of **TD BankNorth Garden**, used at other times for hockey and basketball games.

JAZZ AND BLUES

The city's premier, large concert venue for jazz is **Berklee Performance Center** in Back Bay, which draws on faculty and students from Berklee College of Music as well as touring performers. More intimate settings include **Scullers Jazz Club** overlooking the Charles River in Brighton, the small-hall for aficionados at the **Real Deal Jazz Club** in East Cambridge, and the suave elegance of the **Regatta Bar** just off Harvard Square. No-frills, neighborhood jazz thrives at **Ryles Jazz Club** in Cambridge's Inman Square. The musical parent of jazz, the blues, is also alive and well. **Wally's** in the South End has an ambience that is pure 1940s juke joint, but there's no denying the veracity of the jazz wailing

from its narrow confines. The **Cantab Lounge** in Cambridge's Central Square is a music lover's delight, and features open mic sessions on Mondays and bluegrass on Tuesdays, while the weekends feature live blues, R&B, funk, and soul. The Cantab also runs popular Wednesday night poetry "slams."

FOLK AND WORLD MUSIC

Harvard Square's **Club Passim** is a folk music legend, the hangout in the late 1950s and early 1960s for the likes of Joan Baez and Van Morrison, and still one of the United States' key clubs in the touring life of singer-songwriters. **The Independent** in Somerville's Union Square is a good place to catch unplugged rock, Irish bands, and aspiring troubadours who write their own material Davis Square is a couple of Red Line stops farther out from Harvard station, but well worth the trip for **Johnny D's Uptown Restaurant & Music Club**, where the program offers an eclectic mix ranging from solo singer-songwriters, to zydeco bands, and acoustic and amplified rockabilly. To enjoy some local Caribbean tunes and dancing, one of the the best options is a weekend night at **The Western Front**, which kicks it up near the river in Cambridgeport.

International acts ranging from Afro-pop to ska play at many large venues across Boston in a concert series presented by the music promoters **World Music**.

NIGHTCLUBS AND DISCOS

Boston has a club for just about every type of dance music. Like club scenes everywhere, little happens until late at night; in Boston nothing gets going until at least 11pm. Expect everything from country music and salsa lessons to a weekly Goth night at **An Tua Nua**, near Boston University. **The Grand Canal** near North Station spins techno and house music for a youthful clientele. Located in the rear of a stylish restaurant, **The Gypsy Bar** has a Latin night as well as house and techno music. The extravagant and upscale **Aria** on Tremont Street draws a moneyed Euro-crowd. **Toast Lounge** attracts a gothic crowd for Crypt on Wednesdays, lesbian clubbers for Tuesday's popular Dyke Night, and a multi-gender motley for Heroes on Saturdays. More middle-of-the-road is the **Roxy** in the Theater District, with classy touches such as doormen instead of bouncers, marble walls, and a vast dance floor.

BARS

The legal drinking age in Boston is 21, and you may be asked to show proof of identification *(see p174)*.

Boston has many bars *(see also p151)*, but many, such as those listed below, are specifically themed, offer live entertainment, or place a strong emphasis on being "party" venues. The bar at **Mistral** is typical of the increasingly upscale places springing up in Boston, where the young and the beautiful like to meet and play. More down to earth are some of Boston's Irish bars offering live music and the obligatory pints of Guinness. Among these are **The Phoenix Landing Bar and Restaurant**, a mock Irish pub in Central Square lined with mahogany and featuring English football on cable television as well as Celtic and dance rock performances on weekend nights, **The Burren** that features some of the finest musicians in the city, and the smaller **Druid**, where as the evening wears on, crowds of young professionals give way to recent Irish immigrants.

Bostonians love sports, and the city has dozens of sports bars. The **Cask 'N' Flagon** is adjacent to Fenway Park, perfect for celebrating victory or softening the pain of defeat. At **Kings** big-screen sports TVs vie with bowling lanes, while the **Sports Depot** is just mammoth. The area near North Station is filled with bars catering to Boston Celtics and Boston Bruins fans.

GAY CLUBS AND BARS

Boston's gay scene comes into sharpest focus in the South End and Bay Village, but gay and gay-friendly bars and clubs are found throughout the city. The perpetually packed **Fritz Lounge**, which is attached to the Chandler Inn, is a stalwart South End bar. Boston's longest-running gay club, **Jacques**, features rock acts Friday through Monday and female impersonator cabaret during the rest of the week. The weekly *Bay Windows* newspaper provides wider information as do other Boston listings.

COMEDY CLUBS

Many clubs and bars program occasional evenings of standup comedy, and several specialize in this form of entertainment. The **Comedy Connection** at Quincy Market, brings laughter to the historic hall with an impressive line-up of comedians, who are familiar from their work on national television. **Nick's Comedy Stop** in the Theater District, on the other hand, tends to concentrate more on homegrown talent, grooming performers who often go on to the "big time."

DIRECTORY

ROCK MUSIC

Church
69 Kilmarnock St.
Tel (617) 236-7600.

Middle East
472/480 Massachusetts Ave., Cambridge.
Tel (617) 864-3278 ext. 221.
www.mideastclub.com

Orpheum Theater
1 Hamilton Pl. **Map** 1 C4.
Tel (617) 679-0810.

TD BankNorth Garden
1 Causeway St. **Map** 1 C2.
Tel (617) 624-1000. www.tdbanknorthgarden.com

JAZZ AND BLUES

Berklee Performance Center
Berklee College of Music, 136 Massachusetts Ave.
Tel (617) 266-7455.
www.berklee.edu

Cantab Lounge
738 Massachusetts Ave., Cambridge.
Tel (617) 354-2685.

Real Deal Jazz Club
41 Second St., Cambridge.
Tel (617) 876-7777.
www.concertix.com

Regatta Bar
Charles Hotel,
1 Bennett St., Cambridge.
Tel (617) 395-7757.
www.regattabarjazz.com

Ryles Jazz Club
212 Hampshire St., Cambridge. *Tel (617) 876-9330.* www.rylesjazz.com

Scullers Jazz Club
Doubletree Guest Suites, 400 Soldiers Field Rd., Brighton.
Tel (617) 562-4111.
www.scullersjazz.com

Wally's Cafe
427 Massachusetts Ave.
Tel (617) 424-1408.

FOLK AND WORLD MUSIC

Club Passim
47 Palmer St., Cambridge.
Tel (617) 492-7679.
www.clubpassim.org

The Independent
75 Union Square, Somerville. *Tel (617) 440-6022.* www.theindo.com

Johnny D's Uptown Restaurant & Music Club
17 Holland St., Somerville.
Tel (617) 776-2004.
www.johnnyds.com

Western Front
343 Western Ave., Cambridge.
Tel (617) 492-7772.

World Music
Box Office:
Tel (617) 876-4275.
www.worldmusic.org

NIGHTCLUBS AND DISCOS

An Tua Nua
835 Beacon St.
Tel (617) 262-2121.

Aria
246 Tremont St.
Map 4 E2.
Tel (617) 338-7080.

Grand Canal
57 Canal St.
Map 2 D2.
Tel (617) 523-1112.

The Gypsy Bar
116 Boylston St.
Tel (617) 482-7799.

Roxy
279 Tremont St.
Map 4 E2.
Tel (617) 338-7699.

Toast Lounge
70 Union Sq., Somerville.
Tel (617) 623-9211.
www.toastlounge.com

BARS

The Burren
247 Elm St., Somerville.
Tel (617) 776-6896.

The Cask 'N' Flagon
62 Brookline Ave.
Tel (617) 536-4840.

Druid
1357 Cambridge St., Cambridge.
Tel (617) 497-0965.

Kings
10 Scotia St. **Map** 3 A3.
Tel (617) 266-2695.

Mistral
223 Columbus Ave.
Map 4 D3.
Tel (617) 867-9300.

The Phoenix Landing Bar and Restaurant
512 Massachusetts Ave., Cambridge.
Tel (617) 576-6260.

Sports Depot
353 Cambridge St., Allston.
Tel (617) 783-2300.

GAY BARS AND CLUBS

Fritz Lounge
26 Chandler St. **Map** 4 D3. *Tel (617) 482-4428.*

Jacques
79 Broadway. **Map** 4 F4.
Tel (617) 426-8902.

COMEDY CLUBS

Comedy Connection
Faneuil Hall Marketplace.
Map 2 D3.
Tel (617) 248-9700.
www.comedyconnectionboston.com

Nick's Comedy Stop
100 Warrenton St.
Tel (617) 423-2900.
www.nickscomedystop.com

SPORTS AND OUTDOOR ACTIVITIES

Bostonians have a wealth of recreational opportunities, thanks largely to the city's many spacious parks, its long, well-maintained riverfront, sizeable harbor, and excellent sports facilities. Visitors can enjoy many outdoor activities, whether it is going for an early morning jog on Boston Common, sailing on the

Charles River, taking to one of the extensive cycle paths, or playing a round at a public golf course. In the winter there is also outdoor ice-skating, and farther afield, skiing. For those who watch sports rather than participate, major-league baseball, football, soccer, basketball, and ice-hockey are played at different times through the year.

Rollerblading

WATER SPORTS

During all but the winter months, dozens of small pleasure craft can be seen navigating the Charles River between Cambridge and Boston. At long-established **Community Boating**, only experienced sailors are able to rent sailboats, while farther upriver at the **Charles River Canoe & Kayak Center**, canoes, rowboats, and adult and children's kayaks can be rented.

For those who enjoy swimming or sunbathing, there are several good beaches near Boston, and one supervised beach on the Boston Harbor Islands, reached by ferry from Long Wharf. Carson Beach and the beach at Castle Island in South Boston are two of the closest, while Revere Beach to the north is larger and busier and served by the subway. From June to September swimmers can use the **Department of Conservation and Recreation** outdoor swimming pools.

BICYCLING, JOGGING, AND SKATING

The gentle Boston topography makes sightseeing by bicycle ideal. A number of good trails and bicycle paths crisscross the city, the most popular of which is the Dr. Paul Dudley White Bike Path. This links central Boston with outlying Watertown via a circular 17-mile (27-km) trail that runs along both sides of the Charles River. The Southwest Corridor cycle route links the Back Bay with Roxbury along a section of the Emerald Necklace *(see p103)*, and the recently extended Boston harborfront pathways also attract many cyclists. Farther afield, an old railroad line has been transformed into the Minuteman Bikeway, which runs between Cambridge and Bedford via historic Lexington. **Boston Bike Tours** offers cycle tours along with rental bikes, while other rental stores include **Back Bay Bicycles** and **Community Bicycle Supply**.

In-line skating and jogging are also popular activities in Boston, with riverside esplanades and Boston Common being the favorite areas. If you are looking to buy some gear, try **City Sports**.

Cyclist on the Dr. Paul Dudley White Bike Path

GOLF AND TENNIS

Along with its many excellent private golf clubs, the Boston area also boasts a number of public golf courses, including some municipal links. The **William J. Devine Golf Course** in Franklin Park is the city's public golf course and there is also the nine-hole **Fresh Pond Golf Course** in Cambridge.

The **Department of Conservation and Recreation** maintains a dozen public tennis courts in Boston. Those in North End Park on Commercial Street and Charlesbank Park on the Charles River Esplanade are the most central. Court time can not usually be reserved, so availability is on a first-come-first-served basis.

Sailboats on the Charles River with Back Bay in the distance

WINTER SPORTS

Freezing winter weather sees large groups of heavily clothed ice skaters heading for the Frog Pond on Boston Common. A modest fee is charged for skating, and skate rental is available in the pavilion by Frog Pond, or else a few blocks away at the **Beacon Hill Skate Shop**. Each winter, the Department of Conservation and Recreation also opens its many indoor rinks in Boston and Cambridge to the public, including Steriti Rink in the North End, which also has an indoor bocce court.

Most of the best skiing in New England is found a long way from Boston, in Vermont, Maine, and New Hampshire. Closer options include **Blue Hills Ski Area** in Canton for downhill skiing, and **Middlesex Fells Reservation** in Stoneham for cross-country. These areas depend a lot on the weather, however, and have only a few slopes.

Tentative ice-skaters take to the frozen Boston Common pond

FITNESS FACILITIES

Amenities at most of Boston's large hotels include fitness facilities. Those hotels that don't have facilities on-site usually have an arrangement whereby guests can use a private club in the immediate area. Otherwise, choose from the many other public gyms and health clubs found throughout the city. **Fitcorp** has excellent, modern exercise facilities at numerous city locations, while **Boston Athletic Club** in Downtown has both a well-equipped gym, and also a swimming pool, tennis, and squash courts. Across the river, **Cambridge Athletic Club** offers various racquet sports and a good gym.

DIRECTORY

WATER SPORTS

Community Boating
21 David G. Mugar Way.
Map 1 A3. **Tel** (617) 523-1038. www.community–boating.org

Charles River Canoe & Kayak Center
Soldiers Field Rd., Allston.
Tel (617) 965-5110.
www.ski-paddle.com

Boston Harbor Islands National Park Area
Tel (617) 223-8666.
www.boston islands.com

BICYCLING AND SKATING

Boston Bike Tours
Boston Common. **Map** 1 C4. **Tel** (617) 308-5902.
www.bostonbike tours.com

Back Bay Bicycles
362 Commonwealth Ave.
Map 3 A2.
Tel (617) 247-2336.
www.backbay bicycles.com

City Sports
44 Brattle St., Cambridge.
Tel (617) 492-6000.
www.citysports.com

Community Bicycle Supply
496 Tremont St. **Map** 4 D3.
Tel (617) 542-8623.
www.community bicycle.com

GOLF COURSES

Fresh Pond Golf Course
691 Huron Ave., Cambridge.
Tel (617) 349-6282.

William J. Devine Golf Course at Franklin Park
1 Circuit Drive, Dorchester.
Tel (617) 265-4084.

WINTER SPORTS

Beacon Hill Skate Shop
135 South Charles St.
Map 4 E2.
Tel (617) 482-7400.

Blue Hills Ski Area
Canton, MA 02021.
Tel (781) 828-5070.
www.thenewbluehills.com

Middlesex Fells Reservation
MDC, 4 Woodland Rd., Stoneham, MA 02180.
Tel (781) 662-2340.
www.mass.gov/dcr/parks

FITNESS FACILITIES

Boston Athletic Club
653 Summer St.
Tel (617) 269-4300.
www.bostonathletic club.com

Cambridge Athletic Club
215 First St., Cambridge.
Tel (617) 491-8989.
www.cambridge fitness.com

Fitcorp

1 Beacon St.
Map 1 C4.
Tel (617) 248-9797.

Prudential Center.
Map 3 B3.
Tel (617) 262-2050.

125 Summer St.
Map 2 D4.
Tel (617) 261-4855.

197 Clarendon St.
Map 3 C2.
Tel (617) 933-5090.
www.fitcorp.com

USEFUL ADDRESSES

Boston Parks and Recreation Department
1010 Massachusetts Ave.
Tel (617) 635-4505.
www.cityofboston. gov/parks

Department of Conservation and Recreation
251 Causeway St.
Tel (617) 626-1250.
www.mass.gov/dcr/parks

Spectator Sports

Bostonians watch sporting events with a passion that is unmatched in most other U.S. cities. Boston has had a team in every major professional league for many years, and some of popular sports' greatest athletes have played for home sides. Moreover, such widely known annual competitions as the Boston Marathon and the Head of the Charles Regatta draw amazingly large and enthusiastic crowds, as do the metropolitan area's many college teams, which have long traditions and avid fans.

BASEBALL

No matter whether they win or lose, the **Boston Red Sox** have an emotional following, especially when the New York Yankees come to town. The Red Sox beloved Fenway Park stadium is the oldest in the country, and is famous for its enormous 37-ft (11-m) left-field wall known as the "Green Monster." The small seating capacity, however, means that tickets can be difficult to obtain for the bigger games. Tickets are sold at the gate on the day of the game and are also available from the Fenway Park hotline. The "Bosox" are in the Eastern Division of the American League, one of the country's two major professional leagues. The baseball season runs from early April to the end of September, with championship games in October. In 2004, Boston ended a long drought to win the World Series in dramatic, come-from-behind fashion, and they won again in 2007.

Red Sox baseball player

BASKETBALL

Despite a fluctuating record, the **Boston Celtics** have been the most successful of all of Boston's major-league sports teams. They were the dominant team during the 1960s and 80s, winning 16 National Basketball Association (NBA) championships. Banners hung above their home court, the modern 19,000-seat TD

BankNorth Garden arena, pay testament to this record. Even when not playing to their full potential, the Celtics normally draw big crowds, hoping to see the team rekindle past glories. Tickets are usually available for most games, although they can be pricey – good seats cost at least $50. The season runs from October to April.

AMERICAN FOOTBALL

The home football team, the **New England Patriots** has dominated the sport, winning the Superbowl Championships in 2002, 2004, and 2005. They play against their National Football League (NFL) opponents in the new Gillette Stadium, about an hour's drive south of downtown Boston. Most NFL games are played during the fall on Sundays, or sometimes on Monday evenings to attract a national television audience. Tickets sell out a long way in advance, so the chances of picking one up are remote.

A Boston Bruin waiting for the pass at TD BankNorth Garden

ICE HOCKEY

Five Stanley Cup wins make the **Boston Bruins** one of the most successful teams in National Hockey League (NHL) history, although their recent form has been changeable. The hockey season runs from September to April, with the hard-charging "B's" playing in the NHL's Eastern Conference. End-of-season Stanley Cup Championship games are often sold out well in advance, but for other games, tickets are usually available for between $10 and $175. Games are played at TD BankNorth Garden.

OTHER SPORTS

Boston's major-league professional soccer team, the **New England Revolution**, plays all of its home games at Gillette Stadium after the New England Patriots have finished their season. The soccer season runs from April through to July, and the game is slowly gaining more widespread support, due partly to its increasing popularity as a college sport.

Suffolk Downs is the Boston area's only thoroughbred racetrack, where bets are taken on both live and simulcast races. The year's biggest attraction is the Massachusetts Handicap or "Mass 'Cap" race in July.

New England Revolution playing soccer against Miami Fusion

Greyhound racing takes place at **Wonderland Park** in north-suburban Revere. The track can be reached on the subway's Blue Line, and dog racing is held year-round.

Each August, many of the world's top-seeded players compete in the week-long U.S. Pro Tennis Championships at Brookline's **Longwood Cricket Club**. Despite the suggestive name, no cricket is actually played here.

Boats taking part in the Head of the Charles Regatta in October

Each year on Patriot's Day (a city holiday on the third Monday of April,) the largest event on the sports calendar takes place. The **Boston Marathon** has burgeoned since its inception in 1897, and now approximately 15,000 participants, including many top runners from all over the world, take on the challenge of the 26.2-mile (42.2-km) course. The marathon starts in the town of Hopkinton, west of Boston, and finishes Downtown at the Boston Public Library on Boylston Street. More than half a million people line the entire length of the course to cheer on the runners.

Detail from plaque celebrating the Boston Marathon

The other major event of the sporting year is the **Head of the Charles Regatta**. The world's largest two-day rowing competition is held annually during the third weekend of October on the Charles River. It involves more than 6,000 crew members, who represent clubs, universities, and colleges from around the world. The 3-mile (5 km) course runs upstream from Boston University boathouse to Eliot Bridge. With up to 80 boats in each race, crews set off at short intervals and are timed along the course.

This is a major social event, as well as a sports one, with as many as 300,000 spectators crowding both banks of the river, spread out on blankets and enjoying picnics and beer as they cheer on the rowers.

COLLEGE SPORTS

Boston's major colleges actively compete in a number of sports, with the major events occurring during the winter and fall. The annual Harvard–Yale football game takes place on the Saturday before Thanksgiving and is usually a fun and spirited event, both on and off the field. The sport that Boston colleges are best at, however, is ice hockey, and the biggest event on the calendar is the fiercely contested "Beanpot" hockey tournament. This is held at TD BankNorth Garden over two weekends in early February and involves most of the area's major colleges.

DIRECTORY

BASEBALL

Boston Red Sox
Fenway Park,
4 Yawkey Way.
Tel (617) 267-1700.
www.redsox.com

BASKETBALL

Boston Celtics
TD BankNorth Garden,
1 Causeway St. **Map** 1 C2.
Tel (617) 931-2222
(Ticketmaster).
www celtics.com

AMERICAN FOOTBALL

New England Patriots
Gillette Stadium, Route 1,
Foxboro.
Tel (617) 931-2222
(Ticketmaster).
www.ticketmaster.com
www.patriots.com

ICE HOCKEY

Boston Bruins
TD BankNorth Garden.
(see Boston Celtics).
www.boston
bruins.com

OTHER SPORTS

New England Revolution
Gillette Stadium. (see
New England Patriots).
www.revolutionsoccer.net

Suffolk Downs
Route 1a,
East Boston.
Tel (617) 567-3900.
www.trackinfo.com

Wonderland Park
Route 1a, Revere.
Tel (781) 284-1300.
www.trackinfo.com

Longwood Cricket Club
564 Hammond St.,
Chestnut Hill.
Tel (617) 731-2900.
www.longwood
cricket.com

Boston Marathon
Boston Athletic
Association,
40 Trinity Place
Map 3 C3.
Tel (617) 236-1652.
www.boston
marathon.org

Head of the Charles
www.hocr.org

CHILDREN'S BOSTON

Fun and games
for kids

First-time visitors to Boston may wonder what this city, famous for its history and learning, has to offer families with children. The answer is more than can possibly be explored in one visit, with an enormous variety of children's attractions and entertainment, as well as many helpful services and facilities. Whether you begin your adventure at Boston's acclaimed Children's Museum, head out to sea on a whale-watching expedition, take a specially designed children's walking tour of The Freedom Trail, or visit Franklin Park Zoo, families will soon discover that Boston's unique heritage has as much to interest children as it does adults. A good starting point is the Prudential Center Skywalk (see p98), a 360-degree observatory from where children can locate the city's major landmarks, parks, and attractions. For parents hoping to find some time on their own, a few attractions have supervised children's activities and entertainment, and there are also various baby-sitting agencies.

Boston's Duck Tours – from dry land to the Charles River

PRACTICAL ADVICE

A useful monthly publication, found free at many local children's attractions, is *The Boston Parent's Paper*. This has detailed listings of events, attractions, and activities for kids throughout the Boston region. Children's events are also listed in Thursday's edition of the *Boston Globe*. Short-term baby-sitting can be arranged through **Parents-in-a-Pinch. CVS Pharmacy** (see p117) is open until late for supplies. Boston is easy to explore on foot, but be cautious before crossing streets with children, as Boston's drivers can be very assertive. Boston's subway system (see pp182–3), is free for children under 12 with an adult.

TOURS AND HISTORICAL SIGHTS

There are many tours and historical sights in Boston which children will find both fun and interesting. They can board an amphibious World War II vehicle for a land and water tour of historic Boston with **Boston Duck Tours** (see p175). These drive past the city's historic neighborhoods and landmarks and then splash into the Charles River for a spectacular view of the Boston skyline. Boston's inner harbor and islands can be explored with **Boston Harbor Cruises**, whose cruises also stop at the *U.S.S. Constitution*, commonly known as "Old Ironsides" (see p115). Even more breathtaking are the whale-watching trips, run all through the summer by the New England Aquarium (see pp76–7).

Even if tickets to see the Red Sox games are sold out, baseball fans can still take the 40-minute tour of **Fenway Park** for a behind-the-scenes glimpse of the press box, private suites, and dugouts of this historic ballpark.

The experienced guides of **Boston by Foot** conduct special 60-minute family walking tours of the heart of The Freedom Trail (see pp124–7). History comes alive for children as they walk along the old cobblestone streets, and visit many sites of architectural and historical significance. Tours begin and end in front of the statue of Samuel Adams at Faneuil Hall. This is the gateway to **Quincy Market** (see p64), a lively emporium that sees flocks of tourists and locals alike, attracted by the enormous array of restaurants, shops, and entertainment. Children in particular will enjoy the jugglers, mime artists, musicians, and magicians who perform all around the attractive and traffic-free cobblestone marketplace.

Street entertainer, Quincy Market

MUSEUMS

Known as a pioneer of hands-on interactive learning, **Boston Children's Museum** (see p75) calls itself "Boston's Best Place for Kids," offering four floors of fun-filled education for toddlers to pre-teens in one building and three stories of exhibits in a new adjoining structure. Children can explore a 170-year-old house transplanted from Tokyo, create giant bubbles or conduct experiments in the Science Playground, and learn about healthy, active lifestyles in the new KidPower exhibition. Children aged under three have their own Playspace, a stimulating second-floor area designed especially for them. The **Museum of Science** (see p53) could be another full-day stop, housing over 550 permanent exhibits exploring astronomy, energy, industry, anthropology, and nature. Younger children will enjoy the Human Body Connection, while older kids can explore basic scientific principles in Investigate. All will be impressed by the life-sized Tyrannosaurus Rex and The Computing Revolution, which recreates milestones of computing from giants of the 1940s to the PDAs of today. Attached to the museum there is also a Planetarium and an Omni IMAX film theater.

Few art museums have made their collections so accessible to families as Boston's **Museum of Fine Arts** (see pp104–7). Art classes and workshops are offered for children and adults in several media, including drawing, painting, mixed media, sculpture, and weaving. Family Place is open weekends with art materials, games, and activities for children aged four and up accompanied by an adult. A visitor's guide is available for families. During February and

Playspace activity, Children's Museum

April school vacations, performances and art-making activities are organized throughout the galleries.

The unique history of Boston's African-American community is presented at two sites. The centerpiece of the **Museum of African American History** (see p49) is the oldest black church in the U.S., and the **Abiel Smith School** (see p49) was the first schoolhouse for black children in America. Recently renovated, the schoolhouse has interactive computer stations where children can learn about slavery, the American abolitionist movement, and the Underground Railroad (see p49), as well as more contemporary issues affecting African-Americans in New England. Older children may be interested in the **Black Heritage Trail** (see p49), a 1.5-mile (2.5-km) guided walking tour that visits 14 sites significant to the history of free African-Americans. The **Boston Tea Party Ships & Museum** (see p74), with models of the three brigantine ships involved in the infamous rebellion, may possibly reopen on Congress Street in 2009.

Sports enthusiasts will want to take a trip to the **Sports**

Hands-on exhibit at Boston's Museum of Science

Having fun, Boston Museum of Science

Museum of New England, where interactive exhibits, mini-presentations, and a vast collection of sports memorabilia chronicle the region's sporting history. Children will be fascinated by the life-size wooden statues of Larry Bird, Carl Yastrzemski, and Bobby Orr, and enthusiastically take the chance to try out a variety of sports equipment.

DIRECTORY

PRACTICAL ADVICE

Parents-in-a-Pinch
45 Bartlett Crescent, Brookline.
Tel (617) 739 5437.
Tel (800) 688-4697.
www.parentsinapinch.com

TOURS AND HISTORICAL SIGHTS

Boston by Foot
77 North Washington Street.
Map 2 D2.
Tel (617) 367-2345.
www.bostonbyfoot.com

Boston Harbor Cruises
Long Wharf. **Map** 2 E3.
Tel (617) 227-4321.
www.bostonharborcruises.com

Fenway Park
4 Yawkey Way.
Tel (617) 236-6666.

MUSEUMS

Sports Museum of New England
TD BankNorth Garden. **Map** 1 C2.
Tel (617) 624-1234.
www.sportsmuseum.org

Capybara, some of the many fascinating animals at Franklin Park Zoo

AQUARIUMS, ZOOS, AND PARKS

Visitors are greeted by a group of harbor seals at the entrance to the **New England Aquarium** *(see pp76–7)*, but once inside, all eyes are transfixed by the huge 200,000 gallon (900,000 liter) saltwater tank, which teems with tropical fish, sharks, sea turtles, and even the occasional scuba diver. The gently inclined wheelchair-friendly ramp winds up and around the three-story cylin-drical tank, giving a fascinating view of this simulated marine environment. Young children will also enjoy getting their hands wet in the huge indoor tide pool and watching the penguins and the harbor seals. Families can take a whale watching cruise or just watch a film on the enormous screen in the IMAX Theatre. Animal lovers will want to head directly to **Franklin**

Park Zoo *(see p102)*, with its collection of native and exotic fauna. Don't miss the African Tropical Forest, a re-created savanna with gorillas, monkeys, and pygmy hippos, the Children's Zoo, and Bird's World. For a wildlife trip in the middle of town, no visit to Boston is complete without a ride on the famous **Swan Boats** *(see p46)* in the Boston Public Garden. Immortalized in Robert McCloskey's 1941 children's classic, *Make Way for Ducklings (see p46)*, the pedal propelled boats gently circle a lovely pond as ducks clamor alongside for a snack. Nearby are large bronze sculptures of Mrs. Mallard and family. Crossing Charles Street, visitors will come to **Boston**

Bronze duck sculpture, Boston Public Garden

Common *(see pp46–7)*, which separates Downtown from Beacon Hill and Back Bay. There is a playground here, as well as Frog Pond, which is a huge wading pool in the summer and a skating rink in the winter. Boston's most attractive park, the highlight of the Emerald Necklace, is **Arnold Arboretum** *(see p102)*, in Jamaica Plain. With plenty of opportunity for exploration, it is a good place for children to let off steam.

CHILDREN'S THEATER

Children's theater thrives in Boston. The **Boston Children's Theater** celebrated its 50th season in 2000, with its acclaimed "live theater for children by children." Main-stage productions run from December through April, and its Stagemobile takes performances outside to Boston's parks in the summer. The **Wheelock Family Theater**, another highly acclaimed company, uses multi-ethnic and inter-genera-tional casting, with performances on most weekends from September to May. Fables and fairy tales come to life at the **Puppet Showplace Theatre**, with shows for pre-schoolers on Wednesday and Thursday, and performances for families on weekends from September to May.

Swan Boats on a relaxing cruise around the pond, Boston Public Garden

Marionettes on stage at the Puppet Showplace Theatre

CHILDREN'S SHOPPING

While keeping children entertained can often be a challenge, in Boston you will find that even shopping can hold their interests. With enticing window displays, and stores overflowing with desirable products, do not, however, expect to survive such an outing without spending any money. In Cambridge, **Susie's Gallery** has bright and innovative goods with a sense of whimsy, and **Henry Bear's Park** across the street is especially well-stocked with toys graded by age.

In Harvard Square, **Curious George Books & Toys** carries one of the country's most complete stocks of children's books, while **Calliope** has a menagerie of cuddly stuffed animals and hand puppets. **Newbury Comics** features the best selection of comic books in Boston. **Games People Play** stocks a huge assortment of toys and games. The latest in cool clothing can be found at **Gap**, and there's a wide selection of

outdoor gear at **Patagonia**. It is well worth the trip to Brookline Village for **The Children's Book Shop**, which has an excellent selection of books for infants to young-adults, and to Jamaica Plain for the bubbly **Boing – JP's Toyshop**. Kids will also enjoy the shops, stalls, and street vendors at **Quincy Market** *(see p64)*.

EATING OUT WITH CHILDREN

Though children never seem to tire of fast food, adults generally long for something more substantial and memorable. Both needs can be catered for in many of Boston's restaurants. Children will enjoy sampling Chinese delicacies at **China Pearl** in Chinatown. For pizza in an authentic Italian atmosphere, try the North End's **Pizzeria Regina**. In Cambridge, **The Cheesecake Factory** has an incredibly vast menu of casual fare as well as its eponymous sweets and is sure to please every family member. In the Huron Avenue shopping district in Cambridge, the friendly restaurant **Full Moon** has a play area as well as a varied kid's menu.

Popcorn, a favorite snack

DIRECTORY

CHILDREN'S THEATER

Boston Children's Theater
321 Columbus Ave.
Map 3 C3. **Tel** *(617) 424-6634*. **www**.boston
childrenstheater.org

Puppet Showplace Theatre
32–33 Station St.,
Brookline. **Tel** *(617) 731-6400*. **www**.
puppetshowplace.org

Wheelock Family Theater
200 The Riverway, Brook-line. **Tel** *(617) 879-2000*.
www.wheelock.edu/wft

CHILDREN'S SHOPPING

Boing – JP's Toy Shop
729 Centre St.,
Jamaica Plain.
Tel *(617) 522-7800*.

Calliope
33 Brattle St., Cambridge.
Tel *(617) 876-4149*.

The Children's Book Shop
237 Washington St.,
Brookline.
Tel *(617) 734-7323*.

Curious George Books & Toys
1 JFK St., Cambridge.
Tel *(617) 498-0062*.

Games People Play
1100 Massachusetts Ave.,
Cambridge.
Tel *(617) 492-0711*.

Gap
625 Massachusetts Ave.,
Cambridge.
Tel *(617) 864-7111*.

Henry Bear's Park
361 Huron Ave.,
Cambridge.
Tel *(617) 547-8424*.

Newbury Comics
332 Newbury St. **Map** 3
A3. **Tel** *(617) 236-4930*.

Patagonia
346 Newbury St. **Map**
3 A3. **Tel** *(617) 424-1776*.

Susie's Gallery for Children
348 Huron Ave., Cambridge.
Tel *(617) 876-7874*.

EATING OUT WITH CHILDREN

The Cheesecake Factory
100 Cambridgeside Place,
Cambridge.
Tel *(617) 252-3810*.

China Pearl
9 Tyler St.
Map 4 F2.
Tel *(617) 426-4338*.

Full Moon
344 Huron Ave.,
Cambridge.
Tel *(617) 354-6699*.

Pizzeria Regina
11½ Thacher St.
Map 2 D2.
Tel *(617) 227-0765*.

SURVIVAL
GUIDE

PRACTICAL INFORMATION

More than most American cities, Boston is built to human scale. With the main parts of the city all within a relatively small area, Boston is ideal for the visitor, with walking not only possible, but often preferable, despite a modern and efficient transit system. Boston is also one of the safest cities in the U.S., and one of the most friendly, making it

Trolley bus logo

very easy to feel at home here. So long as visitors take a few sensible precautions, they should enjoy a trouble-free stay. Boston's excellent visitor information centers help people get the most from their stay, and the city also deals better than most with the needs of children and the disabled. Other useful services in the city include many banks and foreign exchanges.

FOREIGN VISITORS

The conditions for entering Boston are the same as for entering the rest of the country. Citizens of the U.K., most western European countries, Australia, New Zealand, Japan, Canada, Mexico, and Caribbean nations (except Cuba) need a valid machine-readable passport but do not require a visa if their stay is less than 90 days and they have a return ticket. Citizens of all other countries need a valid passport and a tourist visa, which can be obtained from a U.S. consulate or embassy.

Discount tickets

VISITOR INFORMATION

Visitor information desks at the airport can provide guides and maps, answer questions, and make hotel reservations. The **Greater Boston Convention and Visitors Bureau** offers a more comprehensive service, and

can help with arrangements before you travel. Major hotels also have helpful guest service desks. All of these places also hold a range of discount tickets offering savings at many of Boston's major museums and attractions, night-life spots, theaters and restaurants.

OPENING HOURS

For the most part Boston's stores keep a 10am to 6pm schedule from Monday to Friday. Most stores also open at weekends, although those open on Sundays often open later. Some gas stations and convenience stores stay open 24 hours. July 4, Thanksgiving, Christmas Day, and New Year's Day are the only retail holidays observed.

ETIQUETTE

Smoking is prohibited in many buildings, all stores, bars, and restaurants in the Boston area. Check for no-smoking signs before lighting

up, or else smoke outside if you are not sure. Tipping is expected for most services: in restaurants tip 15–20 percent of the bill, give $1 per bag to porters, and $2 to valet parking attendants. Bartenders expect 50 cents to $1 per drink.

TAX

In Boston and the surrounding area be aware that taxes will be added to hotel and restaurant charges and most retail purchases, except all clothing items and groceries priced under $175. State sales tax is 5 percent, and hotel tax in the Boston metropolitan area is 12.45 percent.

ALCOHOL AND CIGARETTES

The legal age for drinking alcohol in Boston is 21, and most young people will be required to show photo identification (I.D.) as proof of age in order to get into bars and to purchase alcohol. It is illegal to drink in public spaces, and penalties for driving under the influence of alcohol are severe. The legal age for buying cigarettes is 18, and I.D. may also be required. It is illegal to smoke in public buildings and in all bars and restaurants *(see p139)*.

ELECTRICITY

Electricity flows at 110–120 volts, and a two-prong plug is used. Non-U.S. appliances will need a plug adaptor and a voltage converter. Most hotel rooms, however, have hairdriers as well as dedicated sockets for electric shavers.

Visitor Information Center on Boston Common

◁ Charles River Back Bay

STUDENTS

Students from abroad should purchase an International Student Identification Card (I.S.I.C.) before traveling to Boston, as there are many discounts available to students in the city. The I.S.I.C. handbook lists many places and services offering discounts to card holders, including hotels, hostels, museums, and theaters. The **Student Advantage Card** is a similar card available to all American undergraduates.

International Student Identity Card, recognized student I.D. in America.

CHILDREN

Boston is a reasonably child-friendly city, boasting its own **Children's Museum** *(see p75)*, as well as other museums and attractions that offer interesting hands-on exhibits and activities for children *(see pp168–71)*.

Families with children will find that the casual and fast-food restaurants cater best to their needs, with menus often tailored to children's tastes and appetites. Well-behaved children are welcome at most of Boston's restaurants, however.

SENIOR CITIZENS

Anyone over the age of 65 is eligible for various discounts with proof of age. Contact the **American Association of Retired Persons** for further information. Also, try the international senior travel organization **Elderhostel**, which has programs in Boston.

DISABLED VISITORS

Massachusetts and U.S. law mandate accessibility for persons with handicaps, but wheelchair accessibility is sometimes limited in Boston's historic buildings. Most hotels and restaurants, however, are wheelchair accessible. **Very Special Arts – Massachusetts** provides useful information on disabled-accessible entertainment. For other information contact the **Society for Accessible Travel and Hospitality**.

Disabled sign

Trolley bus outside Trinity Church, Back Bay

GUIDED TOURS

Many city tours depart from the Visitor Information Center on Boston Common, including **Old Town Trolley Tours**, which offers narrated sightseeing tours in an old-fashioned trolley bus, as well as theme tours, such as ghosts or chocolate. For something a bit different try the **Boston Duck Tours**, which use an open-air amphibious vehicle that tours the streets and navigates the Charles River. Also, **National Park Service** rangers offer free walking tours of Boston's parks, the Freedom Trail *(see pp124–7)*, and the Black Heritage Trail *(see p49)*.

DIRECTORY

VISITOR INFORMATION

Greater Boston Convention and Visitors Bureau
2 Copley Place, Suite 105.
Tel (617) 536-4100.
Tel (888) 733-2678.
www.bostonusa.com
Booths at: Boston Common, **Map** 1 C4;
Prudential Center,
Map 3 B3.

Cambridge Office for Tourism
4 Brattle St., Cambridge.
Tel (617) 441-2884 or (617) 497-1630.
Tel (800) 862-5678.
www.cambridge-usa.org
Booth at Harvard Sq.

STUDENTS

Student Advantage
280 Summer St.
Tel (617) 912-2011.
Tel (800) 333-2920.
www.student advantage.com

SENIOR CITIZENS

American Association of Retired Persons (A.A.R.P.)
601 E St. NW,
Washington, DC 20049.
Tel (888) 687-2277.
www.aarp.org

Elderhostel
11 Ave. de Lafayette.
Map 2 D4.
Tel (877) 426 8056.
www.elderhostel.org

DISABLED VISITORS

Society for Accessible Travel and Hospitality
347 Fifth Ave., Suite 605,
New York, NY 10016.
Tel (212) 447-7284.
www.sath.org

Very Special Arts – Massachusetts
2 Boylston St. **Map** 4 E2.
Tel (617) 350-7713.
www.vsamass.org

GUIDED TOURS

Old Town Trolley Tours
Boston Common Visitors' Center. **Map** 1 C4.
Tel (617) 269-7010.
www.trolleytours.com

Boston Duck Tours
Prudential Center.
Map 3 B3.
Tel (617) 267-3825.
www.ducktours.com

National Park Service
15 State St.
Map 2 D3.
Tel (617) 242-5642.
www.nps.gov/bost

USEFUL WEBSITES

Boston CitySearch
www.boston.city search.com

Boston Globe Online
www.boston.com

Personal Security and Health

Hospital sign

Boston's crime rate started to drop in the early 1990s, and the trend has continued ever since. This has made its police force and community relations programs models for other American cities. Nonetheless, it is still prudent to take a few simple precautions and to keep to the tourist areas. The main sights are all located in safe parts of the city with lots of people and where major crime is rare. If you are unfortunate enough to be taken ill during your visit, healthcare in Boston is world class. This does not come cheaply, however, and it is essential to have adequate insurance coverage before you travel.

LAW ENFORCEMENT

The most visible uniformed law enforcement personnel in Boston are the National Park Service or Boston Park Service rangers (usually dressed in olive green or khaki) and the members of the Boston Police Department (BPD), dressed in blue. You will also see City Parking and Traffic officers, who deal exclusively with traffic violations.

Should you encounter any trouble as a visitor, approach any of the blue-uniformed BPD officers who regularly patrol the city streets. Park rangers are often useful sources of information.

GUIDELINES ON SAFETY

Serious crime is rarely witnessed in the main sightseeing areas of Boston. However, avoid wandering into areas that are off the beaten track, during the day or at night. Pickpockets operate in the city and

will target anyone who looks like a tourist. Police officers regularly patrol the tourist areas, but it is still advisable to use common sense, and to stay alert. Try not to advertise the fact that you are a visitor; prepare the day's itinerary in advance, and study your map before you set off. Avoid wearing expensive jewelry, and carry your camera or camcorder securely. Only carry small amounts of cash; credit cards and traveler's checks are a more secure option. Keep these close to your body in a money belt or inside pocket.

Before you leave home, take a photocopy of important documents, including your passport and visa, and keep them with you, separate from the originals. Also make a note of your credit card numbers, in the event of their being stolen. Keep an eye on

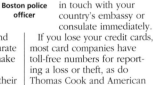

Boston police officer

your belongings at all times, whether checking into or out of the hotel, standing in the airport, or sitting in a bar or restaurant. Keep any valuables in your hotel safe, as most hotels will not guarantee their security if they are left in your room. Also be careful not to tell strangers where you are staying or to let anyone you do not know into your room.

LOST PROPERTY

Although the chances of retrieving lost property are slim, you should report all stolen items to the police. Use the **Police Non-Emergency Line**. Make sure you keep a copy of the police report, which you will need for your insurance claim. In case of loss, it is useful to have a list of your valuables' serial numbers or a photocopy of any relevant documents or receipts as proof of possession. This should be kept separately. It is also useful to try and remember the taxi companies or bus routes you use, as it might make it easier to retrieve lost items. If your passport is lost or stolen, get in touch with your country's embassy or consulate immediately.

If you lose your credit cards, most card companies have toll-free numbers for reporting a loss or theft, as do Thomas Cook and American Express for lost traveler's checks *(see p178)*.

TRAVEL INSURANCE

Travel insurance is not compulsory but strongly recommended when traveling to the United States. It is particularly important to have insurance for emergency medical and dental care, which can be very expensive in the U.S. Even with medical coverage you may have to pay for the services, then claim reimbursement from your insurance company. If you take medication, bring a

Mounted Boston Park Service ranger, Copley Square

Police car

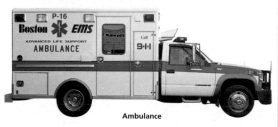

Ambulance

back-up prescription with you. In addition, it is advisable to make sure your personal property is insured and to obtain coverage for lost or stolen baggage and travel documents, as well as trip cancellation fees, legal advice, and accidental death or injury.

EMERGENCIES

If you are involved in a medical emergency, go to a hospital emergency room. Should you need an ambulance, call 911 (toll-free) and one will be sent. Also call 911 for police or fire department assistance.

If you have your medical insurance properly arranged, you need not worry about medical costs. Depending on the limitations of your insurance, it is better to avoid the overcrowded city-owned hospitals listed in the phone book Blue Pages, and opt instead for one of the private hospitals listed in the Yellow Pages. Alternatively ask at your hotel desk or at the nearest pharmacy for information. You can also ask your hotel to call a doctor or dentist to visit you in your room.

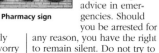

Pharmacy sign

PHARMACIES

If you need a prescription dispensed, there are plenty of pharmacies (drugstores) in and around the city, some staying open 24 hours. Ask your hotel for the nearest one.

LEGAL ASSISTANCE

Non-U.S. citizens requiring legal assistance should telephone their consulate if there is an office in Boston, or their embassy in Washington, DC. These offices will not lend you money but can help with legal advice in emergencies. Should you be arrested for any reason, you have the right to remain silent. Do not try to bribe the police, as this could land you in further trouble.

PUBLIC RESTROOMS

All visitors' centers, museums, and galleries have public restrooms, and invariably offer disabled and baby-changing facilities as well. All restaurants and hotels also have restrooms, but these may be available only to paying customers.

Fire engine

DIRECTORY

LOST PROPERTY

Police Non-Emergency Line
Tel Boston (617) 343-4200.
Tel Cambridge (617) 349-3300.

EMERGENCIES

Police, Fire, Medical (all emergencies)
Tel Call 911 (toll-free), or dial 0 for the operator.

Dental Referrals
Tel (800) 342-8747.
www.massdental.org

Medical Referrals
Tel (781) 893-4610
Tel (800) 322-2303.

Area Hospitals
Tel Call 411 for directory assistance.

PHARMACIES

CVS Pharmacy
155 Charles St., Boston.
Map 1 B3. (Pharmacy open 8am–8pm daily. Store open 24 hours.)
Tel (617) 523-1028.

35 White St., Cambridge.
(Pharmacy open 24 hours.)
Tel (617) 876-5519.

CONSULATES

Australia
150 East 42nd St., 34th floor, New York, NY 10017.
Tel (212) 351-6500.
www.australianyc.org

Canada
3 Copley Place. **Map** 3 C3.
Tel (617) 262-3760.
www.boston.gc.ca

Ireland
535 Boylston St. **Map** 3 C2.
Tel (617) 267-9330.
www.irelandemb.org

New Zealand
37 Observatory Circle, NW Washington, DC 20008.
Tel (202) 328-4800.
www.nzembassy.com

United Kingdom
1 Memorial Drive, Cambridge.
Tel (617) 245-4500.
www.britainusa.com

Banking and Currency

Throughout Boston there are various places to access and exchange your money, from the numerous banks and automatic teller machines (cash machines) to the foreign currency exchanges. The most important things to remember are not to carry all your money and credit cards with you at one time, and to be aware that most banks and currency exchanges are closed on Sundays.

One of Bank Of America's many branches in Boston

BANKING AND ATMS

Generally, most banks are open Monday through Friday from 9am to 2 or 3pm, although some may open earlier and close later. Most banks also open Saturday mornings from 9am to noon or 1pm. All banks are closed on Sundays and Federal holidays *(see p37)*.

Always ask if there are any special fees before you make your transaction. At most banks, traveler's checks in U.S. dollars can be cashed with any photo identification, although passports are usually required if you want to exchange any foreign money. Foreign currency exchange is available at the main branches of large banks, which often have a separate dedicated area or teller window for foreign exchange.

Automated Teller Machines (ATMs) are found throughout Boston. They can usually be found near the entrance to banks, and sometimes inside some convenience stores and supermarkets. Widely accepted types of bank cards include Cirrus, Plus, NYCE, and some credit cards such as VISA or MasterCard. Note that a fee may be levied on your cash withdrawal depending on the bank. Check with your bank before you travel which machines your card can access and the various fees charged. To minimize the risk of robbery, avoid using ATMs in isolated areas, and be aware of the people around you. ATM crime can include someone looking over your shoulder to gain access to your personal identification number (PIN) and then stealing your card from you.

CREDIT CARDS

American Express charge cards

American Express, VISA, MasterCard, Diner's Club, and the Discover Card are accepted almost everywhere in Boston, from theaters and hotels to restaurants and shops. Besides being a much safer alternative to carrying a lot of cash, credit cards also offer some useful additional benefits, such as insurance on your purchases. They are also essential if you want to reserve a hotel or book a rental car. Credit cards can also be useful in emergencies when cash may not be readily available.

CURRENCY EXCHANGE

Foreign currency exchanges are generally open weekdays from 9am to 5pm, but some, especially those in shopping districts, may have extended opening hours.

Among the best known are the American Express Travel Service and Travelex Currency Services, both of which have branches in and around Boston. Major banks also offer exchange services. Most currency exchanges charge a fee or commission, so it is worth looking around to get the best value rates. Hotels may also exchange money, but their fees will be much higher.

TRAVELER'S CHECKS

Traveler's checks in U.S. dollars issued by American Express and Thomas Cook are accepted as payment without a fee by most shops, restaurants, and hotels. It is often simpler to pay by U.S. dollar travelers' checks, where possible, rather than cashing them in advance. Traveler's checks in foreign currencies can be cashed at a bank or with a cashier at a major hotel. Exchange rates are posted wherever currency exchange is offered, along with the commission charges. Check these before you exchange your money – it may be prudent to shop around for the best deal as commission rates can vary.

Personal checks issued by foreign banks are rarely accepted in the United States, so cannot be relied upon as a means of obtaining cash.

Communications and Media

Phone card

Boston's communications infrastructure is modern and well developed. Coin or card operated public payphones are easy to find on many streets and in restaurants, theaters, bars, department stores, hotel lobbies, and gas stations.

News is readily available from Boston's many television and radio stations, newspapers, and magazines, and the postal service is quick and efficient – whether you are sending mail within the United States or abroad.

TELEVISION AND RADIO

The Boston media market is highly competitive, and saturated with television and radio broadcasters. Major network television stations include CBS (channel 4), ABC (channel 5), NBC (channel 7), and Fox (channel 25). Public television station PBS is on Channel 2. Popular radio stations include NPR (National Public Radio) on WBUR (90.9 FM), WFNX (101.7 FM) for rock music, WCRB (99.5 FM) for classical music, and WMJX (106.7 FM) for easy listening.

TELEPHONES

Public telephones are found on some street corners or in stores in the Boston area. Most accept coins as well as phone cards, which can be purchased at gas stations, convenience stores, and newsstands. Credit card calls can also be made by calling 1-800-225-5288. Local calls cost 50 cents for three minutes from payphones, while long-distance call rates vary, and include both a fixed

call charge and a per-minute charge. All numbers with a **1-800, 866, 877,** or **888** prefix, however, are free of charge. Direct calls can also be made from hotel rooms but usually carry hefty surcharges. Unless you are using your own international telephone card, it is better to use the payphone in the lobby.

Directory assistance is available by dialing 411 (local) or 00 (international.) **Operator assistance** is available by dialing 0 (local) or 01 (international.) All operator assisted calls carry a surcharge. For **emergency services** (fire, police, or ambulance) call 911

AREA CODES

The area code for central Boston is **617** or **857**, which must be included when dialing local calls. If dialing out of the local area (but within the U.S. or Canada) dial **1**, then the area code.

For international calls dial **011**, followed by the appropriate country code, the area code (omitting the first 0), and then the local number.

POSTAL SERVICE

Post offices are open from 9am to 5pm, Monday through Friday, and most are open Saturday from 9am to noon. They close on Sundays and for all Federal holidays.

If the correct postage is attached, letters and parcels of less than 16 oz (450 g) can be put in any blue mailbox. Pickup times are written inside the lid. Always use a zip code to insure delivery, and send all overseas mail by airmail to avoid long delays.

NEWSPAPERS

The most widely read newspaper in the Boston area is the *Boston Globe*, which is also thought of as one of the best newspapers produced in the United States. The other local daily widely available around the city is the *Boston Herald* tabloid. Other U.S. newspapers, found at most newsstands, are *USA Today*, the *New York Times* and *The Wall Street Journal*. Thursday's edition of the *Boston Globe*, and the *Boston Phoenix (see p148)*, published on Friday, contain exhaustive listings of entertainment and cultural events in Boston.

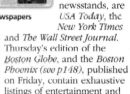

Boston newspapers

DIRECTORY

POST OFFICES

Beacon Hill
136 Charles St.
Map 1 B3.

West End
25 New Chardon St.
Map 1 C3.

Financial District
90 Devonshire St.
Map 2 D4.

Back Bay
390 Stuart St.
Map 3 C3.

Cambridge
125 Mt. Auburn St.,
Cambridge.

North End
422 Hanover St.
Map 2 E2.

Boston post office, Charles Street

GETTING TO BOSTON

United Airlines plane

Arriving in Boston is relatively easy. It is served by Logan International Airport as well as by the smaller satellites, Manchester and T.F. Green Airports, which are both located within 50 miles (80 km) of the city center. Greyhound Bus Lines, Peter Pan Trailways, and Amtrak trains come into Boston's South Station. From here the subway, known as the "T," connects to almost every part of the city. Boston also makes an ideal base from which to take day or weekend trips to the numerous places of interest throughout the New England area.

Control Tower at Boston's Logan International Airport

ARRIVING BY AIR

Situated in East Boston, **Logan International Airport** is the major airport serving Boston, although some international charter flights and several domestic carriers use the less crowded **Manchester New Hampshire Airport** and **T.F. Green Airport** in Warwick, Rhode Island. Both are a bus ride of around an hour from Boston. Boston is served directly by almost all North American airlines and by most international airlines, either directly or in partnership with U.S. carriers. Often the least expensive flights, especially between continental Europe and Boston, require making connections in New York. Frequent direct service is available between Boston and the United Kingdom and Ireland on U.S. carriers as well as British Airways

and Aer Lingus. Logan lies within Boston city limits on an island across the inner harbor from the central city. Harbor tunnel crossings tend to act as a bottleneck, which slows taxi services between the airport and downtown. At busy times, a taxi ride ($20–$30) can take 30 minutes or more, with much of the trip spent in bumper-to-bumper traffic. The least expensive means

Bus from South Station to Logan

($2) of getting from the airport to downtown is via the M.B.T.A. subway (see p172). Free buses connect the airport's air terminals to its subway terminal. There is also a bus service that runs between the airport and Boston's South Station. Arguably the most scenic approach into Boston is the **City Water Taxi** ($10), with stops at Logan Airport, Central and Long wharves.

AIR FARES

For cheap air fares, check with the various airlines and travel agents. The more you shop around, the better deal you will get, and it is worth taking the time to do some research, or to trust a reliable agent to do it for you. For inexpensive consolidated tickets, contact **Expedia.com** online or give **Airline Consolidator. com** a try. Finding the best published fare available at any time can be accomplished online through **Cheap-tickets.com.**

High season runs from June to August as well as around Easter and Christmas, when flights are most expensive. May, September, and October are less expensive, and any other time of the year is considered off-peak. Flights are usually least expensive for travel from Tuesday to Thursday. APEX tickets, usually the best deal, must be booked a few weeks in advance. These tickets however must include a Saturday night.

City Water Taxi, which runs from Logan Airport to Central and Long wharves

PACKAGE DEALS

Boston packages are sometimes available in the U.S. as part of a fall foliage bus tour or through AAA (American Automobile Association). Several airlines arrange packages including travel and lodging. Boston hotels generally post their special event packages on the web site of the **Greater Boston Convention and Visitors Bureau** *(see p175).*

ARRIVING BY TRAIN

A train service between New York and Boston via coastal Connecticut and Rhode Island is provided by **Amtrak**. Conventional train services take 4–5 hours, and arrive and depart from Boston's South Station. A high-speed service which takes 3 hours is now also available but is somewhat more expensive.

In November 2001 a new Amtrak train service between Boston and Portland, Maine was inaugurated. During the summer months, there is a useful stop at Old Orchard Beach in Maine.

ARRIVING BY CAR

Boston is not called "The Hub" for nothing, as most routes in the Northeast converge here. Principal routes from the north are I-95 from the coast and I-93 from northern New England. I-90 comes

Amtrak train waiting to depart from Boston's South Station

in from the west as the Massachusetts Turnpike. I-93 approaches from the south as the Southeast Expressway. I-95, formerly known as Rte 128, circumvents Boston. Highway approaches to the city are markedly improved since the interstate I-93 was moved and re-laid to pass under the city. Exits from the roadway to parts of downtown come up quickly, so check your exit number in advance.

Greyhound Lines

TICKETS

Greyhound Bus Lines logo

ARRIVING BY BUS

Although taking a bus is easily the slowest and usually cheapest way to get to Boston, it need not be unpleasant. **Greyhound Bus Lines** and **Peter Pan Trailways** both serve Boston as long-distance carriers, sharing quarters at the South Station bus terminal. Both offer routes around the country and provide discounts for children, senior citizens, and U.S. military personnel on active duty. Both also offer bargain excursion tickets for unlimited travel within a certain time period for a single fixed rate.

Main concourse of Boston's South Station

DIRECTORY

AIRPORTS

Logan International Airport
East Boston, Massachusetts.
Tel (617) 561-1800.
Tel (800) 23-LOGAN.
www.massport.com/logan

Manchester New Hampshire Airport
Tel (603) 624-6556.
www.flynewhampshire.com

T.F. Green Airport
Warwick, Rhode Island.
Tel (401) 737-8222.
www.pvdairport.com

AIR FARES

AirlineConsolidator.com
Tel (888) 468-5385.
www.airline
consolidator.com

Cheaptickets.com
Tel (312) 260-8100.
www.cheaptickets.com

Expedia.com
13810 SE Eastgate Way,
Suite Bellevue, WA 98005.
Tel (800) 397-3342.
www.expedia.com

PUBLIC TRANSPORTATION

Amtrak
South Station.
Map 2 D5.
Tel (800) 872-7245.
www.amtrak.com

City Water Taxi
Tel (617) 422-0392.
www.citywatertaxi.com

Greyhound Bus Lines
700 Atlantic Ave.
Map 2 D5.
Tel (617) 526-1800.
Tel (800) 231-2222.
www.greyhound.com

Peter Pan Trailways
700 Atlantic Ave.
Map 2 D5.
Tel (800) 343-9999.
www.peterpanbus.com

Getting Around Boston

Public transportation in Boston and Cambridge is very good. In fact it is considerably easier to get around by public transportation than by driving, with the added benefit of not having to find a parking space. All major attractions in the city are accessible on the subway, by bus, or by taxi. The central sections of the city are also extremely easy to navigate on foot.

M.B.T.A. commuter bus, with distinctive yellow paintwork

FINDING YOUR WAY IN BOSTON

The more planning you do before your trip, the easier it will be to locate sights and find your way around the city. The **Greater Boston Convention and Visitors Bureau** *(see p175)* will be a helpful contact point, and your hotel is also likely to be able to offer advice. To find out about any upcoming cultural events, check websites for **Boston CitySearch** and the **Boston Globe** *(see p175)*.

Most of Boston is laid out "organically" rather than in the sort of strict grid found in most American cities. When trying to orient yourself, it helps to think of Boston as enclaves – of neighborhoods around a few central squares. In general, uphill from Boston Common is Beacon Hill, downhill is Downtown. Back Bay begins west of Arlington Street. The North End sticks out from the north side of Boston, while the Waterfront is literally that, where Boston meets the sea.

M.B.T.A. SUBWAY AND TROLLEY BUSES

Boston's subway system is the oldest in North America, but has been vastly expanded and modernized since the first cars rolled between Park Street and Boylston Street

Visitor's Passport, valid on all M.B.T.A. services

on September 1, 1897. The street trolley system began in 1846 with trolleys drawn along tracks by horses. The system was electrified in 1889. The combined subway and trolley lines are generally known as the "T." The "T" operates Monday to Saturday, 5am to 12:45am, and Sunday 6am to 12:45am. Weekday service is officially every three to 15 minutes; though on weekends it is less frequent. There are five lines: the Red Line runs from south of the city to Cambridge and the Green Line runs from the Museum of Science westward into the suburbs. The Blue Line begins near Government Center and goes to Logan Airport and on to Revere while the Orange Line connects the northern suburbs to southwest Boston. The Silver line, a surface bus, runs from Roxbury to Logan Airport, via South Station. Maps of the system are available at the Downtown Crossing M.B.T.A. station.

Admission to subway stations is via turnstiles into which you insert a paper "Charlie" ticket ($2) or plastic "Charlie" card ($1.70). Day or week Link passes ($9/$15) for unlimited travel can be purchased at Downtown Crossing, South Station, Back Bay, Government Center, North Station, and Airport "T" stops.

M.B.T.A. BUSES

The bus system complements the subway system and in effect enlarges the entire transit network to cover more than 1,000 miles (1,600 km). However, buses are often crowded and schedules can be hard to obtain. Two useful routes for sightseeing are Charlestown-Haymarket, (from Haymarket, near Quincy Market, to Bunker Hill) and Harvard-Dudley (from Harvard Square via Massachusetts Avenue, through Back Bay and the South End, to Dudley Square in Roxbury.) Cash or a paper "Charlie" ticket ($1.50) or plastic "Charlie" card ($1.25) is required for the fare.

TAXIS

Finding a taxi in Boston and Cambridge is rarely difficult. They can be found at taxi stands in tourist areas and can be hailed on the street. Taxis may only pick up fares in the city for which they are licensed – Cambridge taxis only in Cambridge, Boston taxis only in Boston. If you need to be somewhere on time, call a taxi company and arrange a definite pickup time and place.

Rates are calculated by both mileage and time, beginning with a $2.25 "pick-up" fee when the meter starts running. In general, the taxis in Boston and Cambridge are more

Boston taxis waiting for fares at one of the city's many taxi stands

expensive than those in other U.S. cities. Taxis to Logan Airport are required to charge customers an airport use fee ($2.25), while those coming from the airport charge for the harbor tunnel toll ($6). Additional surcharges may apply late at night. A full schedule of fares should be posted inside the vehicle.

The driver's photograph and permit and the taxi's permit number will also be posted inside all legitimate taxicabs, along with directions for reporting complaints.

Boston parkland, ideal for walking

WALKING IN BOSTON

Boston is considered North America's premier walking city, partly because it is so compact, and partly because virtually all streets are flanked by sidewalks. It is nonetheless essential to wear comfortable walking shoes with adequate cushioning and good support.

Because Boston is principally a city of neighborhoods, it is often simplest to use public transportation to get to a particular neighborhood, and then to walk to soak up the atmosphere. Walking also allows you to see parts of the city that are impractical to explore by car as the streets are too narrow; for example Beacon Hill, parts of the North End, and Harvard Square.

DIRECTORY

M.B.T.A.

M.B.T.A.
(Route and schedule information)
10 Park Plaza.
Tel (617) 222-3200.
www.mbta.com

TAXIS

Boston Cab Dispatch, Inc.
Tel (617) 262-2227.

Checker Cab Co of Cambridge
Tel (617) 497-9000.

Town Taxi
Tel (617) 536-5000.

Yellow Cab
(Cambridge).
Tel (617) 547-3000.

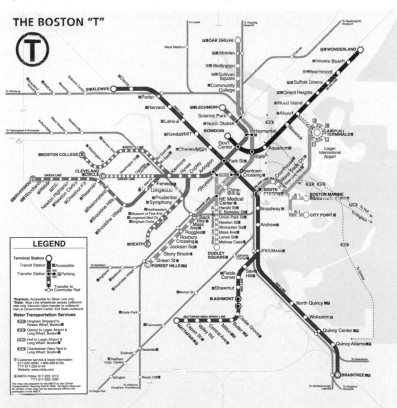

Driving in and Around Boston

Despite heavy traffic and restricted parking, having your own vehicle in Boston can, at times, be an undeniable convenience. For example, visiting some of the outlying sights of Boston, which may be difficult to reach by public transportation, is much easier with a car. Many U.S. visitors to the city arrive with their own cars, and overseas visitors can rent one quite easily. Even so, driving in and around Boston requires patience, good humor, good maps, good driving skills, and the ability to read the road swiftly and take decisive actions.

Boston traffic by night – with the Financial District in the background

DRIVING AND PARKING IN THE CITY

Despite Boston's comparatively small size, its traffic can at times rival a much larger "world city" such as Rome or Hong Kong. Like those cities, Boston has far too many vehicles for its roads, and the city's many one-way streets can prove confusing to everyone except the locals, who will honk at befuddled visitors. Although the work to move the 1-93 under the city is now complete, expect detours as construction continues in the Waterfront area. Use the Street Finder *(see pp188–91)* or other good map (the best show the direction of one-way streets) to help you get around. Also avoid the rush hours of 8–9:30am and 4–6pm and plan your route in advance so you can concentrate on traffic.

Curbside parking is hard to find at the most popular locations, and during morning

"Tow Zone" sign

and afternoon rush hours curbside parking is banned in some areas. If you do manage to find a space on the street, be sure to feed the meter, or you might face a hefty fine. Vehicles parked near fire hydrants, alleyways, in spaces reserved for the handicapped, or at overland "T" and bus stops may be towed away, and can be retrieved only at considerable cost and inconvenience. Parking at meters is free on Sundays and public holidays, and many downtown areas allow parking in loading zones on Sunday as well. Read posted signs carefully. Parking in a public lot or garage can cost more than $10 per hour or $40 per day, but is sometimes the only choice. Valet parking is available at some restaurants, hotels, and malls for a fee. Visitors may consider parking near a "T" or bus stop in the city's suburbs, and continuing their journey into town by public transportation.

RULES OF THE ROAD

The highway speed limit in the Boston area is 55 mph (88 km/h) – much lower than in many European countries. In residential areas the speed limit ranges from 20–35 mph (32–48 km/h). Near schools it can be as low as 15 mph (24 km/h). It is important to obey all signs or you will risk getting a ticket. If you are stopped by the police, be courteous or you may face a larger fine. In addition, all drivers are required to carry a valid driver's license and registration documents for their vehicle.

CAR RENTAL

You must be at least 21 years old with a valid driving license (plus an international driver's license if from outside the U.S.) to rent a car. Drivers under 25 may be charged additional fees. All rental agencies require a credit card or a cash deposit. Collision and liability insurances are recommended, but are sometimes offered free with credit cards. Return the car with a full tank of gas to avoid inflated agency fuel prices. Save paying airport fees by picking up and dropping off your car Downtown.

GAS

Compared to prices world wide, gas (petrol) is less expensive in the U.S. However, with the large engines that are found in older American cars, any savings on

Boston street signs, usually posted very clearly

fuel may be partially offset. Gas comes in three grades: economy, super, and premium. There are many gas stations in and around Boston, which often have self-service pumps. The gas at these is often a few cents cheaper per gallon than at pumps with attendants.

BREAKDOWNS

In the unlucky event of a breakdown, the best course of action is to pull off the road completely and put on the hazard lights to alert other drivers that you are stationary. There are emergency phones along some major interstate highways, but in other situations breakdown services or even the police can be contacted from land or cellular (mobile) phones. In case of breakdown, drivers of rental cars should contact the car rental company first. Members of the **American Automobile**

Cycle path along the Boston side of the Charles River

Association (AAA) can contact the association to have the car towed to the nearest service station to be repaired.

CYCLING

It is perhaps surprising that a city in which driving can be so difficult has an extensive network of bike paths. Cycling is actually a very useful way to see some of the outlying attractions. Cycling on the highways is illegal, and cycling city streets can be hazardous, but dedicated bike paths are generally very safe. Cycle shops and some newsstands carry the Boston Bike Map, which details trails and paths throughout the metropolitan region (see p164).

DIRECTORY

CAR RENTAL AGENCIES

Alamo
Tel (877) 603 0615.
www.alamo.com

Avis
Tel (800) 831-2847.
www.avis.com

Budget
Tel (800) 527-0700.
www.budget.com

Dollar
Tel (800) 800-4000.
www.dollar.com

Enterprise
Tel (800) 736-8222.
www.enterprise.com

Hertz
Tel (800) 654-3131.
www.hertz.com

Thrifty Car Rental
Tel (800) 847-4389.
www.thrifty.com

BREAKDOWN ASSISTANCE

American Automobile Association (AAA)
125 High St., Boston. *Tel* (800) 222-4357 or (617) 443-9300.
www.AAA.com

TIPS AND SAFETY FOR DRIVERS

- Traffic moves on the right-hand side of the road.
- Seat belts are compulsory in the front and the back seats, children under three years old must ride in a child seat.
- You can turn right at a red light as long as you first come to a complete stop, and if there are no signs that prohibit it.
- A flashing yellow light at an intersection means slow down, look for oncoming traffic, and proceed with caution.
- Passing (overtaking) is allowed on any multi-lane road, and you must pass on the left.
- Crossing a double-yellow line, either by U-turn or by passing the car in front, is illegal, and you will be charged a fine if caught.
- If a school bus stops, all traffic from both directions must stay completely and wait for the bus to drive off.
- Driving while intoxicated (DWI) is a punishable offense that incurs heavy fines or even a jail

sentence. Do not drink if you plan to drive.
- Avoid driving at night if unfamiliar with the area. Boston's streets can change from safe to dangerous in a single block, so if you don't know where you are going it is better to take a taxi than to get lost in your own car.
- Single women should be especially careful driving in unfamiliar territory, day or night.
- Keep all doors locked when driving around. Do not stop in a rural area, or on an unlit block if someone tries to get your attention. If a fellow driver points at your car, suggesting something is wrong, drive to the nearest gas station and get help. Do not get out of your car.
- Avoid sleeping in your car.
- Avoid short cuts and stay on well-traveled roads.
- Avoid looking at a map in a dark, unpopulated place. Drive to the nearest open store or gas station before pulling over.

BOSTON STREET FINDER

The key map below shows the area of Boston covered by the *Street Finder* maps, which can be found on the following pages. Map references, given throughout this guide, for sights, restaurants, hotels, shops, and entertainment venues refer to the grid on the maps. The first figure in the map reference indicates which *Street Finder* map to turn to (1 to 4), and the letter and number that follow refer to the grid reference on that map.

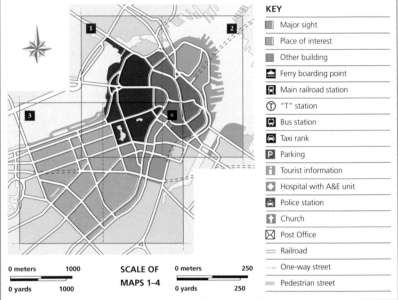

KEY

- 🟩 Major sight
- 🟩 Place of interest
- 🟫 Other building
- ⛴ Ferry boarding point
- 🚉 Main railroad station
- Ⓣ "T" station
- 🚌 Bus station
- 🚕 Taxi rank
- 🅿 Parking
- ℹ Tourist information
- ✚ Hospital with A&E unit
- 🚓 Police station
- ✝ Church
- ⊠ Post Office
- ═ Railroad
- → One-way street
- ▬ Pedestrian street

0 meters 1000
0 yards 1000

SCALE OF MAPS 1–4

0 meters 250
0 yards 250

A

A Street	4 F4
Acorn Street	1 B4 & 4 D1
Adams Place	1 B3
African Meeting House	1 C3
Albany Street	4 D5
Anderson Street	1 B3
Appleton Street	3 C3
Arch Street	2 D4 & 4 F1
Arlington Street	1 A4 & 4 D1
Ash Street	2 D4 & 4 F1
Ash Street	4 E3
Athens Street	4 F4
Atlantic Avenue	2 D5 & 4 F2
Avenue De Lafayette	1 C5 & 4 F2
Avery Street	1 C5 & 4 E2

B

B Street	4 F5
Back Bay Station	3 C3
Battery Street	2 E2
Battery Wharf	2 E2
Batterymarch Street	2 D4
Beach Street	1 C5 & 4 E2
Beacon Street	1 A4 & 3 A2
Beaver Place	1 A4 & 4 D1
Bedford Street	2 D5 & 4 F2
Bell Atlantic Building	2 D4
Belvidere Street	3 A3
Benton Street	3 A5
Berkeley Street	1 A4 & 3 C1
Blackstone Block	2 D3

Blackstone Square	3 C5
Blackstone Street	2 D3
Blagden Street	3 C3
Blossom Court	1 B2
Blossom Street	1 B2
Bond Street	4 D4
Boston Athenaeum	1 C4
Boston Center for the Arts	4 D3
Boston Globe Store	2 D4 & 4 F1
Boston Public Library	3 C2
Boston Tea Party Ship	2 E5
Bosworth Street	1 C4 & 4 F1
Bowdoin Street	1 C4
Bowker Street	1 C3
Boylston Street	1 A5 & 3 B3
Braddock Park	3 B3
Bradford Street	4 D4
Branch Street	1 B4 & 4 D1
Brattle Book Shop	1 C4 & 4 E1
Bridge Court	1 B3
Bristol Street	4 E4
Broad Street	2 E4
Broadway	4 F3
Bromfield Street	1 C4 & 4 F1
Burbank Street	3 A4
Burke Street	3 A5
Byron Street	1 B4 & 4 D1

C

Cambria Street	3 A3
Cambridge Street	1 B3
Camden Street	3 B5
Canal Street	2 D2
Cardinal O'Connell Way	1 B2

Causeway Street	1 C2
Cedar Lane Way	1 B4
Center Plaza	1 C3
Central Wharf	2 E3
Chandler Street	4 D3
Charles Street	1 B2
Charles Street Meeting House	1 B4
Charlesbank Park	1 A2
Charlestown Avenue	1 A1
Charter Street	2 D2
Chatham Street	2 D3
Chauncy Street	1 C5 & 4 F2
Chester Park	3 B5
Chestnut Street	1 A4 & 4 D1
Children's Museum	2 E5
Christian Science Center	3 B3
Christopher Columbus Park	2 E3
Church Street	4 D2
City Square	1 C1
Claremont Park	3 B4
Clarendon Street	1 A5 & 3 C1
Clark Street	2 E2
Clearway Street	3 A3
Clinton Street	2 D3
Clough House	2 E2
Colonial Theater	1 B5 & 4 E2
Columbia	2 D5 & 4 F2
Columbus Avenue	1 B5 & 3 A5
Commercial Avenue	1 A2
Commercial Street	2 D1
Commercial Street	2 E3
Commercial Wharf	2 E3
Commonwealth Avenue	3 B2

Concord Street	3 C5
Congress Street	2 D3
Cooper Street	2 D2
Copley Place	3 C3
Copley Square	3 C2
Copp's Hill Burying Ground	2 D2
Cortes Street	4 D3
Cotting Street	1 C2
Court Houses	1 C3
Court Street	2 D3
Coventry Street	3 A5
Cross Street	2 D3
Cross Street	2 E3
Cunard Street	3 A5
Custom House	2 E3
Cutler Majestic Theater	1 C5 & 4 E2

D

Dalton Street	3 A3
Dartmouth Place	3 C3
Dartmouth Street	3 C2
Davenport Street	3 B5
Dedham Street	4 D4
Derne Street	1 C3
Devonshire Street	2 D5 & 4 F1
Dorchester Avenue	4 F5
Dwight Street	4 D4

E

East Street	2 D5 & 4 F2
East Berkeley Street	4 D3
East Brookline Street	4 D5

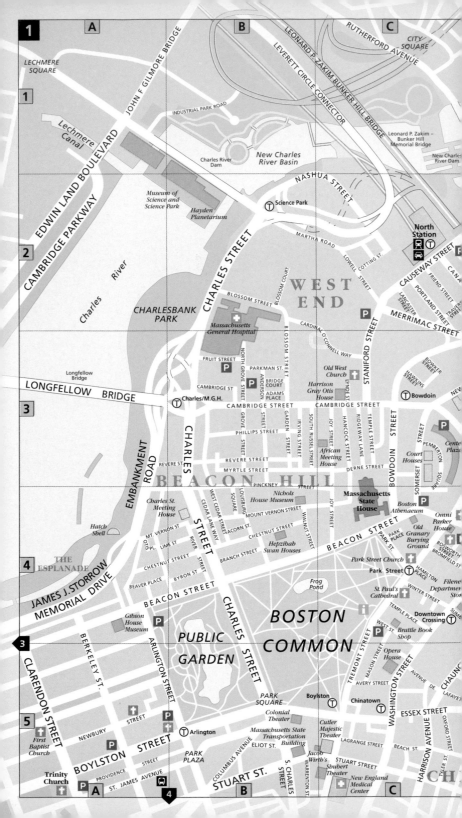

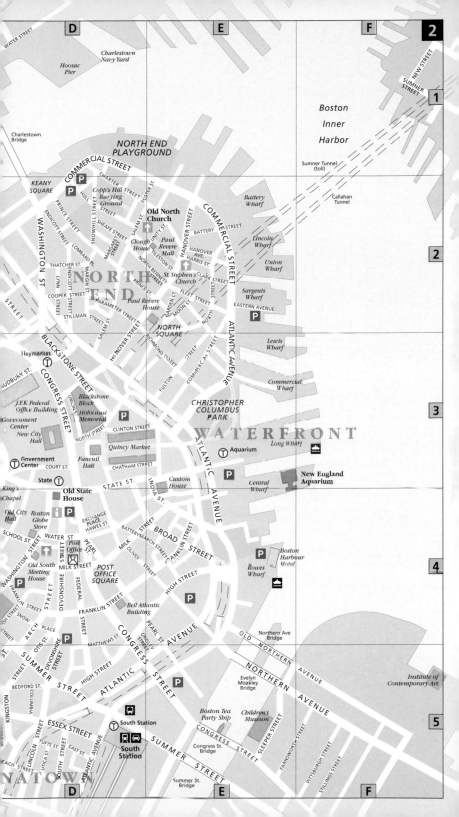

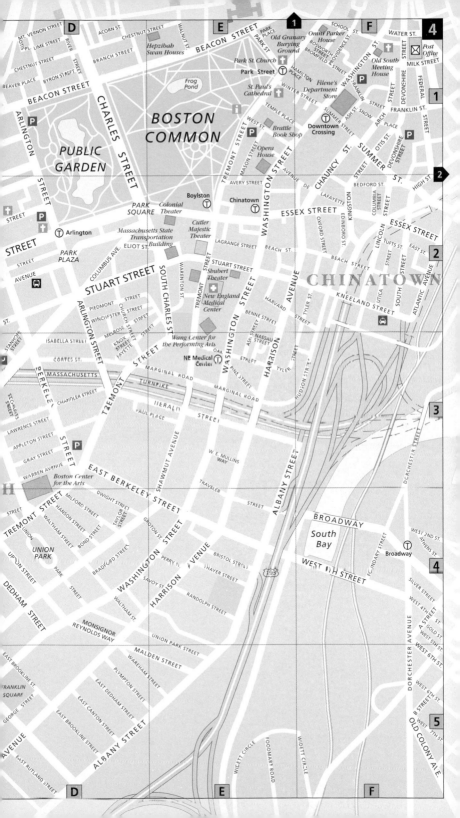

General Index

Acknowledgments

Dorling Kindersley would like to thank the following people whose contributions and assistance have made the preparation of this book possible.

Main Contributors

Patricia Harris and David Lyon are journalists and critics. They review art and restaurants and write extensively about travel, food, and popular culture from their home in Cambridge, Massachusetts. In addition to their books on art and travel, their essays, narratives, and photographs have appeared in a wide variety of online and print publications, including Expedia.com, the *Boston Globe*, the *Los Angeles Times*, *American Craft*, *Arthur Frommer's Budget Travel*, *The Robb Report* and *Boston Magazine*.

Tom Bross has lived in Massachusetts since 1965 and now lives in Boston's North End, virtually next door to Old North Church. During the past 25 years as a freelance travel journalist Tom has written extensively about U.S., Canadian, and overseas destinations for various guidebooks, national magazines, newspapers, newsletters, and on-line publications. His domestic specialties are New England and California; overseas, Germany, Belgium, and Austria. He is, in addition, a professional photographer and spent several years in the 1980s as staff photographer of his home city's American League baseball team, the Boston Red Sox.

Kem Sawyer lives in Washington DC and has written children's books, feature articles, and book reviews. She particularly enjoys writing about history and has written the history feature for the *DK Eyewitness Travel Guide to Washington DC* as well as for this guide.

Additional Contributors

Brett Cook, Carolyn Heller, Juliette Rogers.

Additional Illustrations

Christopher King.

Additional Photography

Peter Anderson, John Coletti, Patricia Harris, David Lyon, Ian O'Leary, Stephen Oliver, Clive Streeter.

Managing Editor

Helen Townsend.

Managing Art Editor

Kate Poole.

Art Director

Gillian Allan.

Design and Editorial Assistance

Mark Bailey, Eleanor Berman, Sam Borland, Jo Gardner, Claire Jones, Esther Labi, Sam Merrell, Katherine Mesquita, Mary Ormandy, Catherine Palmi, Marianne Petrou, Pete Quinlan, Rada Radojicic, Mani Ramaswamy, Lynne Robinson, Sands Publishing Solutions, Meredith Smith, Brett Steel, Rachel Symons, Ros Walford, Hugo Wilkinson.

Proofreader

Stewart J. Wild.

Indexer

Hilary Bird.

Researcher

Timothy Kennard.

Special Assistance

Aimee O'Brien at the Greater Boston Convention and Visitors Bureau, who provided invaluable assistance with many Boston sights. Rosemary Barron for acting as food consultant, and for food preparation.

Photography Permissions

Dorling Kindersley would like to thank the following for their assistance and kind permission to photograph at their establishments:

Courtesy COMMONWEALTH OF MASSACHUSETTS ART: *George Washington* Sir Francis Chantrey, 1827 – 51bl; *Civil War Army Nurses Memorial* Bela Pratt, 1911 – 51ca; *John Hancock Memorial* artist unknown, 1915 – 21cl; *Return of the Colours to the Custody of the Commonwealth*, December 22, 1986, mural by Edward Simmons, 1902 – 51tl; Stained glass window, Main Stair Hall, 1900/details: *Magna Carta seal* 41, *Seal of the Commonwealth* (pre-1898) 50b.

Museum of Fine Arts, Sackler Museum, Harvard Museum of Natural History, the Fogg Art and Busch- Reisinger Museums, and Franklin Park Zoo.

All other churches, museums, hotels, restaurants, shops, galleries and sights too numerous to thank individually.

Picture Credits

t = top; tl = top left; tlc = top left centre; tc = top centre; tr = top right; cla = centre left above; ca = centre above; cra = centre right above; cl = centre left; c = centre; cr = centre right; clb = centre left below; cb = centre below; crb = centre right below; bl = bottom left; b = bottom; bc = bottom centre; bcl = bottom centre left; br = bottom right; d = detail.

Works of art have been reproduced with the permission of the following copyright holders: *Here-There Wall* by Kenneth Noland 1985 (c) DACS, London/VAGA, New York 2006 121bc.

The publisher would like to thank the following individuals, companies and picture libraries for permission to reproduce their photographs.

ALAMY IMAGES: ANDRE Jenny 120bl, 141tl; Alan Myers 123br; William Owens 10cl; Chuck Pefley 11tc; Swerve 10tc, 123tl; Jeff Titcomb 121tr; ALLSPORT USA: 166t/c/b; THE ART ARCHIVE: 87bc; AXIOM: 34cl; LAURA BARISONZI PHOTOGRAPHY/WWW. PHOTOGRAPHERSDIRECT.COM: 122bl; BERKLEE COLLEGE OF MUSIC: Nick

Balkin 97bc; Boston Ballet: Farnsworth/ Blalock Photography 158cr; BOSTONIAN SOCIETY/OLD STATE HOUSE: 53b, 87cb; *Boston Harbor*, 1853, John White Allen Scott. Purchase 1884 – 8-9.

CITY WATER TAXI: 180bc; CORBIS: 24t, Bettmann 25t, 31t/b, 72b, 87cra/bl, 98b; Edifice, Philippa Lewis 126c; Kevin Fleming 10br, 37b, 158b, 184t; Todd Gypstein 170b; Robert Holmes 140cl, 100; Hulton-Deutsch Collection 45t; Richard T. Nowitz 73c; Lee Snider 1; CONCORD MUSEUM www.concord museum.org: *A View of Town of Concord April 19, 1775 (1775-1825)* Artist Unknown, oil on canvas, bequest of Mrs. Stedman Buttrick, Sr. 117cr; CULVER PICTURES, INC.: 22c, 24c.

FOURTHREE MEDIA: Justine Flute 178tl; Getty Images: Photonica 141c; GRANGER COLLECTION, NEW YORK: 9 (insert), 16, 17t, 18t/c/b, 19t/c/b, 20tr/cl/b, 20-21c, 21t/cra/crb, 22t, 23t/c, 25cl, 30t/b, 31c, 39 (insert), 65tl, 75b/c, 83b, 173 (insert).

HARVARD UNIVERSITY ART MUSEUMS: © President and Fellows of Harvard College, courtesy of Fogg Art Museum, Alpheus Hyatt Purchasing and Friends of the Fogg Art Museum Funds *Kneeling Angel* Gian Lorenzo Bernini, c.1674-1675 -112cr; courtesy of the Busch-Reisinger Museum, Gift of Sibyl Moholy-Nagy, *Light-Space Modulator*, Laszlo Moholy-Nagy, 1930 © Hattula Moholy-Nagy/ DACS, London 2006 - 112b; courtesy of Fogg Art Museum, The Hervey E. Wetzel Bequest Fund *Christ on the Cross between the Virgin and Cardinal Torquemada and St. John the Evangelist* Fra Angelico, c.1446 -113b; courtesy Fogg Art Museum, Bequest: Collection of Maurice Wertheim *Skating* Edouard Manet, 1877 - 113cl; HULTON GETTY COLLECTION: 58b; HYATT REGENCY: 130br.

IMAGE BANK: Archive Photos 30c; INSTITUTE OF CONTEMPORARY ART, BOSTON: Iwan Baan 29cr, 66; IRVING

HOUSE: 131c. MAGGIE JANIK/www. photographersdirect.com: 120tc, 122cla. LEBRECHT COLLECTION: The Rodgers & Hammerstein Organization 87t/br; JAMES LEMASS: 6cl, 18 tc, 25crb, 34t/b, 35t/c/b, 36b, 37t, 54, 78, 91crb, 118tl, 119br, 164c, 165, 167t, 168c/b, 172-173.

MARY EVANS: 129 (insert); MASSACH-USETTS TRANSPORTATION AUTHORITY: 183b; MINUTE MAN NATIONAL HISTOR-ICAL PARK: 119cla; MUSEUM OF FINE ARTS BOSTON: Gift of Egypt Exploration Fund *Egypt, Deir el-Bahri* painted wood 24b; HU-MFA Expedition *Shawabtis of Taharka* 28b; 104t; Bequest of Mrs. Beatrice Constance (Turner) Maynard in Memory of Winthrop Sargent *Revere Silver Teapot* 104ca; Egypt Exploration Fund *Inner Coffin of Nes-mut-aat-neru* 104cb; Picture Fund *Dance at Bougival* Pierre-Auguste Renoir, 1883 -105t; Ruth and Carl J. Shapiro Colonnade and Vault *John Singer Sargent Murals* 105c; Francis Bart-lett Donation of 1900 *Head of Aphrodite*, Greek Late Classical or Early Hellenistic period -105b; George Nixon Black Fund *Ewer and basin* 106t; M. and M. Karolik Collection of American Paintings, 1815 – 1865, by exchange, *Boston Harbor* Fitz Hugh Lane 106c; Bequest of John T. Spaulding *La Berceuse* Vincent van Gogh, 1889 – 106b; Maria Antoinette Evans Fund *Babylonia:Nebuchadnezzar II* 107t; Gift by Contribution *Horse, early 8th century, China* 107c; Richard Norton Memorial Fund *Fragment of fresco from villa at Contrada Bottaro* 107b; MUSEUM OF SCIENCE: George Kiley 169t; Andrew Brilliant 169b; Kindra Clineff 28t; NEW

ENGLAND AQUARIUM: 77 cra; Bob Kramer 76t/b, 77t; DAVID NOBLE: 38-39.

OLD NORTH CHURCH, BOSTON: 71cl; OMNI PARKER HOUSE: 56clb; Used by Permission of Orchard House / The Louisa May Alcott Memorial Association: 118c; PAUL O'SHAUGHNESSY: 119ca.

PEABODY MUSEUM OF ARCHAEOLOGY AND ETHNOLOGY/HARVARD UNIVERSITY: © President and Fellows of Harvard College 1976. All Rights Reserved. Photos Hillel Burger 114c. Courtesy Paul Revere Memorial Association: 73t; PUPPET SHOWCASE THEATRE: Marionettes by Paul Vincent Davis 171tl.

SCIENCE PHOTO LIBRARY: Cnes, 1986 Distribution Spot Image 13t. SWISSOTEL BOSTON: © René Staud 130b.

TOPHAM PICTUREPOINT: 25b. UNITED AIRLINES: 180t.

FRONT ENDPAPER: All special photography except INSTITUTE OF CONTEMPORARY ART, Boston: Iwan Baan cr; JAMES LEMASS: bl/bc.

JACKET
Front – Alamy Images: Bill Brooks main; DK Images: Philip Dowell clb. Back – DK IMAGES: Demetrio Carrasco cla, John Coletti tl, bl, Linda Whitwam clb. Spine – ALAMY IMAGES: Bill Brooks t; DK IMAGES: Demetrio Carrasco b.

All other images ©Dorling Kindersley. See www.dkimages.com for further information.

SPECIAL EDITIONS OF DK TRAVEL GUIDES

DK Travel Guides can be purchased in bulk quantities at discounted prices for use in promotions or as premiums. We are also able to offer special editions and personalized jackets, corporate imprints, and excerpts from all of our books, tailored specifically to meet your own needs.

To find out more, please contact:
(in the United States) **SpecialSales@dk.com**
(in the UK) **travelspecialsales@uk.dk.com**
(in Canada) DK Special Sales at **general@tourmaline.ca**
(in Australia) **business.development@pearson.com.au**

Further Reading

Non-Fiction

A Guide to Public Art in Boston: from Newburyport to Plymouth. Carlock, Marty. (Harvard Common Press, 1993.)

AIA Guide to Boston. Southworth, Michael and Susan. (Globe Pequot Press, 1996.)

All about Boston Harbor Islands. Kales, Emily and David. (Hewitts Cove Publishing Co. Inc., 1983.)

Boston Sites and Insights. Wilson, Susan. (Beacon Hill Press, 1994.)

Exploring in and Around Boston on Bike and Foot. Sinai, Lee. (Appalachian Mountain Club Books, 1996.)

Gaining Ground: A History of Landmaking in Boston. Seasholes, Nancy. (Mit Press, 2003)

Imagining Boston: A Literary Landscape. O'Connell, Shaun. (Beacon Press, 1990.)

Paul Revere's Ride. Fischer, David Hackett. (Oxford University Press, 1994.)

The Fitzgeralds and the Kennedys: an American Saga. Goodwin, Doris Kearns. (Simon and Schuster, 1987.)

26 Miles to Boston: the Boston Marathon Experience from Hopkinton to Copley Square. Connelly, Michael. (Parnassus Imprints, 1998.)

Fiction

The Godwulf Manuscript. Parker, Robert. (Delacorte Press, 1974.)

Make Way for Ducklings. McCloskey, Robert. (Viking Press, 1941.)

Mortal Friends. Carroll, James. (Little Brown & Company, 1978.)

The Last Hurrah. O'Connor, Edwin. (Little Brown & Company, 1956.)

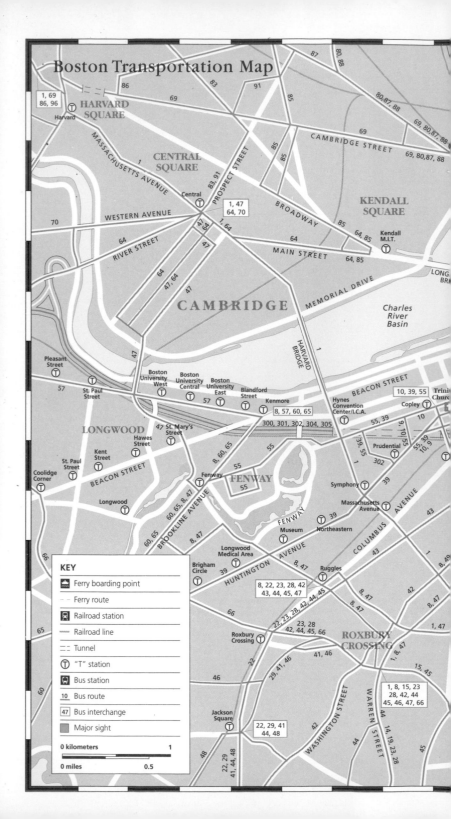